ENTREPRENEURSHIP AND SMALL BUSINESS MANAGEMENT

BY THE SAME AUTHOR

Management of Commercial Banks, Financial Markets and Institutions
Government and Business
Business Environment
Securities and Investment

ENTREPRENEURSHIP AND SMALL BUSINESS MANAGEMENT

DR. C. L. BANSAL
Reader
College of Vocational Studies
University of Delhi

HAR-ANAND
PUBLICATIONS PVT LTD

HAR–ANAND PUBLICATIONS PVT LTD
E-49/3, Okhla Industrial Area, Phase-II, New Delhi-110020
Tel.: 41603490 Fax: 011-41708607
E-mail: info@haranandpublications.com
Website: www.haranandpublications.com

Reprint, 2012

Published by Ashok Gosain and Ashish Gosain for
Har-Anand Publications Pvt Ltd

Printed in India at Saujanaya Printing Press

PREFACE

The role of small business, though overlooked, has always been significant. Large business is highly visible because of its sheer size. On the contrary, the contribution of small business is difficult to evaluate on account of its being complementary and widely scattered. However, there is nothing to belittle its valuable role in India's economic development. The small sector has been the most conspicuous in the field of modern technology particularly telecommunications, computer software, computer aided design, videos and video casettes etc. It accounts for more than 50 per cent of the total industrial production and employs 80 per cent of the total industrial work force. Considering its vast employment potential and significant contribution in economic development, the small sector has begun to be reckoned as a panacea for several of the ills of the developing countries.

Recognising the significance of this subject for upcoming managers and professionals, the subject has been included in the curriculum of M.B.A. examination of several universities. To prepare the youth for self employment, the University of Delhi has started a three-year degree course in "Entrepreneurship and Small Business". The EDPs organised by various professional institutes, trade associations and chambers of commerce lay special emphasis on imparting training in this subject. Notwithstanding the importance of the subject, there is paucity of relevant texts on it. The present book is a humble attempt in the direction of filling up the gap and to provide useful literature covering the theoretical and practical aspects of both "Entrepreneurship" and "Small Business & Industry". In addition to covering the prescribed syllabi of M.B.A. and B.A. (Vocational), chapters of interest to entrepreneurs and practitioners have also been incorporated.

In undertaking the writing of this book, I have received special inspiration from a number of my teachers, friends and colleagues. In this connection, I owe my grateful thanks to Prof. P. K. Ghosh, Prof. G.S. Bhatia (Paniabi University), Prof. Y. P. Singh (Delhi University), Prof. M. Saeed (Jamia Milia Islamia), Prof. D.N. Saxena (PHD Chamber of Commerce), Dr. S.P. Narang (Director, Institute of Company

Secretaries). Dr. Narendra Kumar (MDU, Rohtak), Dr. J.P. Sharma, M/s G.S. Jolly, Satish Bhatia, Kuldeep Ahuja *et al.* I am grateful to my wife and children for their patience and cooperation during the writing of this book.

The author would be amply rewarded if the book is found useful by those for whom it has been written.

C.L. BANSAL

CONTENTS

CHAPTER I

INTRODUCTORY FRAMEWORK OF SMALL BUSINESS

When Adam Smith published 'Wealth of Nations' in 1776, he was describing an economy in which local small business were virtually the only economic entities. Indeed, the era of local economy was the heyday of small business. Rapid technological advances have given a place of pride to large business but the role of small business has continued to remain significant. However, the exact contribution of small business has been rendered difficult because it is widely scattered and complementary to large industries.

Concept of Small Business

Clifford M Baumback regards small business as one which is :

—actively managed by its owners
—highly personalised
—largely local in its area of operation
—of relatively small size within the industry and
—largely dependent on internal resources of capital to finance its growth.

According to 'Committee on Economic Development' a business is small if it meets two or more of the following criteria :

(i) Management of firm is independent in the sense that owners themselves are the managers.
(ii) Capital is supplied and ownership is held by an individual or a small group.
(iii) Area of its operations is local. However, market for its products need not be local.
(iv) The size of the firm in the industry is small as compared to highest unit in its field.

Characteristics of Small Business

1. Privately held or, closely held, if public

There are two broad categories of small business as follows :—

(a) **the very small business** wherein proprietor is the chief worker as in the case of jewellery shops, shoe sellers, grocery stores etc.

(b) **the large small business** where the proprietor mainly directs the work of its employees.

2. **No or few management layers**

A small business must have a few or no management layers.

3. **Style of management**

Small ventures are generally managed in a personalized fashion. The owner has first hand knowledge of what is going on at all levels of business. He participates in all aspects of business decision making.

4. **Limited Resources**

A small business is unlikely to have sufficient resources to be able to dominate its field of business.

5. **Independence**

It means that enterprise's owner-manager has ultimate authority and effective control over it.

6. **Scope of Operations**

Small enterprises serve predominantly a limited segment of local or regional market.

7. **Scale of operations**

They occupy a relatively limited share of a given market.

Because of the above mentioned characteristics, small firms have their special needs and problems. The management approach approriate to a large firm may not be suitable for a small firm. Thomas J. Murray * in his studies have found that executives of large firms who occupied chief executive's position in a small firm found their earlier experiences inappropriate.

Economic Characteristics of Small Business

1. Small business tends towards those businesses which are low in

---

* "The Big Problems of Thinking Small : Taking on the Presidency of a Small Company" *Dun's Review,* Feb 1976, p. 70.

capital and high in labour intensity. Since they cannot afford to acquire capital intensive machinery, they gravitate towards low cost labour intensive businesses.

2. Small business does well where technological innovation is economical.
3. Small business suits businesses involving specialised skills so that the product could be designed to cater to the needs of an individual or few clients.
4. Small business often does well in small, isolated, overlooked or imperfect markets. It has been made possible by the segmentation of mass consumer markets and growing taste for unique products.
5. Small business often operates in little proven or unstable markets or plays the role of filling marginal fluctuating demand.
6. Small business has an edge in developing markets because it can experiment often and react to evolving conditions.

   Unstable markets, i.e., those characterised by unpredictable wide swings in demand or fierce competition are unattractive to big business. Small business often fills this void.
7. Small business survives by being closer to the market place and responding quickly and cleverly to changes in it. It gets the first scent of change which gives it the first chance to act.

Typical Small Business

Majority of small business are characterized by economic tenacity, willingness to endure bleak times, personal energy and resourcefulness of owners. Most small business entrepreneurs tend to seek opportunities in industries that have low entry barriers and about which they have personal knowledge. It is mostly labour intensive and is run in a personal way. The smaller the business, the greater the degree of free intermingling between the owner and third parties. Finances come from family savings accumulated through sacrificing immediate gratification. These are augmented with borrowings from relatives. Family members constitute the top management. When the founder dies, business passes to successor or is dissolved.

Types of Businesses amenable to Small Business

1. **Retailing :** It is the traditional stronghold of small business in any country. These include corner stores, restaurants, bars, hardware shops, home furnishings etc. Many of these are family-run businesses.

2. **Service** such as legal and accounting firms, shops, beauty parlours etc.
3. **Construction activity**
4. **Wholesale business**
5. **Financing, insurance** and **real estate**
6. **Transporation, communication and public utilities.**
7. **Manufacturing**

I. **Large Versus Small Business**

Following are the differences between large and small business :

1. They foster changes differently

Small business fosters change through a cycle of birth and death. The large business pattern of change takes place through expansion and contraction.

2. Their risk-reward investment decisions are assessed differently

Risk/reward is personal in the case of small business and its calculation is circumscribed by the potential fortunes of a single line of business.

In large organisations, risk/reward decisions are made by employee managers without livelihood stake. The judgement includes long range welfare of large perpetual institutions.

3. Their economic power is different

Small business is in no position to influence its immediate economic environment but big business does.

4. They utilise different resources in the economy

Because of its general competitive inferiority, small business must make greater use of secondary resources. But big business due to its superior size has a first call on most of the primary resources.

5. They serve different markets in the economy

Small business serves markets which big business does not wish or cannot serve.

II. **Inter Relationship Between Large and Small Business**

Small business performs several economic roles, offsetting big business vulnerabilities that abets economic disequilibrium. While aggregate small business benefits from serving the supply and distribution needs of large companies, big business profits by shifting the economic fallout arising from economic instabilities and uncertainties to the small business.

Small sector is powerfully affected by developments within the big business sector. This relationship serves the interest of general economic disequilibrium. Economic disruption, e.g., low profits or business failure is better absorbed by scattered cushioning of the small business. Small business economy is more or less self-adjusting. It tends to act as a cushion for the economy in a downturn and as a brake in inflationary periods, e.g., in economic downturn small business responds to the fall in demand with lower prices and lower wages. The nature of inter-linkages between these two sectors are summarised below :—

(i) *Job sub-contracting*, i.e., the large business provides materials and components to small units who process the same into finished part, sub-assembly or component.

(ii) *Purchase sub-contracting*

Here some of or all the material is procured by the small unit who manufactures a specific part or component needed by a particular large unit, or a part which could be used by many similar large units.

(iii) *Complementary*

In this case, the product manufactured by a small company is procured by a large unit as an acccessory or complementary to its main product. Examples of such complementary items are internal aerials, plastic dust cover of a video recorder, electronic passive components etc.

(iv) *Merchandising or commercial* Trading

Many a time, a large organisation may take up for national selling a durable consumer good or a semi-professional product made by a small unit, e. g., sale by a manufacturer of refrigerator or voltage stabilisers manufactured by a small unit.

(v) *Maintenance and Repair Services*

A large unit, instead of having a separate maintenance unit, may assign this work to a small specialised organisation. This kind of sub contracting has good scope in developing countries particularly for hi-tech cousumer products such as personal computers, calculators, digital equipment etc.

(vi) *Ancillarisation*

Many large enterprises have a list of parts/components/ accessories etc. which they procure from small units. Purchases from ancillary units are found to be economical and helpful in the maintenance of production flow.

(vii) *Social benefits of inter-linkages*

Viable interlinkage between small and large industries are justified because of various social benefits e.g. employment generation, decentralisation of industrial benefits, human resource development etc.

Differences in Managing Small and Large Firms

According to John S Deeks*, following are the key differences in the management of small and large firms :

Nature of Difference	*Small Firms*	*Large Firms*
1. Sources of Authority	(a) Traditional (ownership)	(a) Expertize
	(b) Personal	(b) Official
2. Basis of Philosophy	(a) No diffusion between ownership & control	(a) Control without ownership
	(b) No conflict between personal and business objectives	(b) Conflict between individual and organisational objectives
	(c) No distinction between person and role	(c) Clear distinctions between individual and office.
	(d) Integration of work and social values	(d) Values of work place are divorced from both individual and social values.
	(e) Not subservient to economic goals.	(e) Economic performance is the ultimate criterion.

* *The Small firm Owner manager*, Praeger, New York 1976

Nature of Difference	*Small Firms*	*Large Firms*
3. Characteristic Skills	(a) Adaptive	(a) Predictive
	(b) Diagnostic	(b) Prognostic
	(c) Exploitation of change	(c) Control of change
	(d) Tactical facility	(d) Strategic facility
	(e) Pragmatic use of techniques as aid to problem solving	(e) Coordination and control by specialists.
	(f) Social skills applied	(f) Manipulative skills applied largely on an impersonal basis.
	(g) Consequence mitigating decision making	(g) Event shaping decision making
4. Orgasnigation	(a) Informal relationship	(a) Formal relationship
	(b) No divorce between planners and doers	(b) Divorce of planning from doing
	(c) Appointment and promotion often on the basis of birth or personal friendship	(c) Technical qualification is the basis of appointment and promotion
	(d) Everyone prepared to work as much as required	(d) Precise definition of rights, obligations, duties and responsiblities
	(e) Open system of communication	(e) Structured communication system

Due to these differences, the management requirements of small firms tend to be significantly different from those of large firms. But the basic managerial functions and operational activities are essentially the same though these are required to be carried out differently. Moreover, the carrying out of these is the responsibility of just one person, i.e., the entrepreneur. He alone discharges the functions like planning, organising, directing and controlling.

Reasons for the Survival of Small Firms

Inspite of tough competition from large scale firms, small business has survived due to following reasons :—

(i) Personal attention and catering to individual tastes. For instance, in fashion business, small firms alone are suitable.

(ii) Considerations of variety and quality give an edge to small firm over its large competitor.

(iii) Nature of market, i.e., where raw materials and demand are both widely scattered, the small firms are more suitable e.g. brick kiln industry.

(iv) Nature of production process. Particularly simpler production processes are amenable to small firms. It is why khandsari sugar is made in smaller plants whereas crystal sugar is manufactured in big factories.

(v) As ancillaries to large firms. Small firms now-a-days take up production of standardized components required by large firms.

(vi) State assistance and patronage in view of the role played by small industries in planned economic development of the country.

Moreover, small retail shops need limited capital, simple organisational structure and limited managerial skill. Small firms have low establishment charges and low overheads. These reasons explain the existence of small firms along with large firms.

Problems of Small Business

I. *Internal Problems*

(a) Many entrepreneurs leave project formulation and report preparation to professional consultants without trying to understand risk and records of their own project. Many relevant factors particularly marketing escape their notice.

(b) Failure of small entrepreneurs to submit financial statements in time so that financial institutions are not able to reschedule repayment of term loans .

(c) Lack of experience . An entrepreneur may have technical qualifications but may not have sufficient insight into demand potential, financial management, raw material availability etc. He may have been tempted just because somebody else has successfully run a similar unit. Without proper project preparation, training and experience, the entrepreneur is bound to run into rough weather.

(d) Unfair price competition from big firms.

(e) Lack of adequate capital.

(f) Low risk-bearing capacity.

(g) Lack of adoption of modern sales promotion drives.

II. *External Problems*

(a) Difficulty in obtaining variety of approvals and clearances. A large amount of time of a small entrepreneur is spent in complying with the formalities prescribed by regulatory agencies. Added to this, the red tapism dampens the enthusiasm of many a budding entrepreneurs.

(b) Inadequate infrastructural facilities in some of the Government developed industrial estates .

(c) Dependence. Most of the small firms heavily depend on guidance and scrutiny by promotional agencies and banks right from preparation of project profile to final execution. Despite the existence of multifarious agencies comprising every conceivable expertise, there is something seriously wrong with them. For instance, District Industries Centres donot have any authentic data on which to base project report. Even the quality of functionaries manning the DICs is far from satisfactory. They are not familiar with latest developments in a wide variety of production technology, quality standards and modern management techniques.

(d) Non-availability of adequate working capital from banks in addition to delay in sanction or release of working capital.

(e) Cold shouldering of ancillary units by large units.

Below are given some of the suggestions for dealing with the problems faced by small business.

(i) Formation of voluntary cooperative groups :—

Cooperative grouping of small firms will help them increase the size of purchase orders and reap the benefits of large purchases.

(ii) Adoption of modern business practices

Modernisation of business practices will bring efficiency and economy in their trade.

(iii) Taking full advantages of specialised services of wholesalers, financial institutions etc.

Small Business and Innovation

The major feature of modern age is the fast pace with which innovation is rendering new technologies obsolete. Accelerated obsolescene is shortening product lives as also the period during which investment can be recouped. For instance, a sophisticated electronic product may take 8 to 10 years from conception to marketing but the entire ROI must often be realised in only two or three years. Vulnerability of mass production industry to shifting demand and technology is greater now-a-days than in the past.

Innovation is the doing of something in a way that has not been done before. The outcome of innovation may be a product or a business strategy. Scientific phases in innovation process are inherently unstable and sloppy. They advance through a myriad of steps of trial and error. Pure accident sometime plays a role in innovation process.

As part of the innovation process, small business plays a role akin to a low cost extension of big business. Once an advantage is found, it opens the market and sends market signals where larger investments might by merited. A classic example is the case of Milton Reynolds who played a catalytic role in introducing first ballpoint pen. It was nothing more than discovery of an overlooked invention of ballpoint and marketing it in the forties at 12.50 dollars each. In just six months, he multiplied 26000 dollars into after-tax profits of 1.5 million dollars. The truth is that even in the age of atom and genetic engineering, large business depends on complementary and catalytic role of small business entrepreneur to help resolve the disorderly process of innovations. List of innovations introduced by small firms in the 20th century is impressive including double knit fabric, dry chemicals fire extinguisher, heart valve, safety razor, frozen food, soft contact lens, oral contraceptives, vacuum tube etc. Large corporation needs a clear indication of sizable and enduring market potential to justify a significant investment in an innovative production process.

For big business, a commercial failure even of a small nature has far-reaching repercussions. Failure may cause severe setback to the reputation of the corporation and affect its ability to raise equity. Thus big business can not afford to make big gambles. There the innovation process is circumscribed by caution and sense of responsibility to shareholders, society, and perpetuation of corporate institution itself.

Thus small business brings innvoation to the market faster than the big business.

Following are the characteristics of small business innovation :

1. Responding alertly to shifting market conditions.
2. Exploiting overlooked, neglected or rejected opportunities.
3. Keeping fast growing new industries on track.
4. Serving small or specialised markets.
5. Facilitating big business's fast entry into new markets.
6. Providing innovative supplies.

Limitations of small business innovation however is that since large, high risk and long term R & D projects take long to recover original investment, it is beyond the capacity of small business.

Small Sector in India — Some Significant trends

Year	*Number of Unit (lakhs)*	*Production (Rs crores)*	*Employment (lakhs)*	*Export (Rs. crores)*
1985-86	13.53	61228	97	3648
1986-87	14.57	72250	101	4500
1987-88	15.92	84900	107	5895
1988-89	16.98	96600	114	—

CHAPTER II

ENTREPRENEUR AND ENTREPRENEURSHIP

Many of the factors of production would have remained insipid but for the inspiring intervention of the entrepreneur. The desire to establish and operate one's own business is deeply ingrained in the fabric of the personality of an ambitious man. There are those who believe that entrepreneurs are born not made. Some others opine to the contrary. Knowledge about the characteristics of 'entrepreneur' and 'entrepreneurship' is significant not only for resolving this conflict but also to provide guiding hint to those who are thinking of embarking on any new enterprise. By comparing one's personality with the psychological profile of a typical entrepreneur one could discover the chances or otherwise of one's success.

THE CONCEPT OF ENTREPRENEUR

Simply stated, entrepreneur is one who organises and manages a business undertaking assuming the risk for the sake of profit.

The term entrepreneur was first coined by Cantilon, a French baker in mid-18th century to mean, "a person who is uncertainty bearer".* The term appeared in Adam Smith's writings but not very explicitly. J. B. Say regarded him to be 'an organiser who combines various factors of production to produce a socially viable product'. Compared to classical economists, Joseph Schumpeter** analysed the theory of entrepreneurship from a new perspective and regarded the entrepreneur as an 'innovator' with potentialities of doing things in a new way. This innovation could occur in the following five forms:—

(i) Introduction of new goods.

(ii) Introduction of new method of production.

---

* Aitken, Huge J.(ed.), *Exploration in Enterprise,* Cambridge; Harvard University Press, (1965) p. 46.

** *The Theory of Economic Development*; Cambridge; Harvard University Press (1959), pp. 89-105.

(iii) The finding of new product.
(iv) Conquest of new sources of supply of raw materials.
(v) Organisation of industry in a new way, e.g., creation or breaking of monopoly position.

Schumpetrian 'entrepreneur' has been criticised as untrue of the developing countries who need 'imitating entrepreneurs' capable of implementing the innovations made in developed countries. According to Peter Kilby, an entrepreneur in an underdeveloped country performs a wide range of activities including *inter alia* perception of market opportunities, combining and managing factors of production, introduction of production techniques and products etc.

The question is whether the term should be confined to those who start a new business or should it be extended to those who seek out new opportunities and then combine the factors of production to exploit them? Although Schumpeter wanted the term to be restricted to refer to those who carry out innovation (called 'independent entrepreneurs') yet it would not be proper to exclude those who carry out new combinations in order to meet perceived opportunities (called 'corporate entrepreneurs')

Characteristics of Entrepreneurs

Studies have established the existence of some common personal characteristics amongst entrepreneurs. Some of these *inter alia* include: a high level of energy, desire to pursue innovative goals, desire for achievement, a deep involvement in work, optimistic belief in future etc. Given below is a resume of some of the important studies relating to characteristic profile of entrepreneurs.

I David Mcclelland's N-ach Hypothesis *

N-Ach theory emphasises that an entrepreneur is one who is driven by the need for achievement towards accomplishment of tasks that challenge his competence. Such an entrepreneur exhibits the following characterities.

(i) Need for achievement (n-Ach)

It is the prime psychological drive that motivates the entrepreneur. It is a drive within an individual that motivates behaviour towards accomplishment, i.e., in achieving a goal that poses reasonable challenge

---

* Mc Clelland, David C., *The Achieving Society,* Collier Mac Millan, N.Y. (1967).

to an individual's competence. Thus, an easy task would not carry such a challenge. Such an entrepreneur is inordinately energetic but not a gambler. His motivation is the product of a scientific assessment of his energies and the challenge.

(ii) **Desire for responsibility**

Entrepreneur prefers to use his own resources and to be personally responsible for the results. He can perform well in groups particularly when he can influence the results in some specific way.

(iii) **Preference for moderate risk, i.e.**

Seeking high level of performance consistent with the possibility of achievement.

(iv) **Perception of the probability of success**

This consists in collecting and analysing facts and thereafter falling upon his own self confidence for accomplishing the task.

(v) **Future oriented i.e.**

He plans and thinks in the future. He anticipates possibilities that lie beyond the present.

(vi) **Stimulated by feedback.**

Irrespective whether the signals about his performance are good or bad, he draws his inspiration from the feedback.

(vii) **Energetic activity**

He exhibits a high level of energy than an average person and spends a large proportion of his time in finding out novel ways of getting done the set task.

(viii) **Skill in organising**

Entrepreneurs have remarkable skill in organising work and people. They make objective selection of individuals in conformity with their skill in solving specific problem.

(ix) **Attitude towards money**

His attitude towards money is cavelier, i.e., money is not a principal obsession. He values money but not for itself. Money acts as measure of his accomplishment, a token of his achievement rather than as a commodity to be hoarded.

II. Psychological characteristics of an entrepreneur by Albert Shapero*

According to Albert Shapero, an important personality dimension of entrepreneurs is the degree to which they can affect the world around them called 'locus of control'. The people who are **externals** believe that the rewards in life come from forces outside themselves such as luck, fate, power over others etc. On the other hand people who are **internals** believe that they can influence events to their own good or detriment. Such people crave for independence and autonomy. They rely on their own resources. Most of the entrepreneurs lie between these two extremes. But very successful entrepreneurs who were tested for locus of control scored as high internals.

III. John A. Hornaday and John Abond's Study**

Considering that the projective tests developed by McClelland can be administered and interpreted only by a trained psychologist, Hornaday and Abond formulated an objective and structured procedure that could be used by non-psychologists. The test developed by them combines the following :

(a) The Kuder Occupational Interest Survey,

(b) Gordon's Survey of Inter-personal Values, and

(c) A questionnaire drawn from Edward's Personal Preference Scale.

It also employed a standardised interview schedule alongwith a five point scale of personal self-estimation called the "Self Education Scale".

These tests were administered to a group of sixty entrepreneurs who met the following criteria :

(i) they had been successful in the sense that they had started business where there was none before,

(ii) they employed at least 8 persons, and

(iii) they had been in business for at least 5 years.

The results of the study showed that as compared to general population, entrepreneurs rated higher on scales reflecting need for

---

* "The Displaced, Uncomfortable Entrepreneur", *Psychology Today,* Nov. 1975.

** "Characteristics of Successful Entrepreneurs" in *Entrepreneurship & Venture Management*, Clifford M. Baumback and Joseph R. Maneuso (eds), Prentice Hall, Engelwood Cliffs, N.J. 1975, pp. 11-21.

achievement, independence and effectiveness of their leadership. They were low on scales reflecting need for support by others.

QUALITIES (OR QUALIFICATIONS) OF AN ENTREPRENEUR

1. **Mental Ability**: It consists of : (a) overall intelligence, (b) creative thinking, i.e., the ability to adapt to various situations, (c) analytical ability, i.e., ability to systematically analyze the business problems.
2. **Human Relations Ability :** It is demonstrated by emotional stability, skill in interpersonal relations, sociability, tactfulness, empathy (to put oneself in other's place).
3. **Communication Ability**, i.e., skill in conveying information to others so that understanding is created.
4. **Technical Knowledge**, i.e., expertise in such areas as personal selling techniques, operating a complex piece of equipment, analysis and interpretation of financial records etc.
5. **Decision-Making Ability**, i.e., skill in selecting satisfactory course of action from among various alternatives.
6. **Conceptual Ability**, i.e., the ability to comprehend the organisational structure and how each unit fits into the whole. It enables him to recognise opportunities.

MOTIVATIONAL FACTORS FACILITATING THE EMERGENCE OF ENTREPRENEUR

Some of the theories which have attempted to highlight the factors behind the emergence of entrepreneur are described below :

1. NEED ACHIEVEMENT THEORY BY MCCLELLAND

David McClelland developed a theory in 1960 to explain the psychological roots of entrepreneurship. According to him, entrepreneurs are actuated by a high need for achievement. These people are distinctive in several ways. They like to take risk though only a reasonable one. They are highly motivated by challenging and competitive work situations. Thus they (a) take responsibility for solving problems, (b) set moderately difficult goals, and (c) get inspiration from feedback about their progress. Their three-fold needs are :

(i) need for achievement—to excel, to strive and to succeed.

(ii) need for affiliation—the desire to have close interpersonal relationships, and

(iii) need for power over others.

2. PSYCHO SOCIAL THEORIES

(A) Everett Hagen considers entrepreneur to be the product of social changes. Many a time, social changes may cause a loss in the status of certain social groups, e.g., Protestants in the eighteenth century Catholic France. There are five ways of responding to loss of status viz., retreatism, ritualism, innovation, reformism and rebellion. Of these, retreatism is the most important in promoting entrepreneurship. Initially, the people in these social groups may react in a confused way. Since law or social attitudes may prevent them from holding political office, the members of such privileged classes may seek outlets in business.

(B) **Cole** has stressed the significance of such motives as wealth, power, prestige, security etc. in the emergence of entrepreneurs.

On the basis of their motives, **Evans** has distinguished between three kinds of entrepreneurs, namely, 'managing entrepreneurs' whose chief goal is security, 'innovating entrepreneurs' who want excitement, and 'controlling entrepreneurs', i.e., these who want power.

Thomos Begley and David P. Boyd,* however, considered the following to be the most important motivating factors :

(a) high need-achievement orientation,
(b) opportunity to control their own lives (locus of control),
(c) existence of profitable business idea.

Vesper thinks that a would-be entrepreneur must also have access to capital and other production assets, personal contacts and enough of time.

Generally stated, the two major sets of factors affect the emergence of entrepreneur *viz.*, Economic and Non-Economic. Under the economic factors lie (a) the market incentives which present themselves in the form of new social needs, (b) the existence of sufficient stock of capital to finance new enterprises, and (c) the occurrence of institutions such as development banks so as to direct the capital to those who want to use it for entrepreneurial projects.

The Non-Economic Factors consist of : political and economic ideology, social norms and values, legal structure, and social mobility.

---

* 'Psychological Characteristics associated with Performance in Entrepreneurial Firms and Smaller Businesses', *Journal of Business Venturing* 2 (1987), pp. 79-83.

Role of Entrepreneurship (or Entrepreneur)

It may be noted that an entrepreneur is the combination of two skills *viz.*, "an idea person" and "a manager", He is either the orgianator of a new business venture or a manager who tries to improve the organisational effectiveness by initiating productive changes. His role consists of the ability to take up the factors of production and employ them in the production of new goods and services. He perceives opportunities which others donot see or donot care about. As rightly remarked by Jules Buckman, "basically, the entrepreneur sees a need and then brings together the manpower, materials and capital required to meet that need." Akio Morita [the President of Sony], for instance, adapted the company's products to create Walkman personal-stereo. Gulshan Kumar of T-Series skimmed the audio-cassette starved vast Indian market.

1. Introduction of change

An entrepreneur's role lies in introducing the following five broad types of changes :

(a) Initial launching, i.e., original production of goods.

(b) Subsequent expansion i.e. increase in quantity.

(c) Factor innovation, i.e., increase in the supply or productivity of factors mentioned below :

—Financial (procuring capital from a new source or in a new form).

—Labour (upgrading existing labour).

—Material (procuring old material from new source or use of new material).

(d) Production innovation, i.e., hanges in the production process.

(e) Market innovation comprising of changes in the size or composition of the market, e.g., production of new goods, change in the quality or cost of existing goods, discovery of new markets etc.

Essentially, the entrepreneur always searches for change, responds to it and exploits it as an opportunity.*

2. Increasing productivity

Entrepreneurship has a role in raising productivity. The keys to higher productivity are : (a) Research & Development, (b) investment

---

* Peter F Drucher, *Innovation and Entrepreneurship*, Harper & Row, N.Y. (1986), pp. 27-28.

in plant and machinery & human resources, (c) resource allocation from areas of average to above average rate of remuneration of capital and labour, and (d) realization of internal and external economies of scale.

3. Innovation

Entrepreneurship plays a significant role in promoting innovative technologies, products and services. Invention of zipper, titanium, operation of spinning jenny from foot to steam engine, invention of power loom etc., owe to the spirit of entrepreneurship.

Kinds of Entrepreneurs*

1. Innovating Entrepreneurs

He is one who introduces something new into the economy or employs a new technique of production, opens a new market, exploits a new source of raw material and reorganises the whole enterprise. Generally aggressive in experimenting, they are typical of developed countries.

2. Imitating Entrepreneurs

They lap up the innovations originated by innovating entrepreneurs. They are suited to developing countries which are constrained to take up expensive research. Benefits enjoyed by them are, however, the same as those by original innovators. Developing countries need them on account of their capacity to transform the system with limited sources.

3. Fabian Entrepreneurs

They are very catious and skeptical in adopting and implementing any change. They are lazy and shy and lack the will to adopt new methods. Their dealings are determined by custom, religion, tradition and past practices. Avoiding risk, they tend to follow their predecessors. They imitate change only when it becomes clear that they cannot survive without doing so.

4. Drone Entrepreneur

Inert and traditional, they are hurdles in economic development. They struggle to exist, not to grow.

Functions of Entrepreneurs

1. Determination of objectives of the enterprise.
2. Development of the organisation.
3. Securing adequate financial resources.
4. Requisition of efficient technological equipment and its

* Based on a classification by *Clarence* Dank

revision consonant with technical change.

5. Development of market and devising new products to meet anticipated consumer demand.
6. Maintenance of good relations with public autnorities and society at large.
7. Management of human relations.
8. Financial Management.
9. Production Management.

Barriers in the Path of Entrepreneurship

Vesper has listed 12 common barriers in the path of entrepreneurship. These are as follows :

1. Lack of viable concept
2. Lack of market knowledge
3. Lack of technical skills
4. Lack of seed capital
5. Lack of business know-how
6. Complacency (lack of motivation)
7. Social stigma attached to certain vocations
8. Job "Lockins", "Golden Handcuffs" or attachment with the job
9. Time Pressures, Distractor
10. Legal constraints
11. Monopoly-Protectionism
12. Inhibitions Relating to Patents

Some of these barriers are due to peculiar personality traits called 'personality quirks' of the would-be entrepreneurs that make them hard people to work with. Such people tend to distrust others, think themselves as victims of convention bound thinking. Since they wish to control others, they are unable to work effectively with others.

Environmental Conditioning of Entrepreneurs

N-ach depends primarily on the family environment in which an individual grows up. In specific, the following factors are responsible for conditioning of a growing child into becoming an entrepreneur.

(i) Training to attain 'independence and mastery'

Research suggests that children develop high n-Ach when required to meet reasonably high standards of achievement somewhere between the age of six to eight. High n-Ach is promoted when children are trained to take care of themselves and encouraged to develop competence in dealing with people. If pressure to be on their own comes too early, it hampers the growth of the child. This is generally the position in lower class families where the father tends to be authoritarian and compels children to be on their own and to add to family's finances.

(ii) **Supportive family climate**

High n-Ach is also promoted in a supportive family climate. Family encourages children in their efforts. The parents set high but attainable standards of performance. These standards are set covertly without making issue of them. Parents are neither overly protective nor too indulgent. There is general non-interference from parents and father is non-authoritarian. Such type of climate is generally found in middle-class families which supply substantial number of entrepreneurs.

Thus entrepreneurs, by and large, emerge from middle class. Brought up in a supportive family climate, they can gain mastery over their environment and achieve independence at a natural pace.

Entrepreneurship Development (Factors in Failure or Success)

Many of the barriers to entrepreneurship can be overcome through a programme of training and continuing education for the potential and existing entrepreneurs. It will help build up a culture which will encourage the entry of only the deserving entrepreneurs. It will minimise avoidable entrepreneurial wastages or failures besides creating a healthy industry structure on the basis of competence and contribution. Below are discussed the different facets of an EDP.

1. **McClelland's Techniques for testing and identifying Entrepreneurial Characteristics**

In his theoretical exposition, McClelland has described the following to be the characteristics of a high n-Ach entrepreneur :

(a) Innovative ability (continuous creative ability to search for new opportunities)
(b) Ability to deal with unpredictable and unstructured, i.e., to build structure from an amorphous situation
(c) Desire to accomplish
(d) Realism, i.e., setting challenging but practicable goals
(e) Goal, oriented leadership
(f) Objectivity, i.e., pragmatic and rational selection of the course of action
(g) Individualism and self-accountability

(h) Adaptability and flexibility in the wake of changed circumstances

(i) Organisational and administrative ability, i.e., the ability to spot and respect talent and assign responsibility according to a person's genius

There is no specific technique to measure n-Ach level of an individual. McClelland employed statistical technique capable of producing reliable results despite their susceptibility to influence by social environment in which these are administered. These tests involve a special version of Thematic Apperception Test (TAT) to discover the changes in motivation level following deliberate attempts to enhance subjects motivation. The testing procedure is as follows :

(i) The subjects are told that the tasks they are about to perform would indicate their level of intelligence and show how qualified they were to assume position of responsibility.

(ii) At the second stage, they are shown pictures of people-on-work, e.g., two well dressed executives discussing an architectural plan of some kind. Each picture is flashed on the screen for a few seconds.

(iii) The subjects are told to write a story on each picture within an allotted time of five minutes. The stories reflect what the subjects *fantacize* when motivated.

(iv) The stories are compared with stories written by 'control group' which has not been aroused by special conditioning.

It would be seen that the stories written by 'conditioned group' would contain more references to doing excellent job or meeting high standards of performance. It shows that it is possible to bring about a change in the direction of subject's thinking under deliberately created conditions.

Where a person is discovered to write stories containing achievement related statements under normal conditions (i.e., without prior conditioning), it demonstrates his concern for achievement. The number of incidents of this kind appearing in stories could be scored to indicate an individual's n-Ach. Research has shown that a person who scored high on n-Ach in normal conditions would perform better when motivated than those whose n-Ach scores were low under normal conditions. There has been found to be a positive linkage between high n-Ach and entrepreneurial qualities. The type of indication provided by different statements are described below :

(i) **Achievement imagery** (n-Ach) is reflected in the use of words such as *good* or *better* in relation to standards of excellence. Statements of unique accomplishment or of long-term goals such as desire for successful career etc., are the other indicators of achievement imagery.

(ii) **Indicators of affiliation**(n-Affil) consist in statements reflecting desire to establish, maintain or restore a positive emotional relationship with others. Statements that one person likes another or wants to be liked or takes action to mend a broken relationship or statements that describe affiliative activities, e.g., parties, get-together etc., are indicators of affiliation.

(iii) **Indicators of power imagery** (n-Pow) are statements showing emotional concern about getting or keeping control over the means of influencing others or describing an inter-personal relationship in which a superior has control over a subordinate.

2. **Games of Skill**

In these tests, the participants have an opportunity to control the outcome to some extent and can also adjust performance on the basis of feedback of results of their efforts. Some of such games are explained below :

(i) **Ring-toss game**

In this game, the participants are given the liberty to decide at what distance they will stand from a peg to toss rings over it. The distance may range from one to twenty feet and participants are given four rings in each try. In the first two tries, the testees throw the rings from a position they have chosen but at which they must stay for four tosses. That allows them to adjust their distance for the second try according to their performance. In third try, points are awarded for making two or more rings. The farther back the participants stand, higher the score. The fourth try reserves the point scoring. The closer the participants stand to the peg, the larger the point scored. The game discloses people with high 'n-Ach'. Such people prefer moderate risks wherever they can control results through their own efforts. In the third try, they stand at the middle distance where there is appreciable challenges, reasonable chance of success and moderately high pay-off. Even in the fourth trial, he will choose middle distance even though rewards are much less. He does not choose the distance closest to the peg since it does not offer any challenge.

(ii) Another game could be the one like throwing darts at a target which involves situations over which the participant has some control through the exercise of personal efforts and skill. High n-Ach people prefer such games because they donot wish to rely completely on chance.

(iii) Business games that reveal the characteristics of high n- Ach players, e.g., setting of high but attainable goals, use of feedback to adjust their performance, preference to strive for goals that depend on exertion of competence rather than chance, adaptability in the face of rapid change and ability to organise an ill-defined situation.

Development of N-ach Through an Educational Programme

McClelland *et al.* designed an educational programme for developing n-Ach in an individual*. The basic objective of these courses ranging from 10 days to 2 weeks is to help create a powerful belief in the individual that he has the ability to change through his own efforts. The training programme proceeds as follows :

(i) **Making the individual aware of his potential for acquisition of entrepreneurial characteristics**

This is done by requiring the individual to write specific plans for personal change in next two years. He is asked to write detailed specific plans for achieving the goals and the likely difficulties, the proposed ways to tackle them and their emotional responses at various points in the process. He is coached to be specific, realistic and practical in planning.

(ii) **Development of 'Achievement Syndrome'**

The individual is coached to think, talk, act and perceive like a n-Ach oriented person. He learns how to think in terms of standards of excellence, innovative accomplishment and setting long-term goals for achievement, adoption of moderate risks wherein they can depend on their own resources. Through constant use of language of achievement, participants' whole attitude is adjusted to see the world from an achieving point of view.

(iii) **Development of cognitive supports**

It consists in helping individual correlate the new ways of thinking with his earlier assumptions and perceptions. Three fields emphasised during this period include : (a) logical and scientific basis for associating

* David C McClelland, "Achievement Motivation can be Developed", *Harvard Business Review*, Nov.-Dec. 1965.

n-Ach with entrepreneurial success, (b) self-image, and (c) awareness of what is important to him in life.

The natural basis for connecting n-Ach with success in enterprise is presented through theory and data from research. The individual explores the self-concept in the individual and group sessions particularly by answering questions such as : Do I have high n-Ach ? If not, do I want to acquire high n-Ach ? Do I have more potent needs such as *n-Affil* or n-Pow that would make it difficult for one to try to develop n-Ach ? Answer to these enables him to decide whether or not he should embark upon entrepreneurial career.

(iv) **Providing emotional support to help the individual change himself**

The educational experience helps an individual to derive useful hints for improving his perception of self and to reinforce his self confidence. Consequently, the individual becomes able to realise his abilities and to express his major needs.

On the whole, the training helps individuals increase their degree of self-acceptance, confirmation and essentiality. In nutshell, it generates conditions for psychological success. These training programmes have been successfully administered to executives in large American & Mexican firms as well as to businessmen from Bombay and Kakinada (Andhra Pradesh). Except the Mexicans, it was well established in all other cases that those who took the course did better than those who did not.

Benefits of training in n-Ach

(i) Individuals are able to define their own goals.

(ii) Goals are related to the central needs, abilities and values of individuals.

(iii) Individual himself defines the path to these goals.

(iv) The realism in goal setting is demonstrated through achievement of goals.

To summarise, the n-Ach can be achieved in the following ways :

(a) by conditioning oneself to think like an achiever,

(b) by adopting the language of achievement and using it continuously,

(c) by planning for the future and assessing one's level of achievement through timely feedback of performance,

(d) by behaving in a confident and positive fashion.

Small Entrepreneurs in India—Salient Features

In a World Bank sponsored study by Little *etal.*[*] regarding the portrait of Small Entrepreneur in India, the following have been found to be their salient features :

1. **Single-owner entrepreneur** has been found to be the norm who, besides working with his own hands, combines the entrepreneurial functions of initiating the business, making subsequent investments, taking price-decisions, performance of managerial functions of overseeing production and organising sales. With the growth of the firm, two or three working partners could be involved but their presence does not imply that entrepreneurial functions are no longer with a single boss.

2. **Age pattern** has revealed the mean age of entrepreneurs to be 42 and of their enterprise's 12 years. The model entrepreneurial age was over 35 in four out of five industries. The age pattern compares well with that of the Korean entrepreneur (46 years). However, the age-pattern was considerably affected by migrants who had been found to have started at a later age. Migrants were in majority in machine tools, printing and soap manufacturing units.

3. **Educational level**, however, differs for different industries. About 60 per cent of the entrepreneurs in powerlooms and shoes had only a primary education or less. Most in machine tools manufacturing, metal casting and soap had a middle school or high school education while 30 per cent had college education or better. Higher level of education predominated in printing.

4. Turning to **social background,** caste played an important role in two industries, namely, powerloom and shoes. In these and also in soap, the entrepreneur's father was also a proprietor or partner, however small, in about half the cases. On the whole, the social background of small entrepreneur in India has been found to be extraordinarily diverse despite caste affiliations.

5. As to **initial size** and **investment,** most entrepreneurs started in a small way with less than 10 workers and between half to two thirds of the firms in the six industries (machine tools, printing, powerloom, shoes, soap and metal casting) had been started with investment of Rs. 50,000 except a few like metal castings, machine tools manufacturing and printing in which the amount invested was over Rs. 1 lakh.

---

* Little Ian M.D., Mazumdar, Dipak, Page John M (Jr.), *Small Manufacturing Enterprise—A Comparative Study of India and other Economies,* Oxford University Press, 1987 pp. 203-223.

Large initial size and education of the entrepreneur were strongly related. The initial funds came from own savings. But nearly one-fifth of the new firms in machine tools, printing and shoes had got bank loans. Bank loans did not figure in soap and powerlooms.

6. **Growth** was fast in case of those small firms that survived as compared to large firms.

7. **Profitability** (rate of surplus) is very high for shoes (128%), powerlooms (64%), and metal castings (57%). It is high for soap (37%) and normal for printing (29%) and machine tools (20%).

EXERCISE

Selection Test No. 1 **Time : 5 Minutes**

SENTENCE COMPLETION TEST

1. To succeed in life, one needs
   (a) money.
   (b) friends.
   (c) self-confidence.
   (d) good luck.
   (e) skill.
2. If there is a good demand, it requires................to earn in business.
   (a) proper instructions
   (b) quality product
   (c) intensive and good advertisements
   (d) capacity to store goods
   (e) own control over market
3. My main aim in running industry should be
   (a) to keep workers happy.
   (b) to earn good profit.
   (c) to improve quality of products.
   (d) to remain undisturbed by strikes and unrest.
   (e) to work hard.
4. To continue progress, it requires
   (a) hard work
   (b) new and progressive ideas
   (c) honesty and trustworthiness
   (d) education

(e) work systematically and thoughtfully.

5. He became a successful industrialist because
   (a) he knows how to maintain relations.
   (b) he has dependable friends and relatives.
   (c) he has vision and enterprising nature.
   (d) market fluctuations were favourable to him.
   (e) he is a gentleman and a good businessman.
6. He is successful because he
   (a) is highly educated.
   (b) knows value of time and makes plans accordingly.
   (c) has tact to get work done by others.
   (d) has large group of known people.
   (e) has sufficient assets/wealth.
7. He was unsuccessful because
   (a) his friends/acquaintances did not cooperate..
   (b) he did not learn from failures.
   (c) he is extravagant.
   (d) his planning was defective.
   (e) he was a good and gentle person.
8. I want to start a new business because
   (a) I should earn.
   (b) I would be popular in society.
   (c) I want to do something new.
   (d) the state wishes that we should do something.
   (e) I want to serve my caste and society.
9. Slow economic progress of our country is because of
   (a) faulty policies of the government.
   (b) lack of good facilities.
   (c) lack of our own venture.
   (d) labour unrest.
   (e) lack of increasing opportunities.
10. If I will face difficulties in my work then
    (a) I will leave it and will start a new work.
    (b) I will take advice of known and proper person.
    (c) I will think why it happened, and then work again with new enthusiasm.
    (d) I will blame my colleagues.
11. If business fails or there is a loss then
    (a) I shall try to pay less tax to reduce the loss.

(b) I will accept it with sportsmanship and try again.
(c) I will sell goods at cheaper price so that every-thing is sold out
(d) I will join with somebody in partnership
(e) I will try to find out who is responsible for the failure.

Scoring Manuals For Selection Test No. 1
Sentence Completion Test
[Score between 8-11 show high scoring
Score between 6-7 is average scoring
Below 6 is poor]

(1) To succeed in life, one needs : *Self-confidence* (*c*)
(2) If there is a good demand, it requires,
Quality product (*b*) to earn in business
(3) My main aim in running industry should be *to earn* good profit (*b*)
(4) To continue progress, it requires *new and progressive ideas* (*b*).
(5) He became successful industrialist because *he had vision and enterprising nature* (*b*)
(6) He was successful because he *knows value of time and makes plans accordingly* (*b*)
(7) He was unsuccessful because *he did not learn from failures* (*b*)
(8) I was to start new business because *I want to earn (a)*
(9) Slow economic progress of country is because of *lack of our own venture* (*c*)
(10) If I will face difficulties in my work, then *I will take advice of known and proper persons* (*b*)
(11) If business fails or there is loss then *I will accept it with sportsmanship and try again* (*b*).

CHAPTER III

ENTREPRENEURIAL MOTIVATION

This chapter has considered the literature which has endeavoured to unearth the basic urges that make a man an entrepreneur or conversely inhibit the development of entrepreneurial personality. It is significant to understand the socio-cultural environment or psychological factors that stimulate entrepreneurs.

Motivation as the Fountainhead of Entrepreneurship

Entrepreneurship is basically the product of motivation. Motivation is the inner drive that ignites behavioural action to satisfy needs. Each person's behaviour is shaped by a combination of factors such as physiological make-up, work experience, goals, cultural background, educational level etc. The behaviour is always goal directed, i.e., directed towards need-satisfaction. The need-satisfaction process is illustrated below:

Identification of individual needs → causes tension → leads to → motivation to act → Leads to satisfaction

(Leads to satisfaction → back to Identification of individual needs)

Figure 1. Need–Satisfaction Process

Motivation could be either *'positive'* or *'nagative'*. *Positive* motivation occurs when employees strive towards a goal. On the other hand, *negative* motivation arises from fear of failure/ frustration so that the individual is motivated to seek protection. The negative motivation may cause a worker to become apathetic, sabotage the system or leave the company.

MOTIVATION THEORIES

1. Maslow's Need Hierarchy Theory*

The theory suggests that an individual has a hierarchy of needs

* Maslow, Abraham *Motivation and Personality*, Harper & Row, N.Y. 1955.

which he considers to be important. The needs are spread in a sequence of priority so that the lower set of needs must first be satisfied to prompt an individual to work for the realisation of higher level needs. The theory has attempted to explain why employees behave the way they do. With the knowledge of the underlying needs, the management could build up an organizational environment that offers opportunities for higher needs satisfaction so that employees become favourably disposed towards work assignment. The need hierarchy consists of the following five-level needs :

1. Physiological; 2. Safety and security needs; 3. Social needs; 4. Ego; and 5. Self actualization.

The theory proceeds on the assumption that individual needs affect behaviour in accordance with two basic principles namely:

1. Deficit principle

It is a deprived need that motivates an individual. A satisfied need is not a motivator of behaviour.

2. Progressive principle

The needs exist in a strictly ordered hierarchy of prepotency. Only on the satisfaction of lower level needs, the next higher level becomes activated.

The various needs are discussed below:

1. Physiological needs are the basic maintenance needs of every individual. These consist of needs relating to food, shelter, clothing etc. Owner must provide a wage with which the employee could obtain resources to satisfy them. For the entrepreneur, the economic rewards are designed to satisfy his physiological needs.
2. Safety and security needs stem from the need to protect from harm. These can be satisfied in several different ways, e.g., provision of safety equipment or proper physical environment or through job security and pension schemes etc. Successful running of the enterprise is a source of safety for an entrepreneur.
3. Social needs

These needs spring from one's desire to interact with others. These include: (a) need to belong, (b) need to be accepted by co-workers, (c) need to give and receive attention. These are satisfied through affiliation to a group. It can be met through company picnics, cultural programmes or designing of jobs in such a way that facilitates interaction.

Establishment of an enterprise is geared to meet most of the social needs of an entrepreneur.

4. Ego Needs include: (a) self-esteem (self confidence), and (b) personal reputation (recognition). Desire to be independent is another ego need which can be met when employees have some control on how their work is performed. For an entrepreneur, it comes from recognition and appreciation of his work, elevation of status etc.
5. Self-actualization needs are the strongest impelling force for an entrepreneur. The establishment and successful running of an enterprise provides him opportunities of self-expression, achievement and growth.

2. **David McCelland's Acquired Needs Theory**

McClelland assumed that three types of needs are acquired over time and are the result of life experience. These needs are:

(i) Need for affiliation, i.e., the need to establish and maintain friendly and warm relations with others.

(ii) Need for power, i.e., the need to dominate and influence others or control the use of physical objects and actions of others.

(iii) Need for achievement, i.e., desire to accomplish something with their own efforts.

Although all the three needs are simultaneously acting on an individual yet one of these tends to be dominant. It may be mentioned that in an organisation, there could be different types of powers noted below:

(a) Legitimate power which results from the holding of a formal position.

(b) Coercive power which is based on the ability to apply sanctions, e.g., suspensions, discharge, dismissal etc.

(c) Rewarding power is the power to grant or withhold reward such as promotion or wage increase.

(d) Expert power is that which accrues to an individual because of specific knowledge or skill.

(e) Referent power is based on followers' admiration of and identification with the leader.

McClelland identified that achievement motivation is the strongest in the case of entrepreneurs. Characteristics of people with strong achievement needs are :

(i) Establishment of moderate, realistic and attainable goals and taking of calculated risk.

(ii) Preference for situations in which they can take personal responsibility for finding solution.

(iii) Need for concrete feedback on how well they are doing.

The need for achievement exists not merely for the sake of social recognition but for attaining personal accomplishment. To an entrepreneur, what is got lightly has little value and therefore not a motivating factor. An entrepreneur looks for tasks which offer reasonable challenge and involve hard work.

Motivation for starting Industries—the Indian experience*

In a field survey of motivational factors, a variety of responses were noted. These were :

1. Out of a sample of 264 small scale entrepreneurs, 98(37.12%) wanted to do something pioneering and innovative. To make a contribution to the development of a specific state, to introduce an entirely new product in the market, to place their home town on the industrial map of the country, to find an outlet for their creative urge, to make full and effective use of their technical and manufacturing skills and to provide employment to intelligent young men and women in the community were some of the motivating forces in respect of this group.

2. For another 74 (28.03%) entrepreneurs, the principal motivating factor was the desire to be free and independent. This group consisted of those who had earlier worked either as craftmen or sub-professionals/technologists or in managerial or administrative positions. These people wanted to have an independent venture of their own.

3. For 56 (21.21%) entrepreneurs, the main guiding force was the 'bright demand prospects' for the products, the manufacture whereof have been undertaken by them. Familiarity with the products, availability of surplus funds etc. were the other contributing factors.

4. 36 or 13.64% of the entrepreneurs were graduate engineers and had taken over a running concern. Some of the entrepreneurs had been encouraged due to the availability of job-orders from large units.

The exact position is *summed* up in the following table :

* Deolankar, Vivek, 'Entrepreneurship Development in India' in the book with the same title by Samiuddin (Ed.), Mittal Publications, Delhi (1989), pp.17-20.

Nature of Entrepreneurial Motivation for Starting Industries in India (1987)

S.No	Name of the State	Total Number of Sample Entrepreneurs in India	Nature of Motivation			
			Propriatary Concern	Partnership Concern	Cooperative Concern	Private Limited Company
1.	Maharashtra	88 (100)	30 (34.09)	26 (29.55)	20 (22.72)	12 (13.64)
2.	Andhra Pradesh	30 (100)	12 (40)	8 (26.67	6 (40)	4 (12.33)
3.	Karnatka and other States	146 (100)	56 (38.35)	40 (27.40)	30 (20.55)	20 (13.70)
	All Entrepeneurs	264 (100)	98 (37.12)	74 (28.03)	56 (21.21)	36 (13.64)

Note : Figures in parenthesis denote percentage of the total number of entrepreneurs in Col. No. 3
Source : Field Survey

A Quiz for Testing Entrepreneurial Motivation

The quiz is designed to determine your latent qualities. Read each question and respond by indicating 'T' for true or 'F' for false. Be completely honest. Time allotted is 10 minutes.

1. When faced with a problem, I always find a new way of overcoming it.
2. When a decision has to be made, I can make it easily even though I am not sure of the outcome.
3. I have a strong need for social interaction.
4. After learning how to do something right the first time, I don't change my approach.
5. I have a plan of where I want to be financially ten years from now.
6. When I am placed in a new situation at work, I quickly sort out what needs to be done.
7. I see potential problems as challenges.
8. Constantly having to deal with problems wears me down.
9. I revise my goals from time to time in the light of changing situations.
10. It is important for me to know that I have a dependable income.
11. When I am dealing with a problem, I tend to get struck easily.
12. If I were laid off, I know I could find some other source of income.
13. I thrive on the challenge of solving different problems.
14. I don't enjoy being directed by others.
15. I take courses on how to improve what I do.
16. Once I've met a challenge I am usually satisfied, and don't need to look for other projects.
17. I normally start off my day with a list of things to do.
18. I don't enjoy working alone .
19. The fear of losing my job causes me great apprehension.
20. I am not good at dealing with a multitude of problems at the same time.
21. I consider myself to be very resourceful in tight situations.
22. I usually have a plan of action before starting a project.
23. I am good at finding creative ways of solving problems.
24. The idea of being my own boss appeals to me.
25. At times I don't feel completely comfortable with myself.

Scoring Key

1.	Continuous Goal Setting -	5 (T)	9 (T)	16 (T)	17 (T)	22 (T)
2.	Persistent Problem Solving-	7 (T)	8 (F)	13 (T)	20 (F)	23 (T)
3.	Tolerance of Uncertainty-	2 (T)	6 (T)	10 (F)	12 (T)	19 (F)
4.	Desire for Independence-	3 (F)	14 (F)	18 (F)	24 (T)	25 (F)
5.	Innovation	1 (T)	4 (F)	11 (F)	15 (T)	21 (T)

CHAPTER IV

THE START-UP PROCESS OF A SMALL ENTERPRISE

The challenges of starting a new enterprise from the satge of its conception till actual functioning are indeed stupendous and multidimensional as indeed its contribution to the society in various forms such as employment, economic growth, balanced development, equitable distribution of wealth etc. Success is a slave to those who not only correctly percieve the nature and intensity of problems that they are likely to encounter but also plan appropriate remedial actions. This chapter is devoted to studying the following:

(I) The Identification of New Venture Opportunities, and

(II) The Field Problems of starting a new enterprise.

1. Identification of New Venture Opportunities

In the search for new ventures, entrepreneurs explore both (a) external and (b) internal resources. The external sources include:-

(i) Newspapers, trade journals, professional journals etc. which tell about trends in fashions, customs and other social areas.

(ii) Professional magazines catering to particular interests such as electronics, computers, oils and vanaspati etc.

(iii) Trade fairs and exhibitions displaying new products and services.

(iv) Government agencies.

(v) Ideas put forth by others.

Internal resources basically consist of the storehouse of knowledge build up by an individual over the years. An entrepreneur draws upon it and undertakes the following exercise:–

(a) Analysis of concepts in the light of existing problems and their capacity to solve them.

(b) Search of memory to find similarities and elements related to the concept and its problems.

(c) Recombining the elements found in new and useful ways.

Steps in Innovative Process

1. Comprehension of a need

Innovation follows from clear pereption of a need that should be fulfilled. A number of products or services have seen developed from such a perception. These range from xerographic copying machine, credit card, instant photography etc.

2. Collection of data and definition of concept.
3. Outlining the problem.
4. Searching memory for similarities that seem related to the concept and its problem.
5. Evaluating the possibility to combine similarities and related ideas.
6. Reaching tentative solution.
7. Critical scrutiny of solution.
8. Practical implementation.

Sources of Ideas for New Products

1. **Necessity**

   It involves the identification of potential customer needs and then tailoring the product or service to meet them.

2. Hobbies/Personal Interest

For instance, an aircraft designer working for a large company developed a catamaran for his own pleasure. Later he was asked to build a similar catamaran for a friend.Gradually, it took the shape of a successful business.

3. Watching trends in fashions and customs

Alert observers of the fashion scene can capitalise the opportunity thrown by the change of fashion. Demand for handcarfted jewellery, fast foods etc. have made many professionals in these fields.

4. Observing other's deficiencies

It helps improve performance or add desirable features, For instance, development of a key that would identify the person and open the door only to him. It would sound an alarm if the door is forced open or in case an improperly coded key is used.

5. Gap filling

Business opportunities may be found to exist in reply to the question, why is not there a gadget for doing this ? Several products have been developed to fill up a felt gap. For instance, the difficulty of cleaning an old paint brush has led to the development of disposable paint brush with plastic handle into which a polyurethane tapered brush can be inserted and later an discarded after finishing painting.

6. Novel use of known products

With ingenuity, it is possible to think of new uses of existing products e.g. use of flyash-a common effluent in thermal plants, to make bricks and light-weight concrete etc. Similarly, rice hask (a common product in rice sheller) could be used for making hard board.

7. Ancillarisation

An entrepreneurially oriented brain can conceive new ideas or think of improvements in products with which they are familiar: As a consequence, a unit ancillary of an existing industry could be started.

Pitfalls in Selecting New Venture Opportunities

(i) Lack of objectivity

Some entrepreneurs get so obsessed with their idea that they overlook the need to scrutinise its feasbility. No wonder such projects end up as failures.

(ii) Market myopia

A short sighted approach of concentrating on production rather than on marketability could lead to avoidable disaster. An entrepreneur may fail to properly assess the market acceptability of his product. He may not appreciate that no product can become instantaneously profitable or could have an endurable success. Selection of the right time for introducing the product is important for its success. Action taken too soon or too late results in failure.

(iii) Inadequate understanding of technical aspects

Technical difficulties involved in the production of a product is a time consuming and thorough job. Inexperience in this area could prove quite costly and swamp a budding enterprise.

(iv) Improper estimation of financial requirements

Sometimes in their enthusiasm to initiate an enterprise or due to pre occupation with other details, entrepreneurs overlook the financial details. Later it could be the cause of either over capitalisation or under capitalisation.

(v) Lack of product differentiation

To capture the market, the product should have distinctive characteristics in terms of design, utility and other features. Assured superior performance over other products is essential to provide it a competitive edge. Pricing is no problem in the case of such products. Products differentiation is almost essential so that the potential customer could recognise the product merely by looking at it.

(vi) Overlooking legal issues

A shrewd entrepreneur should be alive to meeting the various legal requirements. For instance, workers should be provided with legitimate legal dues, consumers be provided with reliable and safe products; copyright, trade marke etc. should be observed.

Evaluation of New Venture Opportunities

A crucial task in starting a new business enterprise is the systematic analysis and evaluation of its feasibility and long term profitability. Since a number of variables enter the calculations, the exercise is quite a cumbersome one, A U S study relating to the reasons for failure of new ventures has found that most of the factors underlying failure lie within the control of entrepreneur.*

Following have been listed as the reasons for failure of new ventures :

(i) Inadequate market knowledge regarding demand potential, the present and future size of the market, the market share, appropriate methods of distribution.

(ii) Faulty product performance due to hastily taken shortcuts in production, development, quality control etc.

(iii) Ineffective marketing and sales efforts.

(iv) Inadequate awareness of competitors' reactions e.g. price cuts, special discounts.

(v) Rapid product obsolescence due to rapid technological advances in case of certain industries.

(vi) Poor timing of starting the new venture e.g. introducing the product before the market has sufficiently matured.

(vii) Undercapitalization, unforeseen operating expenses, excessive investments and related financial difficulties. Hence, there is the need to undertake a comprehensive feasibility study in the following five areas:

---

* "Why New Products fail". *The Conference Board Record*, Oct.1964. Also John Argent. *Corporate Collapse: The Causes and Symptoms*, John Wiley and Sons, N.Y.(1976).

1. Technical Feasibility

It covers the following:-

(A) Identification of critical technical specifications comprising.

- (a) the functional design of the product,
- (b) adaptability to new customer demand,
- (c) durability,
- (d) reliability of performance,
- (e) safety,
- (f) reasonable utility i.e. aceptable leved of obsolescence.,
- (g) standardization (i.e. elimination of unnecessary variety).

(B) Examination of product quality-cost relationship

In making this investigation, the entrepreneur must understand that there are trade offs between technical excellence and associated cost i.e. a positive relationship exists between technical quality and costs. The following figure shows that the criterion for deciding on the optimum degree of quality of a product is the maximisation of cost effectneness. It is possible

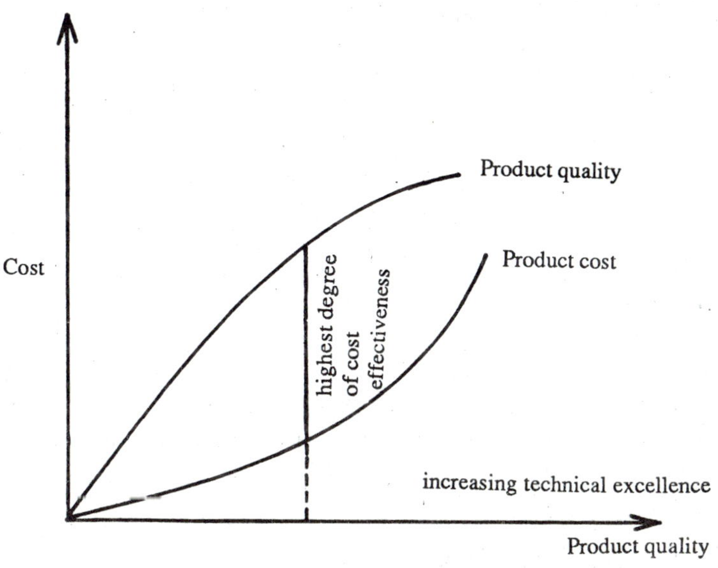

Fig. 2. Relationship between Product Quality and Product Cost

through an increase in the technical excellence of a product to that level at which marginal product quality equals margial cost. This level is reached where slope of product quality and product cost curves are equal.

Quality enhancement should not be carried beyond a particular point because it would cause cost increase and lead to decrease in total market demand (except where the product has a snob value). Thus entrepreneur should avoid unnecessary gold plating when market situation does not justify it.

(C) Product Testing which includes:—

(a) Engineering studies relating to machines, tools instruments work flow etc.

(b) Product development through blueprint, models, prototypes.

(c) Product testing through laboratory testing and field testing.

2. Market Feasibility

The following process may be adopted to assess the market opportunities of a product:

(i) Identifying the market potential*

It involves an estimation of both current demand for the product and projection of future market trends The prospective entre preneur will do well to identify (a) specific end userrs, (b) major market segments, and (c) potential volume of purchases within each market segment Some statistical yardstick may be of quite help in accomplishing this work. To illustrate, a potential manufacturer of helmets may find out the annual production of two wheelers, percentage of helmet users and proportion of demand already met.

(ii) Estimating Cost-volume Relationship to ascertain how various price levels may affect total sales volume

The price must reflect the value of the product. The entrepreneur may not adopt a uniform price structure to take care of the sensitvity of buyer to price changes. The cost-volume analysis would also facilitate the determination of appropriate economies of scales i.e. optimuim size of enterprise which has lowest average per unit cost of production and distribution.

(iii) Sources of market information

Relevant data for market analysis can be gathered from two main sources viz (a) primary sources such as interviews, mailed questionnaire, survey etc, and (b) secondary sources like government agencies, trade

---

* For detailed literature see, Pessemier, Edgah A, *New Product Decision : An Analytical Approach*, McGraw Hill, N.Y. (1966.)

assciatios, chambers of commerce etc. Whereas the former is costly, the latter may not meet the specific requirements of the entrepreneur.

The following kind of data matrix may be quite helpful:

(a) Data relating to general economic trends as revealed by various indicators such as new orders, house activity, inventories, consumer spending.

(b) Market data relating to demand pattern, seasonal variation etc.

(c) Pricing data i.e. range of prices for same, complementary and substitute products; base price; discount structure etc.

(d) Channels of distribution -both wholesale and retail.

(e) Data relating to competitors.

To obtain this data, the entrepreneur may either conduct his own survey or approach a consultant.

(iv) Market testing

It is an important method of establishing the overall feasibility of a new venture, Significanta market testing methods include: (a) displaying the product at trade fairs, (b) test marketing to analyse the receptivity of product, and (c) sample sales. A market test can provide following informaton:

(a) likely sales volume and profitability,

(b) sales volume at different price levels,

(c) soundness of chosen market strategy,

(d) unknown weaknesses that need attention .

The drawbacks of this technigure are: delay in implementation,premature exposure to competitors and expensiveness.

3. Financial Feasibility

It covers the following :

(A) Determination of total financial requirements

It can be done by preparing a financial statement in the following way :

FINANCIAL REQUIREMENT STATEMENT

	Period 1	Period 2
Initial Expenses		
Expenses in product development	—	—
Legal expenses	—	—

Product testing expenditure	—	—
Market and technical feasibility expenditure	—	—
Miscellaneous expenses	—	—
Fixed Investments		
Building	—	—
Equipment and machinery		
Patents	—	—
Other equipments	—	—
Operational expenditure		
Material	—	—
Wages	—	—
Sales promotion, distribution	—	—
Rent, Interest, Insurance, Taxes	—	—
Contingency		
TOTAL		

In making the above estimation, provision must be made for cost escalation that is inevitable due to price changes. Besides, appropriate sales forecasts should also be made to have a clear picture of expenditure. The projection could be weekly or monthly.

(B) Financial resources and other costs

Financial resources could be categorised on the basis of periodicity into :

(i) **Short term resources** i.e. those payable within one year. Trade credit supplies, short term loans from banks or other lending institutions, sale of account receivables etc. belong to this category.

(ii) **Term loans** 'Intermediate term loan's are those available for one to three (sometimes five) years. It includes term loans from banks, lease finance, financial assistance from institutions etc.

Long term loans are those from banks, equity capital and reinvestment of earings.

While considering different sources, it is better to consider specific costs as well as advantages and disadvantages of each. It would be appropriate to compute weighted average cost of the funds as illustruted below :-

1 Method of Finance	2 Proportion (assumed)	3 Cost (assumed)	4 Weighted Cost [2× 3]
Short term debt	20	7%	1.40
Intermediate term debt	10	8%	0.80

Long term debt	20	9%	1.80
Equity	20	10	5.00
	Weighted average cost of capital		9.00

On the basis of average cost of capital, it is possible to ascertain whether there is positive net present value when anticipated cash flow are discounted at average rate of cost of capital.

(C) Cash flow analysis

If the projected sales, associated financial requirements and avai able financial resources are known, the anticipated cash flow can easily determined.

Cash Flow (Projected)

Cash Flow and Financial transaction	Period 1	Period 2
1. **Cash outflow**		
Initial Expenses		
Fixed Investment		
Operating expenses		
Total cash outflow		
2. **Cash inflow**		
Cash sales		
Account Receivables		
Total operating inflow		
3. Net cash flow (2–1)		
4. Desired minimum cash balance		
5. Total amount of funds required [3 (if negative + 4)]		

Sources of Funds

• Short term :	
Net trade credit	—
Commercial loans	—
• Intermediate term loans	—
• Long term loans	—
• Equity	—
Total Financing	

(D). Anticipated Return on Investment

Financial feasibility is adjudged on the basis of satisfactory yield on investment. It can be calculated by relating the average earnings expected over a given period to either the total amount of investment or net worth of the organization (Return on equity). Both are compared with potential yield from alternative investment opportunities to ascertain the acceptability or otherwise of a new venture.

4. Assessment of personnel requirements and organisational capabilities.

Human beings provide the motive force to an enterprise. A proper evaluation of total personnel requirements is an integral part of feasiability analysis. For this purpose, it is necessary to consider the available skills and talents consonant with the organization structure. Then an inventory must be made of the skills needed for effective implementation of new venture. The steps involved in undertaking the exercise relating to determination of personnel requirements and designing the initial organizational structure are described below :—

(a) Ascertaining the anticipated workflow and the various activities (called activity analysis). At this stage, the total range of activities and level of skills are identified.

(b) Grouping the activities into set of tasks that individuals can handle effectively.

(c) Categorisation of various tasks to form the basis of structure of organization.

(d) Determination of inter relationships between different positions and designing of organisational hierarchy.

5. Analysis of competition

In order to ensure survival and growth of the enterprise, it is essential to make competition analysis. Generally, every organisation has to face two types of competition viz., :—

(a) Direct competition from similar products and

(b) Indirect competition from substitutes.

Competition analysis must seek to identify potential competitors, the strategies adopted by them and their impact on proposed enterprise, specific advantages enjoyed by the proposed venture and formulation of strategy in consonance with these advantages. The entrepreneur must guard against being content with neutralizing competitors' strategic advantages. The aim should be to have superior strategies at least durng the initial stages.

Cometitive Analysis Strength*

---

* Adapted from Schollhamer Hans and Kuriloff, Arthur H. *Entrepreneurship and Small Business Managment*, John wiley and sons, N.Y. (1979) p. 84.

Compelitive Strength
[Mesured on scale of 5 (high) to 1 (low)

	Patents	Technology	Location	Services	Price	Conce-sslons
New Venture						
Direct Competion						
Competitor A						
Competitor B						
Indirect Competition						
Competitor X						
Competitor Y						

II. Field Problems of Starting A New Enterprise

Identification of a venture after a thorough analysis of the five major aspects described earlier should not be regarded as the end of all problems. Rather the real problems begin to confront the entrepreneur only now. These problems have been summarised in the following paragraphs :—

(1) **Pre-operator problems**

(a) Problem of selecting an appropriate form of business organisation.

(b) Problems related with the acquisition of basic facilities such as sources of raw materials, power, transport etc.

(2) **Problems during the construction phase.**

These would be connected with :—

(i) acquisition of land;

(ii) construction of building and other aspect of civil works;

(iii) acquisition of machinery and its installation;

(iv) preliminary work about the sources of supply of raw materials, labour and managerial inputs;

(v) Prospecting about marketing;

(vi) preliminary work regarding sources of working capital;

(vii) coordination problem connected with the acquisition of different kinds of assets or completion of jobs;

Unless care is taken to ensure proper sequencing of different activities, the project would have cost over-run and/or time over run. Herein some kind of PERT analysis could be quite helpful.

III. Post Operative Problems of A New Enterprise

Several problems are common to starting any enterprise-whether small or large. They need not always arise but an awareness regarding them could enable their timely avoidance or prevention. Below are given some of the post operative problems.

(i) Lack or absence of profits

(ii) Experience Factor :

(a) Unfamiliarity or lack of experience in product or services line.

(b) Lack of experience in management. There is a vast difference between being a machinist and being able to manage a machine shop.

(c) Overconcentration of experience e.g. focussing only on the area of interest say, sales, finance, production etc and neglecting others.

(d) Incompetence of management.

(iii) Sale Causes

(a) Weak competitive position;

(b) Lack of proper inventory control;

(c) Low sales volume;

(d) Poor location

(e) Decline in demand due to recessionary trends in the particular industry;

(f) Inappropriate marketing strategy;

(g) High production costs and consequent high pricing;

(iv) Expense Causes i.e. failure to control operating expenses that reduce profits and pose a threat to survival of the firm. For instance, borrowing too heavily may force business to close if debts can not be timely paid;

(v) Neglect Causes

Common cases of neglect are : poor health, laziness, family or marriage problems. Entrepreneurs need to establish priorities for themeselves relative to their involvement in the firm. They must concentrate on the objectives of the firm.

(vi) Capital Causes

(a) Low or over estimation of capital needs;

(b) Fund mismanagement;

(c) Cash losses;

(d) Poor debt collection or unfavourable credit terms.

(vii) Customer Causes : i. e. extension of credit on liberal terms.

(vii) Personnel Causes

(a) High rate of absenteeism &/or labour turnover;
(b) Unhealthy industrial relations;
(c) Frequent strikes and lockouts;
(d) Low productivity;
(e) Militant trade unions.

(xi) Natural calamities such as burglaries, earthquakes, fire etc.

(x) Government Regulations
(a) Difficulty of compliance due to excessive cost burden;
(b) Interference and dilatory tactics adopted by government authorities.

(xi) Unmindful expansion so that sufficient business is not generated to sustain expanded capacity.

(xii) Environmental Casues.
(a) Changes in government policy;
(b) Changes in social or political conditions;
(c) Inflationary pressures leading to increases in the input- cost.

(xiii) Production Causes
(a) Technological obsolescene;
(b) Low capacity utilization;
(c) Inability of labour to corectly understand technology;
(d) Non-availability of spares and replacements;
(e) Poor machinery maintenance.

Procedural Aspect of Starting A SSI In India

1. Pre-decision stage

Before embarking on starting a small enterprise, it would be worthwhile to take stock of all the pros and cons including an assessment of one's own aptitudes, propensity to take risk, organizational ability, family background, inherited and acquired skills, financial position, perception about policy environment, educational background, technical skills. This analysis must be done with utmost objectivity and ruthlessness.

2. Selection of the Industries

Having decided in favour of starting one's own business, decide about the line of business to be adopted. It would be guided by the factors mentioned in the preceding para besides the counselling provided by the consultant, the government policy, incentives, infrustructural facilities etc. Another connected issue would be the product selection. This could be done on the basis of comparative analysis of a few selected items with special reference to :—

(a) technical aspects of production,
(b) technology status and contemporary developments,
(c) availability of raw materials,
(d) size and structure of the market,
(e) competitive position,
(f) future demand pattern,
(g) life cycle of the product,
(h) availability of appropriate kind of labour,
(i) government controls, if any.

3. Preparation of the Project Report

Based on the above, the prospective entrepreneur has to prepare a project report. This is a specialist job and consultation of Director of Industries/Small Industries Service Institute may prove useful. These agencies provide guidance on preparing the project report, in the selection of items of manufacture, the incentives available to small units from different agencies.

The broad areas covered in a project reprot are summarised below:—

(I) **Organisational analysis** indicating the form of organisation, the experience, age, qualification pattern of entreporeneur(s) and their financial stake in the organisation, if any.

(II) **Technical analysis** contains a write up on the following :—

(a) the description of the product whose manufacturing is proposed to be taken up,
(b) the manufacturing process supported by flow charts etc.
(c) the plant size, production, schedule, date of installation and of commencement of actual production,
(d) detailed specification of the machinery and equipment, the name of the supplier(s), the quotation, delivery and payment schedules guarantees of performance ,
(e) location of plant and an assessment of its feasibility from the standpoint of raw material resources and markets, scope for future expansion.
(f) plant layout and estimation of cost of erection,
(g) raw materials and utilities required and arrangements for

disposal of effluents,

(i) arrangements for pollution control,

(j) requirements and availability of labour-skilled and unskilled.

III **Financial analysis**

It would involve the making of various financial projections alongwith the assumptions regarding capacity utilisation, input costs, output obtained, inventories, production costs, distribution and administrative expenses. Enumerate the total project cost supported by a break-up, the sources of finance and the porject implementation time table. A good financial analysis must be supported by funds flow and cash flow statement, break- even analysis, return on equity calculations and repayments of loan time-schedule.

IV **Marketing analysis** basically covers an estimation of the demand for firm's products in terms of quantity, quality and value, and firm's specific share thereof. It spells out the impact of starting the enterprise on availability of goods, imports substitution/export potential, generation of employment, balance of payments position, ecology, support to other industries etc.

The appraisal of the project for the purpose of government's approval and financial support etc. depends on a consideration of all the aspects mentioned above. The project report must be supported by evidence of approval from various agencies.

4. Registration of Small Scale Industries

Fortunately, the establishment of small units in our country doesnot require any licence. However, registration of the unit with State Director of Industries and Small Industries Service Institute would be of considerable help in seeking financial assistance, obtaining of machinery on hire purchase basis from the National Small Industries Corporation, allocation of scarce imported raw materials, export promotion etc.

5. Factory site and Raw Materials

Several state governments have developed industrial estates in their respective states. These industrial estates have built up factory sheds as well as common facility services, workshops, electricity, power and water connection etc. Director of Industries is capable of helping in this regard. Machinery–both imported & indigenous cab be procured from for NSIC on hire purchase basis. Financial assistance is obtainable from State Financial Corporations or commercial banks. Non-ferrous materials are canalised thorough STC, and iron and steel through MMTC to the small units on the recommendation of the State Director of Industries.

Formal training in management techniques could enhance an entrepreneurial skills. The necessary theortical framework relating to management aspects is discussed elsewhere in this book.

Project Report Format :

ILLUSTRATIVE PROJECT REPORT OF AN EXISTING COMPANY XYZ OILS

I. Introduction

1.1 XYZ Oils Limited, an existing profit making Company, already owning 25 TPD Vanaspati Plant and 25 TPD Refinery besides two Solvent Extraction Plants of 200 TPD and 150 TPD Capacity and also a hydrogen gas plant for 50 Tons. The works are located at Hazi Rattan Link Road, Bhatinda, Punjab. Besides BCL is also running a 50 TPD Rice Mill and 50 TPD Oil Mill since long.

1.2 The company proposes to under take a modernisation cum expansion of its existing Vanaspati and Refinery units from 25 TPD to 50 TPD each so as to cakes to the overwhelming consumer demand for the company's products marketed under the brand name Rishi (for Vanaspati) and Murli (for Refined Oil). Moreover, the commissioning of new solvent plant will proivde ample oil production enabling the company to dispense with the need to remain dependent on the open market for its oil requirements.

1.3 The estimated cost of the envisaged expansion cum modernisation is Rupees 370 lakhs which is proposed to be financed through a public issue of equity.

1.4 The purpose of this report is to enable the company obtain CCI approval for raising resources of the envisaged magnitude from the capital market.

II. Brief Particulars of the Company

Name of the company	:	XYZ Oils Ltd.
Location of the project	:	
Registered Office and existing plant location	:	
Corporate office	:	

Date of incorporation	:	13-7-1988
Date of commencement of business	:	13-7-1988
Sector	:	Public Limited Company in the private sector

III. Promoters

The company was promoted in 1986 by Shri X alongwith his sons Shri Y and Shri Z. Brief information on the promoters is given in Annexure—I enclosed. Shri X aged 48 years, is a graduate with 20 years of industrial experience in the line of oil extraction. Shri Y, aged, 27 years is a Commerce Graduate and Shri Z, aged 25 years is Mechanical Engineer. The promoters are upto date in filing their income tax and wealth tax returns and there is no pending litigation involving the promoters and/or the company.

IV. Existing Operations

The company was established in 1986 for manufacturing Rice Bran Oil by setting up a Solvent Extraction Plant. Thereafter, the company underwent diversification/capacity expansion from time to time. By 1990, the company possessed the necessary wherewithal to extract oil directly from mustard seeds, cotton seeds and sunflower seeds. Presently, the company has an equity share capital of Rs. 1.50 Crores. During the year ended 31st March, 1991, XYZ earned a net profit after tax of Rs. 50.92 lakhs (cash accruals Rs. 79.50 lakhs) on a turnover of Rs. 3127.07 lakhs. The debt equityratio and the current ratio as on 31st March, 1991 stood at 1.98 : 1 and 1.34 : 1 respectively. The net worth of XYZ is Rs 150.26 lakhs comprising share capital of Rs. 45.50 lakhs and reserves of Rs. 106.76 lakhs. For the period ending 31st March, 1992 the net worth of the company is Rs. 219.22 lakhs based on the valuation done by M/s. ABC Heavy Engineering Pvt. Ltd., as shown in Annexure II, enclosed . As per the unaudited accounts for the year ended 31st March, 1992 XYZ is expected to earn a net profit after tax of Rs. 56.98 lakhs cash accruals Rs. 144.23 lakhs, on a turnover of Rs. 4006.67 lakhs. During the year 1991-92, XYZ has changed the nethod of charging depreciation from written down value (WDV) to straight line (SLM), due to which the company's net profit has increased by Rs. 18.15 lakhs. The products of the company which are marketed under the brand names, 'Maharaj' enjoy sufficient consumer patronage and the demand has always outstripped the supply. The installed capacity of vegetable and refined oil in the country is far lower than the existing demand. The board of directors of XYZ have recommended a dividend of 8% on its equity share capital for the year 1991-92. The board has also declared bonus in the ratio of 1 : 1 during the same period. A summary of the past working results and financial position of XYZ is given in Annexure—III, enclosed. The term debt profile of XYZ is given in Annexure—IV, enclosed. SIDC and PNB have both confirmed company's satisfactory delaings with them. XYZ has not committed any default in payment of its loan obligations to any financial institutions. A summary of the sources and application of funds of XYZ for the past two years is given in Annexure—V, enclosed. From a perusal of the same, it could be gathered that the funds generated have been used mainly for expansion and modernisation. At present the total number of employees of BCL is about 300.

4.1 Other group companies

ABC International Limited is engaged in the exports of extractions for which it has bagged exports awards.

V. Management and Organisation

XYZ is board managed company with Shri Y as the Managing Director. As per the Memorandum and Articles of Association, the board of directors of the company is to consist of not less than 3 and not more than 12 directors including institutional nominees. The present board of XYZ comprises of the following directors :

1. Shri X — Chairman
2. Shri Y — Managing Director
3. Shri Z — Director
4. Shri R — Director
5. Shri K — Executive Director
6. Shri A — Nominee of SIDC

Management of day-to-day operations is looked after by Shri Y who is assisted by competent & experienced professionals. The company has two principal divisions namely technical and commercial each headed by a director. The technical division is supervised by the General Manager. The managers of administrative, accounts, sales and purchase departments respectively report to the director (commercial). The proposed organisation chart for XYZ is given in Annexure - VI.

VI. Capital Structure

The authorised, issued/subscribed and paid up capital of XYZ as on 31st March, 1992 stands at Rs. 500 lakhs and Rs. 75 lakhs respectively. The distribution of share holding as on 31st March, 1992 is given in Annexure - 7 enclosed. The company proposes to raise Rs. 360 lakhs from the envisaged public issue.

VIII. Present Proposal

The comapny is proposing to undertake an expansion cum modernisation of its Vanaspati and Refinery divisions from the existing capacity of 25 TPD to 50 TPD each based on 3 shifts and 300 working days.

7.1 Location

The company has its work located at Road, for the last 6 years. This place is well connected with sources of raw material and market centres both by road and rail. The company has got sufficiently land for envisaged expansion. The present power connection is proposed to be enhanced.

7.2 Manufacturing process

The details of the manufacturing process alongwith the flow charts are given in Annexure - VIII enclosed.

7.3 Technical Arrangement/procurement of plan and machinery

The company is envisaging expansion of its existing vanaspati and refinery from 25 TPD to 50 TPD each by installing continuous deodoriser, continuous neutralisation section, Bleaching section, Thermo Fluid Boiler etc. To procured these equipments, XYZ had approached M/s. ABC Heavy Engineering Pvt. Ltd. who have already set up similar plants on turnkey basis and have recently commissioned 200 TPD Solvent Extraction Plant successfully. The major production is based on Mustard, Sunflower, Cottonseeds, Rice Bran and OIl Cakes. M/s. ABC Heavy Engineering Pvt. Ltd. have already supplied technical know-how for vanaspati and refinery to other manufacturers which are working satisfactorily. XYZ has chosen ABC for their proven expertise in the field. The details of the plant and equipments to be procured are provided in Annexure - IX.

7.4 Raw materials

Owing to the commissioning of company's new solvent extraction plant, the basic raw material namely edible oil, sunflower/cottonseed/mustard/rice bran oil etc. would be available internally. The increased demand shall be met within the present production capacity of the existing solvent extraction plants. Presently, XYZ is selling the oils to outsiders. With the implementation of envisaged expansion cum modernisation, the company would be come capable of making in house use of it present edible oil production.

7.5 Utilities

a. Power

XYZ has sufficient sanctioned power connection for meeting the existing requirements. As regards additional power requirements, the company would make application to SEB. An adequate provision has been in cost estimates towards this end.

b. Water

XYZ has got sufficient number of tubewells to meet the total requirements of the plant.

c. Fuel

Rice husk is used as fuel which is abundantly available internally and also from outside suppliers.

d. Effluent Disposal

The company has got NOC from the Pollution Board. The company presently has a water treatment system which will be upgraded alongwith the present plants and it will not require any major cost inputs.

e. Manpower requirements

The company has got the requisite number of competent persons to look after their respective fields. The detailed organisational structure is shown in Annexture - X, enclosed.

f. Schedule of implementation

The envisaged expansion cum modernisation is expected to the completed by March 1993.

VIII. Cost of Project

The details of the cost of project estimated at Rs. 370 lakhs are given in Annexure - XI enclosed. A summary thereof is given hereunder :

(Rs. in lakhs)

1.	Buildings	15.00
2.	Plant and machinery	115.00
3.	Thermal fluid boiler	10.00
4.	Power connection	05.00
5.	Silo for storage	15.00

6.	Civil works	15.00
7.	Public issue expenses	40.00
8.	Working capital margin	155.00
	Total	370.00

The cost of building is based on estimates submitted by machinery suppliers. The cost would be mainly towards laying down of foundation and building a shed for housing refinery. The cost of plant and machinery, thermal fluid boiler, Silo for storage and civil works are based on quotations given by M/s. ABC Provision of Rs. 40 lakhs has been made for meeting capital issue expenses. The margin money for working capital placed at Rs. 155.00 lakhs has been worked out on the basis of applicable inventory norms and margins stipulated by banks. The additional requirements of margin money, if any, would be met by XYZ from its internal accruals.

IX. Means of Financing

The entire cost of the project estimated Rs. 370 lakhs is proposed to be financed as follows :

- — Public issue of Rs. 300 lakhs alongwith a premium of Rs. 60 lakhs (calculated on the basis of a premium of Rs. 2 per share.)
- — The short fall in the premium amount, if any shall be met by the company from internal accruals.

X. Status of Government Approvals

Clearance of SEBI— To be obtained

NOC from State Pollution Control Board— Obtained

Sanction of power— To be obtained

XI. Marketing and Selling Arrangements

The products manufactured by the company are consumer items which are generally in short supply (see Annexure - XII). The company has got its depots in the states of Punjab, Haryana, Rajasthan and U.P. besides the Union Territory of Delhi.

XII. Profitability

Statement showing the projected cost of production and profitability and assumptions thereof for the 10 operating years for XYZ is given in Annexure XIII and XIV respectively. The projected production and profitability for XYZ as a whole, cash flow and balance sheet are given in Annexure - XV, XVI, and XVII respectively.

12.1 Important performance indicators

The important performance indicators for the optimum year of production viz........... for the company are given below :

(Rs. in lakhs)

Total sales/other income
Gross profit before interest
and depreciation
Net profit after tax
Gross profit to sales %
Net Profit to sales %
Cost of raw material to sales %
Capital employed to value of output
Return on capital employed
Breakeven (%)
Cash breakeven
Proposed dividend

CHAPTER V

STRUCTURAL ALTERNATIVES (FORMS OF ORGANISATION]

One of the foremost decision to be made by the entrepreneur is the one relating to legal structure of the enterprise. This structure is separate from organizational structure which is used to denote management roles and relationships depicted on the organizational chart. The choice of a particular form affects the rights, duties, obligations of owners as well as the tax incidence. The alternative forms of organisation are described herein. The main forms of ownerships organisation are :

(1) Sole Proprietorship
(2) Partnership
(3) Joint Stock Company
(4) Cooperative Society

Considerations in the Selection of a Particular form of Organisation

1. Ease of Formation

From the entrepreneur's point of view, the ideal form of organisation is one which can be brought into existence with the least difficulty. In other words, it must not involve much legal expense in formation and legal complexities.

2. Facility of raising required capital

There should be no difficulty in arranging the requisite amount of capital for the form of organisation chosen. In addition to convenience of raising capital, the entrepreneur must be assured of the safety of investment, fair return and transferability of investment.

3. Limited liability

The degree of risk of a business depends on its nature. The form of organisation will depend on the risk involved. For instance, the risk is the highest in sole-proprietary firm followed by a partnership firm. In case of a joint stock company, however, the liability is limited.

4. Relationship between ownership, control and management

The extent to which an entrepreneur will take interest in business depends on the extent of his control on management. However, sometimes close relationship between ownership and management may discourage adventure and enterprise. For instance, ownership, control and management are directly vested in the owner of a sole proprietory firm.

5. Flexibility

A good form if organisation is one which can adapt itself to changed circumstances. It should be capable of expansion or contraction depending on exigencies such a characteristic is found in sole proprietorships..

6. Stability and continuity

Unless the form of organization is capable of continued existence, it would be difficult to formulate any future plans for it with a degree of confidence. A joint stock company perfectly meets this test.

7. Scale of operation

Also impinges on the choice of a form of organisation. To illustrate, a departmental store is better organised as a joint stock company on account of complexity of its operations.

8. Retention of business secrets The form of organisation chosen should enable the entrepreneur to retain vital secrets. A sole proprietor is the sole repository of all the secrets of his business.

9. Government Regulation

Various forms of organisation have different degrees of government controls applicable to them. The entrepreneur should select that form which has minimum control. Of the various forms of ownership, joint stock company is subjected to the largest types of controls.

10. Lighter tax liability

Other things being equal, the ideal form of organisation is that which attracts the minimum amount of tax liability.

In practice, the choice of a form of organisation is made by balancing the following considerations.

(i) The type of business-whether trading, manufacturing, commercial.

(ii) Expected volume of business.

(iii) Size of business.
(iv) Degree of control over management.
(v) Extent to which entrepreneur can assume risk.
(vi) Life span of business.
(vii) Likely tax advantages.
(viii) Financial requirements.
(ix) Degree of government regulation

1. Sole Proprietorship

This is the oldest form of organisation and outnumbers all other forms. In it, the business is conducted by an individual who retains legal ownership of the entire business in his own name although employees may be hired. It requires least amount of documentation for its inception. Its degree of stability is rather precarious. The proprietor makes most of the business decisions. In the event of loss, the entire fortune of the proprietor can be jeopardized.

The sole proprietor is a person who carries on business exclusively by and for himself. He is the supreme judge of all matters pertaining to his business subject only to the general laws of land and to such special legislation as may affect his particular business. He not only introduces his own capital as well as skill and intelligence but is also solely responsible for the results of its operations.

Thus its salient features consist in :—

1. Single ownership
2. One man control
3. Undivided risk
4. Unlimited liability
5. No government regulation
6. No separate entity from its owner.

Merits of Sole Proprietorship

1. There is **ease of formation and dissolution.** Any person capable of contracting can set up such an organisation. Dissolution of business is equally easy provided creditor's' claims are satisfied.
2. There is a **direct relationship between efforts and rewards**. The entrepreneur has sufficient incentive to put forth his best in the management of the business.
3. Freedom from or a minimum of legal formalities.
4. There is **no problem of coordination** because the entrepreneur himself takes the decisions. On account of his personal **relationship**

with the employees, he can secure teamwork from them.

5. **Maintenance of secrecy** about business matters is another characteristic of this business which guards him from competitors.
6. **Promptness in decision-making** enables the entrepreneur to exploit opportunities as arise from time to time. The entrepreneur does not have to consult another persons in deciding his business affairs.
7. **Flexibility in management** set-up as per the changed circumstances give this enterprise an edge over other forms of organisation.
8. Due to his good personal resources, he may enjoy a **favourable credit standing** among suppliers and bankers etc.

Limitations of sole proprietorship arise from :—

1. **Limited financial resources** compel this size of the enterprise to remain perpetually small. It makes difficult for him to reap the advantages of economies of scale.
2. **Limited managerial skill** of the individual entrepreneur renders it difficult for him to handle modern complications.
3. **Unlimited liability of the owner** discourages expansion. In the event of loss, not only the business but private assets shall also be used to pay off creditors' claims.
4. **Uncertainty of continuance** because life of the firm is linked with that of the properietor. Even where the business passes to entrepreneur's successors, they may not be equally capable.

Thus, this form of organisation is suitable in the following cases :—

(a) Where the capital required is small and the risk is not heavy
(b) Where prompt decision making is essential
(c) Where customers require personal attention
(d) Where business is subject to changes in fashions and tastes.

Hence household and personel service concerns, retail shops, professional firms are suited to sole proprietorship.

Expansion of Business—Whether to Take a partner or Engage a Servant

On the expansion of business, the sole proprietor may have to choose between hiring a servant and taking a partner. The pros and cons of each alternative are given below :—

Merits of Engaging a servant

1. Maintenance of **freedom of decision-making.**
2. For the **performance of specialised tasks** i.e. where specialised

skill is necessary.

3. **Maintenance of control** is easy over a servant than a partner.
4. **Easy to discharge** in case of incompatibility of views between the proprietor and the servant.
5. No interference in managerial policies.
6. No claim of the employee on business profits so that the owner remains the sole-claimant thereof.

Demerits of engaging a servant

(i) Permanent expense.
(ii) No assistance in case of capital problem.
(iii) Lack of personal devotion.
(iv) No increase in goodwill.

Taking A Partner-Advantages

1. Incentive to work on account of claim on profits.
2. Contribution of capital.
3. Personal and joint responsibility.
4. No additional expenses.
5. Proper advice.

But it is difficult to remove a partner in case of conflict. Thus the decision will depend on specific requirements of business. Where capital is needed, take a partner. On the other hand, if the need is to have a specialist, engage an employee.

2. Partnershiip

Expansion of business calls for more capital, enhances the risk and needs managerial capabilities than an individual is capable of. A wealthy man may lack managerial skill and a qualified manager may suffer from shortage of capital. They can however join hands as partners and tide over their respective problem. Partnership has thus grown out of the limitations of sole proprietorship.

The formation and running of a partnership organisation is governed by the Indian Partnership Act, 1932. Section 4 of the Act defines partnership as, "the relation between persons who have agreed to share the profit of a business carried on by all or any of them acting for all."

Characteristics of Partnership

1. Association of two or more persons

There must at least be two persons who should join together as partners whether by means of an oral or written contract (called Partnership Deed). Both of them must be legally competent to enter into contracts.

2. Contractual relationship

Formation of partnership agreement requires that the persons joining as partners must be competent to contract under the relevant law. The partnership agreement brings about contractual relationship between the persons involved.

3. Existence of business

The purpose of forming a partnership firm must be to carry on a business or trade

4. Profit Motive

The object of the business must be to earn profit. If business is carried on for a charitable purpose, it would not be considered to be a partnership.

5. Mutual Agency

The partnership business must be carried on by all or any of the partners acting for all the other partners. In other words, each partner acts in a dual capacity i.e. both as a principal and an agent. Each partner is an agent of the other partners and can bind them by his acts while acting in the ordinary course of firm's business. Similarly, other partners can bind him by their acts.

6. Sharing of profit/losses

Sharing of profit/losses in an agreed proportion or in an equal proportion in the absence of an agreement.

7. Unlimited liability

Each partner has unlimited liability for firm's debts. In case of loss, not only his share of profits but also private assets become liable to discharge the claims of creditors. But the liability of partners is joint and several .

Minimum and Maximum Number of Partners

The Partnership Act has not stipulated any thing about the maximum number of partners although it has specified the minimum number of partners to be two. But section 10 of the Companies Act, 1956 has provided that in case the number of partners exceeds 20 in case of general business, and 10 partners in case of banking business, the association must be registered as a company or it would become an illegal association.

General Features of Partnership

1. Formation

There are no special problems regarding formation of partnership. There could be either a verbal or written agreement about this. In the latter case, the contract is called a Partnership Deed. It contains rights, duties and obligations of partners. But there is no compulsion as to registration of the firm. However, an unregistered firm suffers from certain disabilities. For instance, the partners of an unregistered firm or the firm itself cannot file a suit in a court of law to enforce their respective contractual rights. Consequently, the registration of the firms is considered essential.

2. Financing

The capital of the firm is contributed by the partners. Sometimes a partner may be admitted to partnership without requiring him to contribute any capital. It may be due to his special skill or goodwill. Moreover, the contributions of partners need not necessarily be in proportion to their profit sharing ratio. The contribution of excess capital by a partner may be given interest.

3. Control

The control of the firm's affairs vests in the partners collectively. Major decision are taken with the unanimous consent of all the partners. However, the sleeping (or dormant) category of partners do not participate in the firm's affairs though they may continue to share in the profits.

4. Management

Legally, each partner can bind the other partners by his acts done in the ordinary course of business. Similarly, each partner is bound by the acts of other partners. In practice, partners allocate specific areas of management between themselves. For instance, one may look after manufacturing, another purchases and the third marketing and so on.

5. Taxation

Tax is charged in the hands of the firm only.

Essentials of Ideal Partnership

1. Existence of **mutual understanding** between partners.
2. Manageable number of partners i.e. between 5 to 7.
3. Common approach to conducting partnership business. Contrasting and contradictory views may lead to sharp and irreconciliable differences.
4. Sincerity and good faith, each contributing his best.
5. Balancing of skills and talents so that there is no concentration of skills in any one area leading to problems in others.
6. Adequate long term capital.
7. Sufficiently long duration.
8. Partnership Deed containing rights and obligations.
9. Registration of partnerships to avoid subsequent difficulties.

Merits of Partnership

1. Ease of formation without much expenditure or legal complexities.
2. Large capital and managerial resources.
3. Facility of alteration in the business.
4. Balanced judgement due to participation by all in decision making.
5. Democratic organization due to involvement of all the partners.
6. Advantage of direct supervision.
7. Incentive for hard work.
8. Emphasis on cooperation.
9. Benefit of division of work.

Demerits of Partnership

1. Suspicion due to maintenance of secrecy about accounts.
2. Unlimited liability.
3. Uncertainly due to likelihood of dissolution in the event of a partner's insolvency, death, insanity or notice.
4. Mutual conflict due to divergence of views.
5. Possibility of loss from principal-agent relationship.
6. Liability of a partner even after dissolution of firm.

Implied Authority of A Partner

1. Sale and purchase of materials

2. Engaging servants on behalf of the firm.
3. Contracting and payment of loans.
4. Making, accepting, endorsing negotiable instruments in firm's name.
5. Issue of valid discharge to debtors.

   But as a partner, he can not do the following :–
   - (i) Opening a bank account with firm's money in one's own name.
   - (ii) Purchase of immovable property.
   - (iii) Withdraw a suit filed by the firm.
   - (iv) Enter into partnership with other firms on behalf of the firm.
   - (v) Submitting the firm's disputes to arbitration.
   - (vi) Transfer his rights as a partner to another.

Dissolution of Firm

1. Dissolution by agreement (Section 40)
2. Compulsory dissolution in the following circumstances :—
   - (a) If all but one partner are declared insolvent.
   - (b) If the business of the firm has become illegal (Section 41)
   - (c) On the expiry of he stipulated time for which the firm had been established.
   - (d) On the completion of the task for which firm had seen established.
   - (e) On death or insolvency of a partner.
   - (f) On notice of dissolution by a partner.
3. Dissolution by the court in following cases :—
   - (i) Lunacy of a partner
   - (ii) Permanent incapacity of a partner
   - (iii) Misconduct by a partner
   - (iv) Breach of agreement by a partner
   - (v) Where firm cannot be carried on except at a loss.
   - (vi) Where a partner is guilty of fraud.

3. Joint Stock Company

The joint stock company has emerged due to the limitations of earlier forms of organisation and the highly increased demands made by large scale industry.

Definition

Lord Justice Lindley has defined a company as "an association of many persons who contribute money or money's worth to a common stock and employ it in some common trade or business and who share the profit or loss arising therefrom. The common stock so contributed is denoted in money and is the capital of the company. The persons who contribute it or to whom it belongs, are members. The proportion of capital to which each member is entitled is his share. Shares are always transferable although the right ot transfer them is aften more or less restricted.''

Characteristic of a company are : (i) Separate legal existence, (ii) Artificial personality, (iii) Separation of ownership from management, (iv) Limited liability, (v) Perpetual succession irrespective of whatever happens to members, (vi) Common seal, (vii) Transferability of shares, (viii) Separate property, (ix) Capacity to sue and of being sued.

A careful consideration of these characteristics will show that a joint stock company has several advantages over partnership. Separate personality, limited liability and perpetual succession are the most important of these advantages.

Type of Companies

Of the various types of companies, the most suitable for a small business is the 'Private Limited Company''. It has the followig characteristics.

(i) The maximum number of its members is restricted to 50 (excluding the past and present employees).

(ii) It does not invite outside public to subscribe to its shares.

(iii) It restricts the right of transferability of its shares.

A private company enables the owner to keep the number of members within manageable limits, raise adequate finances, get specialised people and at the same time maintain his control on the management (due to non-transferability of shares). The continuity of the company is not affected by any adverse happening to the owner.

Closely Held Public Company

Where the business undergoes further expansion, the enterpreneur may find it advisable to change the private company to closely-held public company. A closely held public company resembles a private company. Its shareholding is restricted among members of owner's family, relatives or group of friends. It ensures the continuance of control over management in the owner-group's hands without having to lose the advantages of a joint stock company form of organisation. Subsequently, the company may approach the public for making a share issue if there arises a need to raise substantial amount of funds. In the forthcoming years, the joint stock company is expected to become a popular form of organisation with the small business too. After all, small is not that small as it is thought to be. The company form would be best suited to those lines of business activity which require huge capital outlay and maximum stability.

Merits of a comapny form of orgtanisation are noted below :—

1. Greater financial strength due to comparatively large number of members.
2. Considerable scope of expansion to reap the advantages of large scale organisation and production.
3. Transferability of ownership.
4. Limited liability.
5. Diffused risk.
6. Stability.
7. Tax Advantages

Brief Procedure of Incorporation.

1. Collecting the requisite number of persons i.e. 2 in case of private company and 7 in case of a public company. They shall subscribe their names to the Memorandum of Association and Articles of Association, if any.
2. Choosing a name for the company.
3. Preparing and filing the following documents with the Registrar of companies of the state where the registered office of the company is to be located accompanied with the requisite fees.
   (a) Memorandum of Association duly signed by subscribers.
   (b) Articles of Association, if any, duly signed by subscribers to the memorandum.
   (c) The agreement which the company proposes to enter into with any individual for appointment as managing director whole time director or manager.
   (d) A list of the directors who have agreed to become the first directors of the company and their written consent to act as directors and take up qualification shares (Sec. 266).
   (e) A declaration stating that all requirements of the Companies Act relating to registration have been complied with. Such declaration shall be signed by any of the following :—

(i) an advocate of the Supreme or High Court ; or
(ii) an attorney or pleader entitled to appear before a High Court, or
(iii) a secretary or chartered accountant in whole time practice in India who is engaged in the formation of the company, or
(iv) a person named in the Articles as a director, manager or secretary of the company.

Within 30 days of the date of incorporation, the company must notify to the Registrar the place of situation of its registered office.

The Registrar of Companies scrutinises the documents filed with him. If he is satisfied with the compliance of requirements, he retains the documents and issues a certificate of incorporation.

4. Cooperative Organisation

A cooperative orgainsation is essentially an association of persons who have joined together on a voluntary basis for the furtherance of their common economic interest. In India a cooperative society must be registered under the relevant Societies Registration Act. These are basically based on mutual help, democracy in functioning and service motive. Shares of a cooperative society are not transferable. It is not a popular form of orgainsation in the area of small business despite its suitability to small and medium scale enterprise. However, some cooperative organisations in Gujrat and Maharashtra have made a respectable headway and established themselves in the field of milk products, household articles etc. Indian Farmer's Fertilizer Cooperative is one of the biggest enterprises based on cooperation.

Organisation Structure in A Selected Number of States in India—A Survey

In a study by Vivek Deolankar* in 1987 on the basis of secondary data provided by Director of Industries and District Industries Centre from three states namely Maharashtra, Andhra Pradesh, Karnataka and some other states, the following conclusions were derived.

Of the total sample of 264 entrepreneurs, 158 (69.84%) were found to be proprietary concerns of single man ownership : the next popular form was partnership comprising of 106 entrepreneurs (i.e. 40.16 %). None was found to be organised as a cooperative society or a joint stock company. Thus the typical form of organisation has been the proprietary ownership.

Consider the following table :

* Samiuddin (ed.). **Entrepreneurship Development in India.** Mittal publications, Delhi (1989).

Break up of the Organisation Structure of Entrepreneurs in India (year 1987)

S.No	Name of the State	Total Number of Sample Entrepreneurs in India	Organisational Structure			
			Proprietory Concern	Partnership Concern	Cooperative Concern	Private Limited Company
1.	Maharashtra	88 (100)	52 (59.09)	36 (40.91)	nil	nil
2.	Andhra Pradesh	30 (100)	16 (53.33)	14 (46.67)	nil	nil
3.	Karnatka and other States	146 (100)	90 (61.64)	56 (38.36)	nil	nil
	All Entrepeneurs	264 (100)	158 (59.84)	106 (40.16)	nil	nil

Note : Figures in parenthesis denote percentage of relivail number of entrepreneurs to the total number of entrepreneurs in respect of the otate as shown in Column. 3.

Source : Field Survey

CHAPTER VI

CONCEPTUAL BACKGROUND OF SMALL INDUSTRY

The urge for rapid economic growth was natural after the attainment of political independence. In any programme of economic development, industrialisation occupies a central position because of the close relationship between the two. The choice however is not that easy : Difficulties crop up particularly when it comes to choosing between the small and large industries, and specially as regards the role of small enterprises in socio-economic development. Fortunately, the policy makers clearly recognised and laid emphasis on the development of the decentralised sector comprising of the cottage and village and small scale industries so that these could acquire sufficient velocity to become self supporting. Their development was to be integrated with that of the large scale industry. The government assumed the responsibility of establishing the basic, long- gestation, highly capital intensive industries. It included industries like iron and steel, heavy engineering. aluminimum, machine building, basic chemicals, cements etc. Their establishment was designed to provide essential inputs to other vital sectors of the economy including agriculture, power, trasnport etc. The government also undertook the development of basic industries which donot make heavy demands on scarce capital resources but generate increased employment opportunities and ensure diversificationof industries. As a consquence of these efforts, the number of SSI units in the country as on 1st May, 1990 stood at 1.7 millions accounting for 45 percent of the total industrial output and more than 30 percent of the the total exports.*

Reasons for the Significance of Smalll Sector

(i) Development of small industries facilitates the effective mobilisation of capital and labour resources.

(ii) They contribute towards better utlilisation of local resources and skills which might otherwise remain unutilised.

---

* The Hindustian Times, N. Delhi (12.5 1990)

(iii) Small industries are a means to carry industrialisation to rural areas and decentralisation of industries.

(iv) Small industries being labour oriented are capable of generrating more employment.

(v) Small industries help in raising standards of living of people in rural areas. They mobilise savings of people, provide employment and make available consumer goods. They raise capital income and consumption levels and also help in equitable distribution of income.

(vi) They are necessary to maintain and retain traditional skills and handicrafts.

(vii) Compared to large industrial establishments, small industries involve shorter gestation period and make lesser demands on scarce capital resources.

(viii) They help large and medium industries by meeting their requirements as well as through ancillarisation :

(ix) They are the only medium for diversification of rural economy and for peaceful and concurrent socio-economic development of all classes of people.

Various Forms of Small Scale Enterprises

Small enterprises can take a variety of forms as depicted below :—

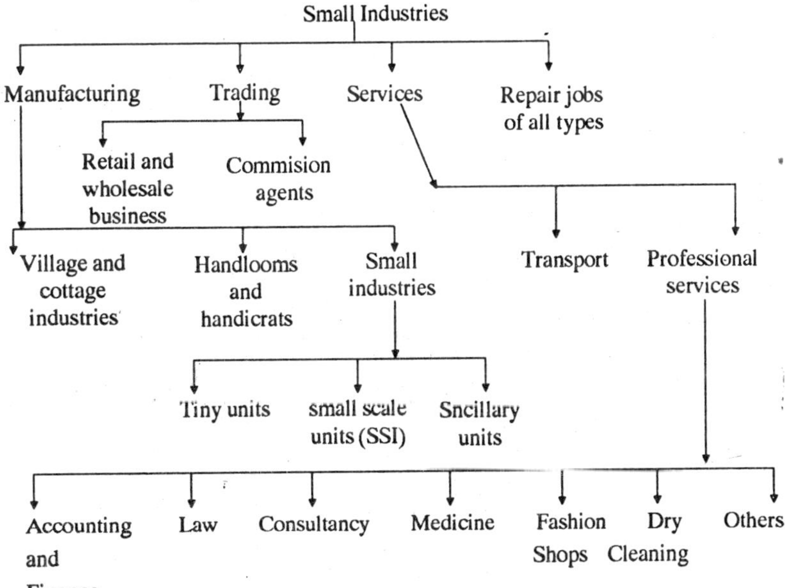

Concept of Small Industry

Indisputably, it is not easy to put small and large firms or industries into watertight compartments. But the confusion gets worse confounded because of the application of vastly different criteria for marking off a small business from a large business. The different criteria used in defining a small industrial unit can possibly be the following :

(i) Aggregate assets or fixed assets, or
(ii) Total investment in plant and machinery, or
(iii) Value of turnover/production, or
(iv) Number of persons employed, or
(v) A combination of the above.

The position in different countries as regards the criteria of defining small industry is summed up in the following table :—

	Criterion	Countries
1.	Investment (Plant & Machinery)	India, Indonesia
2.	Employment (not more than)	USA, UK (100)
3.	Investment and Employment	Japan, Korea, & Phillipines
4.	Per Capita Investment	Indonesia (not more $1000), India (village Industry-not more than Rs. 15,000)
5.	Turnover/Production	UK (commercial) ; China
6.	Employment and turn over	Korea (commerce)
7.	Investment and turn over	Malayasia (Small Business)

In India, the definition of small industry is based on investment in plant and machinery. Moreover, on the basis of location, small units are further categorised into 'Tiny' and 'Village Service Industries'.

It may be noted that the expression "small industry" is used mainly in relation to those units engaged primarily in manufacturing although a few servicing activity may also be included. It doesnot however include (as in Japan and U.K.) trading-whether wholesale or retail.

The scope of activities performed and the relevant terminology used in different countries are summarised in the following table:—

	Country	Terminology	Scope
1.	Japan	Small Enterprises	Manufacturing, Mining, Services, Trading (Wholesale & retail)
2.	Korea	Small Enterprises	Manufacturing, Repair and Maintenance
3.	USA/Canada	Small Business	Manufacturing, Service, Trading & Commerce

4.	UK	Small Firms	Manufacturing Trading, Construction, Mining Transport
5.	India	Small Industry	Manufacturing, Repair, & Services

From the above table, it becomes clear that the scope of activities included in the expression "small industry" is quite restrictive. Small scale industry need not include mere smoke stacked chimneys. Rather, the scope of this expression may be extended to a wide spectrum of activities particularly in the service sector such as beauty shops, restaurants, advertising activities, software packaging etc. Moreover with the extension of industrialisation to rural areas, it is not clear why the scope of small industry should not be made to include such activities as growing fingerlings in ponds, cultivation of mush-rooms, poultry, dairying etc. The better expression, therefore, is 'Small Enterprise" or "Small Business" as is the case with other countries.

Position in India

The small sector in India has been broadly categorised as follows :—

1. **Traditional Industries Sector** which is based on traditional skills.It may be sub-divided into the following :—

(A) Village Industries

These are the units situated primarily in rural areas. But the definition of village industry will depend on the agency which gives the composite loan for fixed and working capital.

The Khadi and Village Industries Commission has defined "Village Industries" as :

(i) units in settlements with population upto 10,000 producing goods/rendering services, with fixed capital investment of Rs. 15000,

(ii) any other non-manufacturing unit established for the sole purpose of providing, maintaining, assisting or servicing (including mother unit) or managing any village industry.

The village indusiries are engaged in producing consumer goods and other utilitarian products mainly by hand or with the help of small tools. Instances of such industries are potteries, leather products, handwoven textiles, silk materials and so on.

(B) Handicrafts

These are highly selective goods involving high skill and workmanship e.g. wood and ivory carving. metal work, carpet making, bidri work etc.

The "Village Industries" come under the jurisdiction of Khadi and Village Industries Commission (KVIC). On the other hand 'Handicraft' fall within the purview of the All India Handicrafts Board (ALHB).

2. Small Scale Industries Sector

This sector comprises of units using sophisticated technology as well as artisans' workshopos engaged in repairing implements, machinery, vehicles etc. This sector comes under the jurisdiction of All India Small Scale Industries Board consisting of :—

(i) Small Industries Development Organisation (SIDO) headed by the Development Commissioner Small Scale Industries. It is the main policy implementation agency.

(ii) Small Industries Service Institutes providing the external service.

The power looms also come under the category of small scale industries. Broad categorisation of small sector is as follwos :—

(i) Small Scale Industries.

(ii) Ancillary units.

(iii) Tiny Units and.

(iv) Service Establishments.

Definitions

1. Small Scale Industrial Undertaking (SSI)

A small scale industrial undertaking means :

Any industrial undertaking in which investment in plant and machinery-whether held on ownership terms or by lease or by hire purchase, does not exceed Rs. 60 Lakh.

However, unit which undertakes to export a minimum of 30 percent of its production latest by third year may be regarded as small scale industrial undertaking even if its investment in plant and machinery is upto Rs 75 lakhs.

2. Ancillary Industrial Undertaking

A unit is treated as an ancillary unit if it has the following features:—

(i) The investment in plant and machinery-whether held an ownership terms or by lease or by hire purchase does not exceed Rs. 75 lakhs.

(ii) The undertaking is engaged or proposes to engage in the manufacture or production of parts, components, sub-assemblies, tooling or intermediates or the rendering of services, or it supplics or renders or proposes to supply or render 30 percent of its production or services, as the case may be, to one or more industrial undertaking.

However it is clarified that if it is a subsidiary of or is controlled or owned by any other industrial undertaking, then it would not be deemed to be ancillary unit.

Units providing servicing facilities e.g. sand blasting, machining, pressure cleaning, grinding etc. are recognised as ancillaries. Moreover, one small industry can function as ancillary to another.

3. Tiny Units

It means all service-oriented enterprises having investment in plant machinery to the extent of Rs 5 lakhs and which are located or are going to be located in rural areas and towns with a maximum population of not exceeding 5 lakhs. These cover units such as laundry, zeroxing, repair and maintenance of consumer durables, car repair garages, hatcheries, poultry forms etc. Thus in the case of tiny unit i.e. service establishments, besides investment in plants and machinery, the criteria of location has also been introduced.

Consider the following table :—

	Category of unit.	Ceiling on investment in P & M (in Rs lakhs)
(a)	Small scale units	60
(b)	Export oriented small scale units (i.e. those undertaking to export 30 percent of their production by the third year)	75
2.	Ancillary Units	75
3.	Tiny units	5 (but these be located in rural areas or towns having population not exceeding 5 lakhs)

Method of Determining Investment in Plant and Machinery

While calculating the ceiling of investment in all the above mentioned unit i.e. small, ancillary and tiny, the following methodology shall be adopted.

1. The items to be included

The original price paid by the owner irrespective whether plant and machinery is new or second hand. In the case of imported machinery besides the cost, import duty, customs clearance charges, sales tax and shipping charges shall be included.

2. The items to be excluded :
   - (a) Cost of equipments such as tools, jigs, dies, moulds, spare parts for maintenance.
   - (b) Cost of installation of plant and machinery.
   - (c) Cost of R & D and pollution control equipments.
   - (d) In the case of imported machinery such charges as cost of transportation from port to site, demurrage, premium for import entitlements etc.
   - (e) Cost of generating set.
   - (f) Cost of transformers installed as per regulations of State Electricity Boards.
   - (g) Cost of gas producing plant.
   - (h) Bank and service charges paid to NSCI or to State Small Industries Corporation.

Women Entrepreneur Promoted Enterprises

The definition of small unit as recommended by National Commission on Women Entrepreneurs and adopted by All India Small Industries Board in December 1987 is as follows :—

"An enterprise owned and administered by a women entrepreneur having a minimum financial interest of 51 percent of share and giving at least 50 percent of the employment generated in the enterprise to women".

Role of Small Scale Industries in Economic Development

Small scale industries occupy a prominent place in the Indian economy due to the following factors

1. Employment generation

Being labour intensive, small industries have tremendous employment potential. They provide employment to agricultural labour which remains idle during certain months. A sum of Rs. one lakhs invested in fixed assets in a small industry provides employment to 16 persons which is about five-time that of the large establishment in which the same amount has been invested. It is responsible for 80 percent of the total employmenin the industrial sector. This sector has provided employment to 175 lakhs persons as at present.

2. Capital requirement

Annual Survey of Industries (1974-75) has revealed that fixed capital investment per employee in case of small industry was Rs. 3706 as compared to Rs. 27757 in a large industry. Moreover, gestation period of a small industry is quite small. Quick returns justify the promotion of this sector as capital is scarce in India. Although net output per worker in large industry is more than double than that of a small industry worker yet investment in large industry is seven times as high.

3. Share in Industrial Production

The small industries contribute more than 51 percent of the total industrial production. Over 5000 products are being manufactured in the small scale sector. These comprise consumption items as well as sophisticated item such as TVs, electronics, hearing aids etc.

4. Export Promotion

Small units have done a yeoman's service by creating demand for traditional items in foreign markets and thus have kept the traditional skills alive. They account for 30 percent of the total value of exports. During 1987-88, this sector exported item worth Rs. 3000 crores. It constituted 91 percent of the non-traditional exports. Items exclusively exported by this sector include: sports goods, processed tobacco, marine products, leather goods etc.

5. Dispersal of Industries

Small industries are an effective instrument for the development of rural and semi-urban areas. District Industries Centres (DICS) are playing an important role in dispersing industries in the entire length and breadth of the country.

6. Development of entrepreneurial class

More than 90 percent of the small units have an investment in plant machinery of less than Rs 2 lakhs. It has helped develop a class of entrepreneurs who can channelise their savings in this sector. Successful running of small units tones up their spirit of self reliance and of entrepreneurship in the society as a whole.

7. Ancillarisation

Small industries are responsible for a substantial amount of ancillary production as evidenced by Rs. 370 crore worth of purchase made by the large sector from it every year.

8. Healthy balance between urban and rural areas

Migration from rural to urban areas necessitates the investments in social overheads like hospitals, schools, transportation etc. Principal causes of rural migration are disguised unemployment and lack of employment opportunities. To stem it, small industries should be developed in rural areas so that a healthy balance is maintained between both the areas.

9. Small industries are also effective vehicles for providing self-employment to a large number of technically qualified and unemployed graduates.

CHAPTER VII

POLICY SUPPORT TO SMALL SECTOR IN INDIA

It is a truism that small industries constitute the backbone of a developing country like India. This chapter has considered the policy environment for small-scale enterprises in the context of India's overall industrial policy.

1. Industrial Policy Resolution 1948

To create conditions for the growth of cottage and small industries, the Industrial Policy Resolution 1948 ascribed them an important role in the larger context of national policy. These were to be the industries particularly suited for better utilisation of local resources and for achievement of self- sufficiency in respect of certain consumer goods.

The Karve Committee (1955) and the International Perspective Planning Team ((1953-54) also emphasised the need to develop small scale and village industries to meet the following objectives :—

(i) To create large scale employment at relatively small capital costs.

(ii) To mobilise unused resources of capital and skills.

(iii) To ensure a more equitable distribution of national income including regional dispersal of industries.

(iv) To counter the tendencies towards concentration of economic power by widening opportunities for new entrants in medium and small sized units.

The primary responsibility for developing small industries has been entrusted to State Governments by the constitution. The Central Government frames broad policies for the development of the small sector besides coordinating the efforts of the state governments. To accelerate the process of development of small industries, the Central Government set up Small Industries Development Organisation (SIDO) in 1954 under the Ministry of Industries. Besides, six All India Boards were set up in place of a single Cottage Industries Board so as to deal with separate groups of industries. It may be noted that SIDO is designed to perform industrial extension service through Small Industries Service Institutes in each state. It also conducts training programmés for the development of technical and managerial personnel. The Central Government set up National Small Industries Corporation in 1955 for the promotion of small industries by taking following steps : (i) supply of machinery on hire purchase basis, (ii) running of Prototype Production and Training Centres, (iii) distributing scarce raw materials, (iv) undertaking export marketing, (v) assisting in stores purchase programme of the Central Government etc.

The Mahalnobis model which formed the basis of second five year plan and was adopted during this period gave justification for the existence of small scale industry on account of its ability to supply the increased demand for consumer goods with very little investment and greatly increased employment.

Thus, the 1948-policy laid the basic administrative foundation for the coming years.

2. Industrial Policy Resolution 1956

The 1956 resolution is an important landmark in the industrial history of India. It provided that besides continuing the policy of supporting cottage, village and small industries by differential taxation or direct subsidies, the aim of the state policy will be "to ensure that decentralised sector acquires sufficient vitality to be self supporting and its development is integrated with that of large scale industry. The State will, therefore, concentrate on measures designed to imporve the competitive strength of the small scale producer". To achieve this goal, 128-items were reserved for exclusive production in the small sector. It also reserved 166 items for exclusive purchase by the government from the small sector. The list could be expanded in accordance with the requirements of smal sector.

In 1959, the Small Scale Industries Board constituted a working group to examine and formulate a plan for the development of small industries during the Third Plan. The Study Group recommended the provision of following for securing small industries development.

(a) Technical Assistance
(b) Technical and Managerial Training
(c) Provision of factory accomodation
(d) Financial assistance including facilities to obtain machinery

on hire purchase basis.

(e) Supply of raw material and power.

(f) Marketing of products of the small industry.

These were aimed at helping rapid development of small units and making them more capable to withstand competition from large units.

In the Third Plan Period (1961-66), intensive development of small industries was taken up in selected project areas, known as "Rural Industries Projects". Industrial Estates Programme was oriented towards promoting industries in small towns and rural areas as a part of policy of industrial dispersal.

Administrative Reforms Commission Report on Small Scale Sector, 1969.

The ARC recommended the following :–

(i) Constitution of an autonomous small scale industries commission to guide the development of small industries including handloom and handicrafts.

(ii) Establishment of an apex financial institution at the centre to cater exlclusively to the needs of the small scale sector.

(iii) Establishment of well equipped laboratories for testing raw materials, components and quality inspection.

(iv) Greater emphasis on technical guidance and consultancy services provided by the Small Industries Service Institutes (SISIs).

3. Industrial Policy, 1977

The policy categorically emphasised that its main thrust will be on effective promotion of cottage and small industries widely dispersed in rural areas and small towns.

Salient Features

I. The policy classified small sector in three categories :–

(a) Small scale industries comprising of industrial units with an investment of upto Rs. 10 lakhs and in case of ancillaries with an investment in fixed assets upto Rs 15 lakhs. A total of 504 items were reserved for production in small sector.

(b) Tiny Units :

These were the units with an investment in machinery and equipment upto Rs 1 lakhs and situated in towns with a population of less than 50,000 according to 1971 census.

(c) Cottage and household industries which provide self employment in large numbers.

All the three categories were to be developed simultaneously. The purpose of classification was to devise specific policy measures for each category.

II. Special measures sought be taken to implement the policy:–
   (a) Reservation of production of 504 items in the small sector with further scope of expansion;
   (b) Special assistance to tiny sector and cottage and household industries;
   (c) Establishment of District Industries Centres in all districts of the country to serve as a focal point of development for small and cottage industries;
   (d) Special marketing arrangements through the provision of services like product standardisation, quality control, market surveys etc;
   (e) Encouragement to traditional sector for technological up gradation.

III. Objectives of the policy were :—
   (a) to provide increased employment;
   (b) to encourage gradual progress in the techniques of production in the unorganised sector without causing any large scale technological unemployment.
   (c) to promote production of large variety of goods including consumer goods through labour intensive methods by correlating them with the production programme of large scale sector;
   (d) to encourage and give support to small industries with special emphasis on tiny sector and
   (e) to ensure a more equitable distribution of national income and balanced regional development.

IV. Promotion of Khadi and Village Industries by means of detailed plans and adoption of modern management techniques. The list of items under the purview of KVIC was to be expanded.

   To meet clothing needs of masses, the developoment of handloom sector will be ensured.

V. Development and integration of appropriate technology in consonance with the requirments of broad programme of all round rural development.

—

VI. Indigenous technology

Government's endeavour is to ensure that future development of industries be made with indigenous technology. Full scope will be given to the development of indigenous technology for the efficient production of increased quantities of goods which the society urgently needs.

4. Industrial Policy 1980

(i) The policy spelt the need for intensifying the promotion of small industries through integrated industrial development and fostering complementarity between large and small sectors. Siginificant element of the policy was the raising of investment limits in various categories as follows :—

(a) Tiny Units : Rs 2 lakh (from Rs. 1 lakh)
(b) Small Scale Unit : Rs. 20 lakh (from Rs 10 lakhs) and
(c) Ancillaries : Rs 25 lakhs (from Rs 15 lakhs)

II. Concept of nucleus plants

The District Industries Centres were replaced by "nucleus plants" in each industrially backward district so as to promote as many ancillaries and small and cottage industries as possible. The nucleus plants were to concentrate on assembling the products of ancillary units and to produce inputs needed by large number of small units.

III. Marketing Support and Reservation of items for small industries was to continue.

IV. Financial support to small units by strengthening existing arrangements and making necessary changes to facilitate availability of credit to growing units in small sector.

V. Village Industries i.e. suitable industries in rural areas will be accelerated to generate economic viability in the villages without disturbing ecological balance. Handloom, handicrafts, khadi and other village industries will receive greater attention to achieve faster rate of growth in the village.

VI. Building up buffer stocks of critical inputs.

Socio-Economic Objectives

The basis objective of new policy is to ensure balanced growth of economy with spheres earmarked for large, medium and small and cottage industries sections. The detailed objectives were as follows :—

(a) Optimum use of installed capacity;

(b) Maximum production and achievement of higher productivity;
(c) Higher employment generation;
(d) Correction of regional imbalances through preferential development of industrially backward areas;
(e) Strengthening of agricultural base by according preferential treatment to agro based industries and promoting optimum inter sectoral relations;
(f) Faster promotion of export -oriented and import substitution industries;
(g) Promoting economic federalism with an equitable spread of investment and disposal of returns among widely scattered small but growing units in rural and urban areas;
(h) Consumer protection against high prices and bad quality;
(i) Establishment of an early warning system to avoid sickness and take appropriate remedial measures;
(j) Merger of sick units with healthy which are capable of managing the former and restoring their viability.

Seventh Plan (1985-90)

The seventh Plan focussed on up-gradation of technology and modernisation to improve competitiveness of small industry ; strengthening/creation of tooling and workshop facilities for development of prototype design, new product and processes. Ancillarisation was to be given greater emphasis. To provide common service facilities in fields like heat-treatment, electroplating and leather processing, facilities available with SISI or mobile workshops were sought to be modernised and upgraded. More items of mass consumption were to be brought under quality control inspection Comprehensive marketing support was to be provided to small units through market counselling, research, special studies, participation in trade fairs and exhibitions etc. Creation of facilities for optimum utilisation of existing capacities and growth and development of export oriented industries had been the other areas emphasised.

5. Industrial Policy, 1990

Salient features of this policy are given below :—

(i) Investment ceiling for small scale industries was raised from Rs 35 lakhs to Rs 60 lakhs and for ancillaries from Rs 45 lakhs to Rs 75 lakhs. The small units which undertook to export 30 percent of their annual production by the third year were to be permitted to step up their investment in plant and machinery to Rs. 75 lakhs.

(ii) Investment ceiling for tiny units had been increased from Rs 2 lakhs to Rs 5 lakh provided the unit is located in an area having a population of 50,000 as per 1981 census.

(iii) 836 items were reserved for exclusive manufacture in the small sector though efforts were to be made to identify more items.

(iv) A new scheme of Central Investment Subsidy had been mooted exclusively for small industries in rural and backward areas and capable of generating high level of employment.

(v) Implementation of the programme of technology upgradation.

(vi) Establishment of Small Industries Development Bank (SIDBI) to ensure timely flow of credit for small sector.

(vii) Identification of locations in rural areas endowed with adequate power supply and attracting suitable entrepreneurs to set up tiny and small units.

(viii) Special emphasis on training of women and youth under Entrepreneurial Development Programme (EDP) and to establish a special cell in SIDO for this purpose.

(ix) Expansion of the activities of Khadi and Village Industries Commission and Khadi and Village Industries Board.

(x) Growers to be encouraged to set up agro-processing industries which will receive high priority in credit allocation from financial institutrion.

(xi) Delicensing of all new units with investment of Rs 25 crore in fixed assets in non-backward areas and Rs 75 crore in centrally notified backward areas. Similarly delicensing shall be done in the case of 100%. EOUs set up in EPZs upto an investment limit of Rs. 75 lakhs.

(xii) Location policy shall apply to small industries except-for location in and around metropolitan cities with population above 4 million. In metropolitan cities, location shall not be permitted within 20 kms calculated from the periphery of metropolitan area except in prior designated industrial areas and for non-polluting industries.

6. Industrial Policy 1991

The basic thrust of this policy is to ensure India's development as part of the world economy rather than in isolation. The government would promote the development and utilisation of indigenous capabilities as well as its upgradation to world standards. As per the policy document placed before the Parliament, "Goverment will continue to pursue a sound policy framework encompassing encouragement of entrepreneurship, development of indigenous technology, dismantling of regulatory system, development of capital markets and increasing competitiveness for the benefit of the common man. The spread of industrialisation to backward areas of the country will be actively promoted through appropriate incentives, institutions and infrastructure investments".

Government has undertaken to provide enhanced support to the small sector so that it flourishes in an environment of economic efficiency and continues technological upgradation. The policy has also done away with industrial licencing except these specified. The licensing exemption is particularly designed to help many small and medium entrepreneurs who had been unnecessarily hampered by it.

Major objectives

1. To build on the gains already made.
2. To correct distortions that may have crept in.
3. To maintain a sustained growth in productivity and gainful employment.
4. To attain international competitiveness.

The pursuit of these objectives will be tempered by the need to preserve the environment and ensure efficient use of available resources. All sectors of the industry whether small, medium or large belonging to the public, private or cooperative sector will be encouraged to grow and improve on their past performance. Government's policy will be continuity with change.

Small Indusrtries During Various Five Year Plans

An idea about the significance attached to small industries during successive plans can be formed by glancing through the total public sector outlay in this particular sector. The position is summarised below:

Table showing Public Sector Investment in Village and Small Industries

Plans and Period	Small Industries (Rs. million)	Village and Small Industries (VSI) Rs. million	Small Industries as percentage of VSI
First Plan (1951-56)	52	337	15.4
Second Plan (1956-61)	560	1800	31.1
Third Plan (1961-66)	1131	2408	47.0
Annual Plan (1966-69)	535	1261	42.4
Fourth Plan (1969-73)	962	2426	39.7
Fifth Plan (1974-78)	2217	5925	37.4
Annual Plan (1979-80)	1048	2557	41.0
Sixth Plan (1980-85)	6161	19519	31.6
Seventh Plan (1985-90)	11205	27527	40.7

Source : (i) Table 12.3 of Sixth Plan document
(ii) Table 4.3 at P-104 of Seventh Plan document Vol. II

To recapitulate the provisions made for small industries during various plans, the following may be perused :–

1. The First Plan focussed on establishing separate All India Boards for formulating plans for the development of small scale industries besides reservation of certain items for exclusive production in this sector.

2. Keeping in view the recommendations of Karve Committee, the Second Plan (1955-61) emphasised the wide dispersal of small units throughout the country so as "to extend opportunities, raise income and standards of living and achievement of a more balanced and integrated rural economy." During this plan, sixty industrial estates were set up and prohibition were prescribed on the expansion of certains large industries like vegetable oil, rice milling, leather footwear etc.

3. The Third Plan (1961-65) stressed on" improvements in the techniques of production without affecting employment". Out of the Rs. 264 crore earmarked for the development of small and cottage industries, only Rs. 240.76 crore could be utilised. The three annual plans during 1966-69 provided for an expenditure of Rs. 132.55 crore. On the eve of

4th plan (1969-74), 346 industrial estates had been completed, and small units set up in them had provided employment to 87,200 persons with annual production of Rs 99.25 crore.

4. Like the Third Plan, the Fourth plan could use only Rs 250 crore out of the allocated Rs 293 crore. Thrust of this plan was: (i) administration of credit facilities under the State Aid to Industries Act, (ii) training and common service facilities, (iii) Quality marketing and consolidation of Industrial Estates Programme.

5. The Fifth Plan (1974-79) had as its principal objective the development of different small industries so as to facilitate the attainment of the goal of removal of poverty and inequality in consumption standards through the creation of large scale opportunities for fuller and additional productive employment and impovement of skills. However, the estinated expenditure on village and small industries stood at Rs 388 crore as against the provision of Rs 510 crore.

6. During the sixth plan (1980-85), various programmes were designed to subserve the different goals inter alia: erection of additional employment opportunities; fuller utilisation of existing capacities, development of entrepreneurial skills and expanded efforts on export promotion. These targets were sought to be achieved as follows:–

(i) Increase in the number of items reserved exclusively for small sector to 847.

(ii) Liberalisation of procedures and condition of financial assistance from commercial banks and other financial institutions.

(iii) Large import facilities to meet requirements of imported inputs.

(iv) Reservation of 409 items for exclusive purchase from small Industries.

(v) Provision of comprehensive range of consultancy services in technical, managerial, economic and marketing areas through SIDO.

(vi) Establishment of Council for Advancement of Rural Technology in October 1982 for providing necessary technical input to rural industries.

7. The Seventh plan (1985-90) contributed to the improving of economical and occupational profile of rural, semi-urban and weaker sections of urban communities, as well as regional dispersal and structural diversification, Special attention was paid to the upgradation of technology to improve competitiveness; increased ancillarisation,

provision of design development and testing facilities and integrated and comprehensive marketing support.

8. The Eigth plan has advocated a strategy based on employment generation as the motive force for growth. In this strategy, small and village industries have been assigned an extremely important role. The plan of action for the development of these industries is as follows:–

(a) Since the thrust on employment and poverty alleviation will generate additional demand for mass consumption goods, this demand will be met by employing labour-intensive forms of manufacture .

(b) The objective of consciously developing rural and backward areas can be properly achieved by providing incentives for development of village/household enterprises including khadi, and village establishments, handlooms, handicrafts, sericulture etc.

(c) There is need to explore avenues for securing proper integration of small scale producers for getting inputs on terms comparable to their competitors. For this purpose continuance of subsidies and reservation policy shall have some justification.

(d) The growth of labour intensive industry cannot be ensured without an integrated application of industrial policy, technology policy and fiscal policy.

(e) Provision has to be made for inducting into the small scale sector, a measure of technological dynamism so that production efficiency is improved and products can find a place in the market an a competitive basis.

The overall endeavour of the plan will be to ensure that small industry sector should not only act as a source of productive employment and livelihood to millions of families but that it must also result in the generation of an entrepreneurial revolution in the community as a whole.

Policies and Measures for Promoting Small Industries

Government policy regarding small industry aims at :–

(a) encouraging and facilitating the entry of new entrepreneurs into this sector;

(b) supporting the growth of this sector in a variety of ways;

(c) protecting the small units from intensive competition from medium and large sector;

(d) solving the problems and hurdles in the way of this sector;

(e) ensuring that small units pay due regard to such aspects as the need for productivity enhancement, technology upgradation and export development.

The various measures designed to achieve the above objectives are described below:–

1. Reservation Policy

Reservation has been visualised as an instrument for helping small sector to attain sufficient vitality and competitive strength for its proper integration with the large scale sector. But it was not until 1967 that reservation was eventually resorted to. Begining with 8 items in 1968, it has gone upto 836 items in May 1990. The implications of this policy are as follows:–

(a) The large scale sector is precluded from taking up the production of items included in the reservation list.
(b) The large units accepting an export obligation of 75 percent of their total production are allowed to take up a reserved item for production.

It is however doubtful whether artificial prop of reservation can provide adequate incentive to the small sector to grow. It is argued that reservation may have justification only if it is for a specific period. The supporters of reservation argue however that in its absence, small sector would not have grown to present status.

2. Purchase Assistance and Price Preference

Allied to the policy of reservation is that of exclusive purchase from the small sector. About 434 items have been reserved for exclusive purchase from the small sector by the DGSD –the main purchasing arm of the central government and a few other departments/ministries. A purchase preference is also allowed in accordance with the following three lists:

(a) List I comprising of 409 industrial products which DGSD has to purchase to the extent of 100 percent.
(b) List II having 3 items for purchase upto 75 percent of its requirements by the DGSD.
(c) List III having 28 items for purchase upto 50 percent of the requirements by the DGSD.

Apart from purchase prerference, other facilities provided to small sector in government procurement by DGSD are ;

(i) No registration fee and facility of single point registration by

NSIC.

(ii) Forms for registration are supplied free of charge.

(iii) Security deposit upto a specified limit is dispensed with in respect of units registered with the NSIC under Single Point Registration Scheme.

At the end of March 1989, 15297 small scale units were enlisted with NSIC under Single point Registration Scheme. During this period, the total orders secured by SSI from DGSD and other central government departments were of the order of Rs 740 crore.

Besides purchase preference, small unit products are accorded a price preference of 15 percent.

3. Concessions in Central Excise

Consession in central excise duties is one of the most significant concessions enjoyed by the small sector. Clearences upto the value of Rs. 20 lakhs per year are completely exempt from central excise. In case a unit manufactures items which fall in more than one tariff, the exemption limit is extended to Rs. 30 lakh p.a. Clearances beyond Rs. 20 lakhs per year and up to Rs. 75 lakhs are taxed at concessional rate. Between Rs. 75 lakhs to Rs. 200 lakhs of clearances are taxed at 100 percent of the normal rate. Beyond Rs. 200 lakhs, there is no concession at all.

4. Sales Tax Exemption/deferment

State government have drawn schemes for exemption/deferment of sales tax on products of new units as well as of units undergoing expansion or diversification. In the case of Haryana, for instance, the exemption or deferment of sales tax is allowed upto a particular ceiling calculated as a percentage of capital investment. The period during which this deferment is allowed is also prescribed. Consider the following table

Sales Tax Exemption/ Deferment in Haryana in Respect of SSIs.

Zones	Ceiling in terms of percentage of fixed capital investment (FCI)		Time limits
	New Industrial Units	Units undertaking expansion/diversification	
A	150 % of FCI	100 % of FCI i.e. fixed capital investment	9 years from the date of commercial production

B	125 % of FCI	100 % of FCI	7 years from the date of commercial production
C	100 % of FCI	100 % of FCI	5 years from the date of commercial production

Zone A Centrally and state notified backward areas viz. Mohindergarh, Bhiwani, Hissar, Jind(except Rajand block) and Sirsa district.

State declared backward areas: Kalka, Naraingarh, Ambala tehsil, Ambla district, sub tehsils of Jhajjar, Meham and Rohtak of Rohtak district. Tehsil Gohana of Sonepat District and Mewat region of Faridabad and Gurgaon districts i.e. Hathin, Nagina, Nuh, Punhana, Ferozepur Jhirka and Tauru blocks.

Zone B : Rest of the area except those mentioned in A. & C.

Zone C : Faridabad and Ballabhagarh Complex Administration areas.

5. Supply of Raw Materials

To assist the small sector in procurement of raw materials, small Industry Development Organisation (SIDO) of the central government maintains a close liaison with suppliers and canalising agencies on the one hand and with the State Director of Industries on the other. The state Director of Industries assists SIDO in working out a realistic estimation of the demand of various important raw materials like iron and steel, HR Coils, non-ferrous materials such as copper, nickel, lead, tin and aluminium.

National Small Industries Corporation also provides assistance in procuring raw materials through:

(i) Import of OGL items for actual users in SSI sector.

(ii) Procurement of canalised items in bulk against release orders of the concerned canalazing agencies in favour of the SSIs.

(iii) Procurement and supply of raw materials from local sources in case units face difficulty in lifting raw materials in bulk.

6. Capital Subsidy for small units in rural and backward areas capable of generating higher level of employment.

7. Financial incentives

To help small units get finance on priority basis in adequate quantity and on concessional terms, the following arrangements have been made.

(i) **Term finance** is provided by such primary lending institutions as: State financial Corporations (SFCS), State Small Industsry Development Corporations (SSIDCs), Commercial Banks including Regional Rural Development Banks. To motivate them to give priority in lending to SSIs, the IDBI provides them with refinance facilities to the extent of 75-100 percent depending on the nature of the scheme. The refinance facility is provided at quite concessional rates.

(ii) **Working capital financing** is done by commercial banks under the overall guidance of the RBI.

(iii) Under the IDBI's Single Window Scheme, SFCS and SSIDCs provide both terms loan and working capital (upto Rs 25 lakhs) to new and tiny units whose project costs donot exceed Rs 5 lakhs.

(iv) In August 1987, the central government launched "**National Equity Fund**" for providing equity assistance to tiny and small scale industries. The scheme is aministered by the IDBI through nationalised banks, SFCs & SSIDCs. Under it, small and tiny units located in villages or towns having a population not exceeding 5 lakhs are provided Soft loans upto Rs 75000 per project at a nominal service charge of 1% per annum. To avail this facility, the eligible unit is required to bring in a minimum cash contribution of 10 percent of the project cost. The borrower need not furnish any security.

(v) **Margin Money Scheme** was started in 1982 to nurse units in incipient sickness stage. Such units are provided loan assistance upto Rs. 50000 but not exceeding 50 percent (75 percent in case of tiny units) of the margin money required by a unit to avail of the additional loan from financial institutions or banks under the rehabilitation programme. In exceptional cases, the limit of assistance may be increased to 75 percent (90 percent in case of tiny units).

(vi) National small Industries Corporation provides assistance to SSIs in kind. Its schemes include: supply of machinery on hire purchase basis, equipment leasing, and technical advice in regard to choice of machines.

(vii) **Specific financial assistance schemes** have been drawn up by state governments to assist high priority sectors. For instance, Haryana government has schemes for engineering personnel, physically handicapped, SC/STentrepreneurs, women entrepreneurs, EOUs, small hospitals/nursing homes, hotels, educated unemployed, ex-servicemen etc.

(viii) Small Industries Development Bank of India (SIDBI) has been set up to take up several functions performed by IDBI.

8. Establishment of institutional infrastructure for undertaking promotinal work.

A network of institutions have been set up by the central and state governments to undertake promotional and developmental work. They provide assistance in such areas as selection of product line, preparation of project report, guidance into technical and engineering aspects, preparation of designs and drawings, training, export and marketing.

ANCILLARISATION AND ITS ROLE

Quite a number of policy measures have thus been taken to develop small industries. Preservation of SSIs as ancillaries to large industries is one of them. The experience of Japan and other .western countries has revealed the existence ofgreatdeal of inter dependence among large, medium and small industries. Since large industries do not manufacture everything in-house, they procure a large number of items and services from outside industries. This has introduced the concept of ancillarisation or sub contracting.

The object of ancillarisation is the same as that of small scale industries namely decentralization of economic power, dispersal of industries, increased employment with comparatively lower investment, specialised capacity creation. The Government of India attached considerable importance to the ancillarisation programme and a special cell was created during the early 60s to promote SSIs as ancillaries to large industries. Consequent upon the efforts of various agencies, the number of small/ancillary units and purchase, made from them rose from 550 units and Rs 80.57 crores in 1977-78 to 16166 units and Rs. 448 crores respectively in 1985-86.

In the highly technologically advanced world of today, inter- dependence between varaious cataegories of industries is inevitable. Ancillarisation is particularly significant in high- tech assembly oriented industries like automobiles, transportation, communications, industrial machinery etc. In the case of these industries, the percentage of components bought from ancillaries range between 50 to 90 percent. Anullaries provide scope of vertical transfer of technology from large to small industries.

Following are the advantages of ancillarisation to large industries:

(i) Savings in investment.

(ii) Avoidance of unnecessaray capacity creation for items sub-contracted.

(iii) Lessening of inventories.

(iv) Lower competitive prices due to lower overhead in ancillaries.

It must be noted that inter sectoral dependence and cooperation as is envisaged in the case of ancillaries and large industries requires observance of equity and fairness to each other. This should not be considered as a relationship of charity from big to small but as one based an " enlightened self- interest" and "mutual benefit."

CONCLUSIONS AND SUGGESTIONS

Due to concerted efforts of both the central and state governments, the small industries sector has emerged as a dynamic sector of the national economy. It employs over 11 million persons and annual production in this sector is of the order of 107 billion rupees. The contribution of this sector as depicted in the following table:

Table showing the growth of small scale industries over the years:

	1985-86	*1986-87*	1987-88	1988-89
Number of unit (lakhs)	13.6	14.8	15.8	17.0
Production at current prices (Rs. crores) Percentage increase during the year	61,226 21%	72250 18%	87300 21%	106875 22%
Employment (in lakhs) Percentage increase during the year	96 7 %	101 6%	107 6%	113 6%
Exports at current prices (Rs. Crores) Percentage increase during the year	2753 8%	3617 31%	4535 25%	N.A.

Source: Annual Report for 1988-89 of small Industries Development Irganisation.

Despite a remarkable growth of the small industry sector, the following suggestions need a careful consideration.

1. The small and medium industry must be considered as a con-

tinuum. In terms of technology employed, skills required and location, there is hardly any distinction between them whereas there is significant and qualitative difference between the "small" and "village" industry. It would be better to look at the problems of the small and medium units in an integrated manner and to encourage small units to graduate to medium status in a reasonable period of time.

2. The service sector which is likely to become key sector of the small enterprises is at present limited to non-metropolitan locations i.e towns with less than 5 lakhs of population In fact, such services are more needed in the new urban complexes growing all over. There is the need to remove the limitation on location to motivate young entrepreneurs to organise much needed services to the community.

3. The development of small industry is diffused through a multiplicity of agencies both at the centre and state levels. Besides the Small Industry Development Organisation (SIDO) and its many asoociate institutes such as the Tool Rooms, NISIET, NISEBUD, IDEMI etc., there are agencies such as National Small Industry Corporation & its network of PTDCs. Then there are agencies serving the small sector, though not exclusively, such as the National Productivity Council for People's Action & Rural Technology (CAPART) in the Ministry of Rural Development and the National Research and Development Corporation (NRDC) in the Department of Science & Technology.

The situation is equally worse at the state level. Besides the State Director of Industry, there are SIDCs for distribution of scarce raw materials, SFCs for grant of term loans, Infrastructure Corporations to provide developed land and other facilities at reasonable cost, Trading Corporations to render marketing asisstance, and sectoral corporations in leather, Handlooms, Electronics, Handicrafts etc. Only at the district level, there is a unified structure in the form of DICs who can provide meaningful support to emerging entrepreneurs. But their effectiveness is vitiated by the lack of expertise at the centre. On account ot these factors, the small forms suffer, as the Olton Report of UK mentioned, from unintended disadvantages. Of course, the Devolopment Commissioner SSI does atempt to coordinate the policies towards the small sector, but quite often his is a voice in the wilderness.

To provide an effective focus at the policy making levels, it is necessary to set up a Department of Small Industry in the Ministry of Industry which will formulate a coherent policy frame and supervise its implementation in place of a host of agencies whose functions have begun to overlap. Such a deparatment will have authority to represent effectively the problems of small units in the inner counsels of the government. For instance, in the U.S.A., the Small Business Administrator reports directly to the president and is enjoined by an Act to submit an annual report to the Congress on the share of small Business in the government procurement programme. In Japan, the Small Enterprise Agency is located in the prestigious Ministry of International Trade and Industry, and a Small Enterprise Council—an advisory body, operates in the prime Minister's office. It would be advisable if DCSSI were to report to Parliament on specifie aspects such as the extent of employment created, dispersal of small industry in backward areas, the degree of ancillarisation and the share of small industry in government purchase programme.

4. For a continuous interaction between small sector and the government, there is the need to set up a Small Industry Commission on the lines of similar bodies that are already functioning in the departments of Atomic Energy, Electronics, Space, Oil and Natural Gas, Khadi and village Industries etc. It may have members from industry, Technology, finance and Management. This suggestion was given way back in 1969 by the Administrative Reforms Commission. The suggestion is more relevant today in view of the rapid growth of the small sector producing as many as 5000 products.

It is necessary to redefine the tiny units and hand over many of them to the Khadi and village Industries Commission which has greater sympathy with activities having accent on welfare rather than growth. Thus craft-oriented and artisan based units wherever located may be looked after by the KVIC while the modern small, tiny and service units may be looked after by the Small Industry Commission.

5. The credit provided by various financial institutions to small indusrty is nerely 26 percent of the total credit to the industrial sector although small industry accounts for 50 percent of the production. However the problem is not that of flow of credit to small sector but in the mental barriers existing in the minds of bank officials who fail to recognise that the norms applied to large units may not always be valid for the small sector. In the small sector what is more important than cash flow statements is the 'entrepreneur' himself with his sense of dedication and commitanent to the project besides the personal qualities which he brings to bear on the project. The bank manager must be a good judge of people than projects.

6. Then there is the problem of sickness. The incidence of sickness among small units has risen from 5.31 percent on 1979 to 11.58 percent in 1984. The total number of sick units stood at 1,30,606 in June 1986. Of course, some amount of sickness is unavoidable yet a poor country like India can not afford such collosal wastage. In this connection, banks can play a crucial role by developing an 'early warning system'to detect the onset of sicknes and to take measures to prevent it. An objective analysis also needs to be made into the factors responsible for it and the policy measures to tackle the same.

7. Reservation of items for the small sector must be done on the basis of its proven capability to produce them economically and qualitatively. Once this is done, they must be assured of credit, raw materials and technology.

8. Increased complexity of products has made it essential to provide meaningful technology support to small sector. Rather than giving general and vague advice and treating the entrepreneur as a part of the crowd, the need is to introduce individual unit based plant counselling. It could be ensured through field visits by the technical personnel of the promotional agencies. The areas in which counselling is needed by small units are : pollution control, low-cost automation, energy conservation, industrial desigin and packaging, quality control and testing, approprate technology etc. Alongwith the need to introduce new technology through close alliance with R & D institutions, there is also the need to upgrade and modernise the existing units.

9. The Administrative Reforms Commission 1969 has recommended the formulation of a suitable law for the small industries. Again in 1971 a committee appointed by the Ministry of Industry under the chairmaship of Shri A.R.Bhat has recommended a simple legislation for small industries which would palce the key elements of the support programme such as reservation, price preference, ancillarisation, limited liability for partnership etc. on a statutory basis. The U.S.A. had enacted the Small Business Act as early as 1953. Japan framed a basic law in 1963 for the growth and development of small enterprises.

Thus, in the fourth decade of planned development, the small sector is poised to play an even larger role in the economy. Even the growth of large scale industry is critically dependent on the existence of a healthy and dynamic small industry sector.

CHAPTER VIII

INSTITUTIONAL SUPPORT TO SMALL INDUSTRIES

To promote the development of small sector, an elaborate organisational infrastructure has been set up both at the central and state level. The present chapter studies the various institutions and the role and functions performed by each.

INSTITUTIONAL INFRASTRUCTURE SET UP BY THE CENTRAL GOVERNMENT

Ministry of Commerce & Industry
Department of Small Scale Industries & Agro and Rural Inds.

↓

Small Industries Development Organisation (SIDO)
Development Commissioner SSI [DCSSI]

↓

Small Industries Service Institutes (SISIs)

Main Offices	= 27
SISIs Branches	= 31
Extension Centres	= 37
Total	95

Product Development Centre (PDCs)

Product-cum-Process Development Centre (PCPDCs)	= 3
Production Centres	= 4
Total	7

National Small Industries Corporation (NSIC)

Headquarter	= 1
Regional offices	= 4
Prototype Dev.-cum-Trg. Centre	= 4
Total	9

Specialised Institutions

—Central Institute of Tool Design, Hyderabad
—Central Tool Room & Trg. Centre, Ludhiana
—Central Tool Room & Trg. Centre, Calcutta
—Central Institute of Hand Tools, Jalandhar
—Hand Tool Design Development and Training Centre, Nagpur
—Institute for Design of Electrical Measuring Instruments (IDEMI)
—Integrated Trg. Centre, Nilokheri

—National Institute for Entrepreneurship and Small Business Development (NISEBOD)
—National Institute of Small Industry Extension Trg. (NISIET)
—Product-cum-Process Dev. Centre Foundry and Forging), Agra
—Sports Goods and Leisure Time Equipment, Meerut
—Electronic Service & Trg. Centre, Nainital.

Institutional Infrastructure at the State Level

Directorate of Industries
(Director of Industries)

District Industries Centres (DICS) 422

State Small Industries Development Corporations

The responsibility of developing the small industries is vested primarily in the states. However, for the development of industries in a coordinated manner, a department has been created in the Ministry of Industry of the Central Government. Below are discussed the principal organs dealing with the promotion and development of small sector.

1. Small Industries Development Organisation (SIDO)

It is the apex level organisation headed by the Development Commissioner under whom are the various Directors for looking after Industrial Development and Raw matertials, Chemical Industries, Industrial Estate, Economic Investigations and Statistics, Industries Management and Training, and Secretary, Small Scale Industries Board. It functions through 27 offices, 31 Small Industries Service Institutes, 37 Extension Centres, 3 Product-cum-Process Development Centres, and 4 Production Centres.

SIDO functions as a policy formulating, coordinating and monitoring agency for the development of small industries. The scope of its activities covers all the small industries except those falling within the purview of specialised boards and agencies like KVIC, Coir Board etc. Its main functions are : *coordination, industrial development* and *extension services.* Its coordinating functions are as follows :

(a) evolving an all-India policy for the development of small scale industries;

(b) coordination of the policies and programmes of various state governments;

(c) liasioning with relevant central ministries, planning commission, state governments, financial institutions etc;

(d) coordinating the programme for the development of industrial estates.

For the purpose of *industrial development,* it performs the following functions :-

(a) To secure reservation of items for production by the small-scale sector.

(b) To assess the requirements of and make arrangements for the supply of indigenous and imported raw materials and components.

(c) To collect data on consumer items which are imported and encourage the establishment of new units in those areas by giving coordinated assistance.

(d) To approve the production programmes of specifically selected industries and of such items as come under the Common Production Programme.

(e) To assist and advise the Controller of Imports and Exports as regards the issue of licences for imports or the restricting thereof.

(f) To prepare schemes, project reports and other technical literature of interest to prospective entrepreneurs.

(g) To render support for the growth of ancillaries.

(h) To encourage small units to participate in Governemt Stores Purchase Programme and give them the necessary guidance, market advice and assistance.

SIDO's *extension services* cover the following :

(a) Provision of *technical services* for improved technical process, production planning, selection of machinery use of modern machines, preparation of factory layout and design etc.

(b) Provision of *consultancy and training* in various disciplines to help improve the competitive strength of small entrepreneurs and to become aware of the latest developments in their respective areas. Such services are given in the field of management costing, documentation, personnel management etc.

(c) Provision of *economic investigation and infromation services* such as conducting industrial potential surveys, feasibility studies, market studies, industrial prospects services etc.

(d) Provision of training facilities to help small industries overcome their drawbacks and improve their productivity.

(e) Provision of marketing assistance.

2. Development Commissioner, Small Scale Industries [DCSSI]

It may be noted that the Central Government had set up an All India Board known as Small Scale Industries Board (1954) to take up the responsibility of overall planning, coordination and development of small-scale industry in the country. The Board has representatives of Central and State Governments, financial bodies, institutions, Federation of Small Industries Association, trade etc. The Board discusses questions relating to provision of credit facilities, raw materials, revision of definition of small industry for assistance purposes, dispersal of industries, review of programmes relating to growth of the small sector. To implement the policies laid down by the Small Scale Industries Board, an officer of the rank of Joint Secretary but with the designation of Development Commissioner is appointed in the Ministry of Commerce and Industry. He controls the activities of National Small Industry Corporation and Small Industries Service Institutes. He is represented in different Licensing Committees, Development Council and other bodies and seeks to safegurard the interests of small-scale sector.

3. Small Industries Service Institutes

They occupy a pivotal place in the central network. They are responsible for providing consultancy and training to small entrepreneurs— both existing and potential. These institutes employ regular staff for imparting training. The activities of the SISIs are coordinated by the Industrial Management Training Division of the DCSSI's office. The activities of the SISIs supervised by a Director at the headquarters. The training is imparted in such areas as : Industrial Management, Marketing Management, Personnel Management, Financial management, Production mamagement besides technical courses.

4. National Small Industries Corporation (NSIC)

It was set up in 1955 to supply machinery and equipment to small entrepreneurs or a hire purchase basis and assisting them in procuring government orders. It has three main branches at Bombay, Calcutta and Madras. Its main functions are given below :-

(i) To provide machines on hire purchase basis.

(ii) To participate in stores purchase programmes of the government.
(iii) To develop small units as ancillaries of large industries.
(iv) To arrange the marketing of products of small industries and promoting exports.
(v) To develop prototype of machinery and equipment for transfer of technology and know how for commercial production.
(vi) To distribute basic raw materials through raw materials depots.
(vii) To import and distribute components and parts to actual users in specific industries.
(viii) To undertake the construction of industrial estates.
(ix) To provide training in selected trades and technologies through its 4-prototype development training centres.

Starting from a scratch, the corporation has succeeded in creating proper industrial infrastructure. It has also infused confidence in small entrepreneurs to prepare schemes of modernisation and diversification.

5. Prototype Development and Training Centres

There are 4-PDTCs at New Delhi, Rajkot (Gujarat) Howrah (West Bengal) and Madras (Tamilnadu). Their main functions are :

(a) To develop and design prototypes of machines, implements and components as are suitable for production by the small-scale industrial units.
(b) To provide common facilities and technical know-how.
(c) To provide training to workers of small units.

6. Specialised institutions

(i) Central Institute of Tool Design, Hyderabad

It was set up in 1968 with the help of UNDP and ILO to help small industries by imparting training to technical personnel in the design and manufacture of tools, jigs, fixtures, dies and moulds. Its other functions are :

(a) To provide consultancy and advisory services including assistance in the design and development of tools.
(b) To recommend measures to standardise tools, and tooling elements, components of jigs, fixtures, dies etc.
(c) To provide tool room facility.

The management of the Institute has been entrusted to a governing council comprising of representatives of government and industry. The Development Commissioner (SSI) is the ex-officio Chairman of the governing council.

(ii) Central Tool Room Training Centres

These are located at Ludhiana, Calcutta, Bangalore and New Delhi to provide tool room services and facilities in design, manufacture and training.

(iii) Central Institute of Hand Tool (CHIT) has been set up at Jalandhar to provide improved technology, raw materials, design and testing for handtools industry.

(iv) Institute for Design of Electrical Measuring Instruments Bombay (IDEM) for providing technical consultancy regarding the design and development of electrical and elecronic instruments, calibration and testing, tool designing and tool fabrication, prototype fabrication and training. It was set up in 1969 with the assistance of UNDP.

(v) National Institute of Entrepreneurship and Small Business Development (NISEBUD), New Delhi

It has been set up in 1983 to coordinate research and training in entrepreneurship development besides specific training programmes suited to various categories of entrepreneurs. It serves as an apex national level institute. It provides a forum for interaction and exchange of views between various agencies engaged in entrepreneurial development.

(vi) National Institute of Small Industries Extension Training (NISIET), Hyderabad. It was started in 1956 on an experimental basis to develop manpower for small sector. Its functions are :

(a) To provide training to persons engaged in small industries.

(b) To undertake research programmes relating to development of small industries.

(c) To enter into technical assistance agreement with international or other organisations for provision of services for the development of small industry.

It runs courses in business management for entrepreneurs and semi-managerial persons of small industries.

Other important national institutes are :

(vii) Sports Goods and Leisure Time Equipment, Meerut.

(viii) Electronic Service and Training Centre, Nainital.

(ix) Central Machine Tools Institute, Bangalore.

(x) Central Institute for Plastics Engineering and Tools, Madras under the Ministry of Petroleum and Chemical.

(xi) National Institute of Foundry and Forging Technology, Ranchi.

STATE LEVEL ORGANISATIONS

1. Directorate of Industries

It is a state level executive agency for the promotion and development of Village and Small Industries sector. It acts under the overall guidance of SIDO and concerned central institutions. It performs both regulatory and developmental functions. It acts through a network of District Industries Centres, industries officers at sub-division level an extension officers at block levels. Functions of directorate of industries are :

(i) Registration of small-scale units and recommending cases of large and medium industries to appropriate authorities.
(ii) Provision of financial assistance under State Aid to Industries Act.
(iii) Distribution of scarce and indigenous raw material to industrial units.
(iv) Establishment of industrial estates/industrial cooperatives.
(v) Grant of Essentiality Certificates for import of raw materials.
(vi) Provision of technical consultancy and training of entrepreneurs.
(vii) Development of infrastructure.
(viii) Undertaking industrial surveys and collection of information.
(ix) Overall administration of village and small industries sector and maintenance of close liasion with central and state organisations concerned with industrial development.
(x) Arranging concessions and incentives.

2. Small Industries Development Corporation

Objectives :

(i) To procure and supply scarce raw materials.
(ii) To provide machinery on hire purchase.
(iii) To provide marketing assistance.
(iv) To set up joint ventures in small sector.
(v) To promote entrepreneurship through various schemes.
(vi) To set up trade centres.

3. Specialised Corporations

States have also set up specialised agencies of the following kind :

(i) Industries Infrastructure Corporation/Industrial Area Development Board to plan and develop industrial estates and industrial areas.

(ii) Agro-Industries Corporations for the following :

(a) supply of agricultural machinery and equipment on hire purchase basis;

(b) development of agro-based industries;

(c) supply of agricultural inputs like fertilizers, pesticides etc.

(iii) Electronic Development Corporation for the promotion of industries in the field of electronics including joint and public sector enterprises.

(iv) Leather Industries Development Corporation and similar other commodities corporations.

(v) Rural Industries Marketing Corporation for Marketing village industries' products and provisions of variety of services needed by village industries and tiny units.

(vi) Technical Consultancy Organisations sponsored by IDBI/IFCI/ICICI for providing technical consultancy services.

4. **State Financial Corporations to provide long and medium-term loans for acquisition of fixed assets.**

DISTRICT INDUSTRIES CENTRES (DICs)

Structure and Role

With a view to providing integrated administrative framework at the district level for industrial promotion, a scheme of establishing District Industries Centres was started in 1978. It is aimed at providing all assistance and support to entrepreneurs at various stages. It is a unified agency. As at the end of March 1989, a total of 422 DICs serving 431 districts were in operation.

Structure : DIC consists of (i) one General Manager, (ii) Four Functional Managers of whom three would be in the areas of economic investigation, credit, and village industries. The fourth functional manager may be entrusted with responsibility in any of the area like raw materials/marketing/training etc. depending on the specific requirements of each district, and (iii) three Project Managers to provide technical service in the area relevant to needs of the district concerned. Their role is to facilitate modernisation an upgradation of technology in the small sector.

At the sub-divisional level, there could be 'Assistant Director of

Industries' and an Industry Promotion Officer. But this position does not obtain in every state.

Functions and Role of DICs

DICs ' role is mainly promotional and developmental. To attain this end, it has to provide all services and support to small and village industries. Their functions are as follows :

1. Conducting Industrial Potential Surveys

It conducts surveys for assessing industrial potential keeping in view the availability of resources in terms of material and human skill, infrastructure, demand, products etc. Based on these assessments, it provides investment advice to entrepreneurs.

2. Preparation of Action Plan

On the basis of endowments and possibilities, it is required to prepare an action plan that can be effectively implemented in the concerned district.

3. Guidance to Entrepreneurs

It has to guide entrepreneurs in identifying appropriate machinery and equipment, sources of supply and procedure for procuring imported machinery, assessing raw material requirements. It also interacts with various authorities for the supply of scarce and critical raw materials.

4. Appraisal

It has to appraise the prospects of various proposals received from entrepreneurs and formulates creditworthy schemes. Then it helps entrepreneurs obtain credit and monitors the flow of industrial credit in the district.

5. Marketing Assistance

Under the marketing assistance programme, it organises and collects marketing information, guides entrepreneurs in marketing their products, assesses the possibility of ancillarisation and export promotion, and suggests appropriate marketing strategies to entrepreneurs.

6. Contact with R & D Institutions

It contacts R & D institutions for updating current processes and undertake product development appropriate to small industries.

7. Special Schemes

It has been given the operational responsibility for special schemes to provide self employment to educated unemployed youth.

8. Artisan Training

It is also responsible for conducting artisan training programmes. It also functions as the technical arms of DRDA in administering IRD and TRYSEM programmes, designing and implementing training programmes and identifying appropriate opportunities and projects for the beneficaries.

9. Development of rural and cottage industries and maintaining effective liaison with related agencies

Thus the overall task of DICs is to promote industries in the district. This is done through the delivery of a package of assistance meaningfully and expeditiously, identification of opportunities and provision of guidance to entrepreneurs. The DIC also prepares an Action Plan which is coordinated with District Credit Plan prepared by Lead Bank in the district.

ADDRESSES OF SMALL INDUSTRIES SERVICE INSTITUTES, BRANCH SSIs AND EXTENSION CENTRES

Annexure—B

Andhra Pradesh

1. Small Industries Service Institute,
   Narsapur Cross Road,
   Balanagar,
   Hyderabad-500 037.
2. Br. SSI,
   F-19 to 22 D-Block,
   IDA, Autonagar,
   Vishakhapatnam-530 012
3. S. I. S. I. Extension Centre,
   A-1, Industrial Estate,
   Santhanagar,
   Hyderabad-500 018
4. S. I. S. I. Extension Centre,
   B-2, Industrial Estate,
   Vijayawada-7.

5. S. I. S. I. Extension Centre,
   Papanaidupet, Near Renigunta,
   Chitoor District-517 526

Assam

6. Small Industries Service Limited,
   Industrial Estate,
   Bamunimaidan,
   Gauhati-21.
7. Branch S.I.S.I.
   Link Road,
   Lane No. 14,
   Silchar-6. (Assam)
8. Br. SSI,
   Amalpatti,
   Diphu (Post),
   Karbi Angolong (Dist.),
   Assam.
9. Br. SSI,
   Pologround Road,
   Tezpur (Post),
   Sonitpur (Distt.),
   Assam
10. S.I.S.I. Extension Centre,
    Parbatghigaon,
    Tinsukia
11. S.I.S.I. Extension Centre,
    Rajabari,
    Jorhat-2.

Arunachal Pradesh

12. Branch S.I.S.I.,
    Near R.K. Mission Hospital,
    Itanagar-791 113.

Bihar

13. Small Industries Service Institute,
    Industrial Estate, Patna-13.

14. Small Industries Service Limited,
Bela Industrial Estate,
P.O. R.K. Ashram,
Muzaffarpur.
15. Small Industries Service Limited,
Industrial Estate,
Kokar, Ranchi.
16. Branch S.I.S.I.,
Katras Road,
Dhanbad-826 001

Delhi

17. Small Industries Service Institute,
Opposite Okhla Industrial Estate,
New Delhi-110 020
18. S.I.S.I. Extension Centre,
Balsahyog,
Connaught Circus,
New Delhi-110 001

Goa

19. Small Industries Service Limited,
Audhi Mapari Building,
P.O. Box No. 334,
Margao-403 601.

Gujarat

20. Small Industries Service Limited,
Harsiddh Chambers,
4th Floor, Ashram Road,
Ahmedabad-14.
21. Branch S.I.S.I.,
1/5, Jagannadha Plot,
Rajkot-360 001.
22. Branch S.I.S.I.,
Masat Industrial Area,
Silvasa (Dadar Nagar Haveli).
23. S.I.S.I. Extension Centre,
Bundar Road, Bhavannagar.

24. S.I.S.I. Extension Centre,
    Dwarakpuri Road, Near Ram Mandir,
    Jamnagar.
25. S.I.S.I. Extension Centre,
    No. 10, Central Road,
    Udyog Nagar,
    Udhana 394 210 (Surat)
26. S.I.S.I. Extension Centre,
    Chaklashi hagol,
    Near Kalkaata Temple,
    Nadiad.

Himachal Pradesh

27. Small Industries Services Institute,
    Janak Kuti, Chambaghat,
    Solan-178 218.

Haryana

28. Small Industries Services Institute,
    Kothi No. 113, Sector-13,
    Urban Estate,
    Karnal-132 001.
29. Br. Small Industries Services Institute,
    I.T.I. Campus
    Bhiwani-125 001.
30. S.I.S.I. Extension Centre,
    Behind S. D. College,
    Ambala-133 401.
31. S.I.S.I. Extension Centre,
    Near Civil Hospital,
    Rewari-123 401.

Jammu & Kashmir

32. Small Industries Service Institute,
    181, Karan Nagar,
    Srinagar-190 010.
33. Branch S.I.S.I.,
    Industrial Estate,
    Pathankot Road, Jammu (Tawi)-180 003.

Karnataka

34. Small Industries Services Institute,
Rajaji Nagar,
Bangalore-560 044.
35. Branch S.I.S.I.,
Mahabaleshwar,
Mangalore-575 003.
36. Branch S.I.S.I.,
C-I Industrial Estate,
Gulbarga.
37. Small Industries Services Institute,
Indl. Estate,
Gokul Road,
Hubli-580 030
38. S.I.S.I. Industrial Extension Centre,
Yadavagiri,
V.V. Mohalla,
Mysore-370 002.
39. S.I.S.I. Extension Centre,
Udyambag,
Khanpur Road,
Belgaum-590 008.

Kerala

40. Small Industries Services Institute,
Kanjjany Road,
P.O. Ayyanthali,
Trichur-680 011.
41. S.I.S.I. Extension Centre,
Shornur-679 112
42. S.I.S.I. Extension Centre,
A. S. Road,
Kemmady,
Alleppy North-688 007
43. S.I.S.I. Extension Centre,
Govt. Arts College,
P.O. Kallai, Calicut-673 018

44. S.I.S.I. Extension Centre,
    Attingal,
    Trivandrum District,
    Pin-695 101
45. S.I.S.I. Extension Centre,
    Mudavoor,
    Muvatupuzha,
    Ernakulam District.

Madhya Pradesh

46. Small Industries Services Institute,
    10, Industrial Estate,
    Pologround,
    Indore-452 003.
47. Branch S.I.S.I.
    Opposite Chattisgarh Club, Civil Lines,
    Ranipur-492 001.
48. Branch S.I.S.I.,
    Industrial Estate,
    Tansen Road,
    Gwalior-474 002
49. Branch S.I.S.I.
    37, Housing Road,
    Bada Bazar Colony,
    Rewa-486 001
50. S.I.S.I. Extension Centre,
    Industrial Estate,
    Adhartal,
    Jabalpur-482 004
51. S.I.S.I. Extension Centre,
    Makoriam,
    Ujjain-456 001

Maharashtra

52. Small Industries Services Institute
    Kurla Andheri Road,
    Sakinaka, Bombay-72
53. Small Industries Services Institute
    Sadar, Nagpur-425 007

54. Branch S.I.S.I.,
32-33, MIDC Indl. Area,
Chikalthana,
Aurangabad-10
55. S.I.S.I. Extension Centre,
Samaj Kalyan Bldg.
Shankarshet Road,
Swargate, Pune-411
56. S.I.S.I. Extension Centre,
P-31, FTS Buildings,
MI.D.C. Shiroli,
Kolhapur-416 122

Manipur

57. S.I.S.I.,
Shed No. C-17 & 18,
Bit No. 23,
Industrial Estate, Takyelpet,
Imphal-795 001

Meghalaya

58. Branch S.I.S.I.,
Industrial Estate Near Meter Factory,
Short Round Road,
Meghalaya,
Shilong-793 001
59. Branch S.I.S.I.,
Hawa-Khana Road,
Tura-794 001

Mizoram

60. Branch S.I.S.I.,
Kelish House,
Republic Veng.,
Aizwal-1

Nagaland

61. Branch S.I.S.I.,
Industrial Estate,
Dimapur,
Nagaland-797 112

Orissa

62. Small Industries Services Institute,
    Kanika Road,
    Tulsipur, Cuttack-753 008
63. Branch S.I.S.I.,
    C-9, Industrial Estate,
    Rourkela-4
64. Branch S.I.S.I.,
    Rayagada,
    Koraput, Orissa.
65. S.I.S.I. Extension Centre,
    Industrial Estate,
    Jharsugura, (Sambalpur),
    District Sambalpur-768 202

Punjab

66. Small Industries Services Institute,
    Industrial Area-B,
    Ludhiana-141 003
67. S.I.S.I. Extension Centre,
    11-A, Industrial Estate,
    Batala-(Punjab).

Rajasthan

68. Small Industries Services Institute,
    M. I. Road,
    Jaipur-302 001
69. S.I.S.I. Extension Centre,
    Industrial Estate,
    Shed No. A-1/A-3,
    Jodhpur
70. S.I.S.I. Extension Centre,
    Industrial Estate,
    Shed No. A-1/A-3,
    Pratap Nagar,
    Udaipur-313 001
71. S.I.S.I. Extension Centre,
    Industrial Estate,
    Shed No. A-1/A-2,
    Kota-324 007

Sikkim

72. Small Industries Services Institute,
Tadong Housing Colony,
P.O. Tadong,
Gangtok,
Sikkim-737 102

Tamil Nadu

73. Small Industries Services Institute,
65/1, G.S.T. Road,
Guindy,
Madras-600 032
74. Branch S.I.S.I.,
Patel Road,
Coimbatore-641 009
75. Branch S.I.S.I.,
Plot No. 76, CGE Colony,
Tirchendur Road,
Tuticorin-628 003
Tamil Nadu

Tamil Nadu

76. S.I.S.I. Extension Centre,
Industrial Estate,
Madurai-625 001
77. S.I.S.I. Extension Centre,
Peria Agraharam P.O.,
Erode-6398 005

Pondicherry

78. S.I.S.I. Extension Centre,
Thattanchavadi
Pondicherry-605 009

Tripura

79. Branch S.I.S.I.,
21, Harish Thakur Road,
Agarthala–799 001

Uttar Pradesh

80. Small Industries Services Institute,
Industrial Estate,
Kalpi Road, Fazalganj,
Kanpur-282 005
81. Small Industries Services Institute,
A-208, Kamla Nagar,
Agra-282 005
82. Small Industries Services Institute,
E-17-18, Udyog Nagar,
Allahabad
83. Branch S.I.S.I.,
Industrial Estate,
Varanasi-2
84. Branch S.I.S.I.,
Bareily Road,
Haldwani
Nainital (U.P.)
85. S.I.S.I. Extension Centre,
Suraj Kund Road,
Meerut-250 001
86. S.I.S.I. Extension Centre,
S. N. Marg,
Firozabad-282 203

West Bengal

87. Small Industries Services Institute,
111 & 112 B. T. Road,
Calcutta-700 035
88. Branch S.I.S.I.,
Industrial Estate,
J.P. Avenue,
District Burdawan,
Durgapur, W. Bengal
89. Branch S.I.S.I.,
Ektisal,
Industrial Estate, Shed No. 3 & 4,
Siliguri,
Jalpaiguri-734 402

90. Branch S.I.S.I.,
R. J. Tagore Road,
Suri, Birbhum,
W. Bengal
91. Branch S.I.S.I.,
Port Blair.
92. S.I.S.I. Extension Centre,
Block-D,
Industrial Estate,
District Nadia.
Kalyani-741 235
93. S.I.S.I. Extension Centre,
Naturn Chatti,
Bankura-722 101
94. S.I.S.I. Extension Centre,
47, South Tangra Road,
Calcutta-700 046
95. S.I.S.I. Extension Centre,
58/5-B, I.B.T. Road,
Manicktala,
Calcutta-700 002

Annexure-C
TESTING CENTRES

Regional Testing Centre

1. Regional Testing Centre,
SISI Campus,
Saki Naka, Kurla,
Andheri Road,
Bombay-400 072
2. Regional Testing Centre,
111/112, B. T. Road,
Calcutta-700 035
3. Regional Testing Centre
Capt. Sahid Gour Marg,
Okhala Industrial Estate,
New Delhi-110 020

4. Regional Testing Centre
SISI Campus,
65/1, G. S. T. Road,
Guindy, Post Box No. 3146,
Madras-600 032

FIELED TESTING STATIONS

1. Assistant Director I/C.
Field Testing Station
Near Grinding Bldg.
Industrial Estate,
Batala-143 505
2. Assistant Director I/C.
Field Testing Station,
Laboratory Building, Bais Godam,
Jaipur-(Rajashthan)
3. Assistant Director I/C.
Field Testing Station,
G. T. Road, Asmalkha-132 101
4. Assistant Director I/C.
Field Testing Station,
Shed No. 8, Woollen Hosiery Complex,
Dehradun (U.P.)
5. Assistant Director I/C.
Field Testing Station,
South Wing Block-111
Behela Industrial Estate,
620, Diamond Harbour Road,
Calcutta-700 034
6. Assistant Director I/C.
Field Testing Station,
Shed No. S-3/52, Sector-A,
Lane-B,
Mancheswar Industrial Estate,
Bhuvaneshwar-751 010.
7. Assistant Director I/C.
Field Testing Station,
Indira Nagar,
Agartala-799 005

8. Assistant Director I/C.
   Field Testing Station,
   145-45 B, L.I.G. Quarters,
   G.I.D.C. Udhav,
   Ahmedabad-382 415
9. Assistant Director I/C.
   Field Testing Station,
   47-E, Industrial Area,
   Govindpura,
   Bhopal-23.
10. Assistant Director I/C,
    Field Testing Station,
    Shed No. 57,
    Industrial Area, Shiroli,
    Kolhapur-416 122
11. Assistant Director,
    C/o Director SSI,
    Industrial Estate,
    Patna.
12. Assistant Director,
    Field Testing Station,
    S.I.S.I. Campus,
    Rajaji Nagar,
    Bangalore-560 044
13. Assistant Director,
    Field Testing Station,
    Industrial Estate,
    Sanath Nagar,
    Hyderabad-500 018
14. Assistant Director I/C.
    Field Testing Station,
    C.F.S.C. Building,
    Industrial Estate,
    Changanesery-685 106

[illegible] Assistant Director I/C.
Field Testing Station,
Industrial Estate,
Thattanchavadi,
Pondicherry.

16. Assistant Director I/C.
Field Testing Station,
Industrial Estate,
Madurai-625 007
17. Assistant Director I/C.
Field Testing Station,
Industrial Estate,
Borogui, Tinsukhia (Assam).

Process-cum-Product Development Centres

1. Process-cum-Product Development Centre for Ceramics and Glass Industries Kumhartoli,
2nd Lane, Purulia Road,
Ranchi-834 010 Bihar
2. Process-cum-Development Centre (Sport Goods And Leisure Time Equipments),
Delhi Road,
Meerut City-250 002
3. Process-cum-Development Centre (Foundry & Forgings)
F-166, Kamla Nagar, Agra (UP)

Annexure-D
PRODUCTION DEVELOPMENT CENTRES

Production Centre

1. Production Centres,
Attingal, Trivandrum District,
Kerela-605 104
2. Production Centre,
Mudavoor, Moovatupuzha,
Ernakulam District, Kerala.
3. Production Centre,
Industrial Estate,
Eddumanur,
Kottayam District,
Kerala-686 631
4. Production Centre,
Manjadi, Tiruvalla,
Alleppy District, Kerala-689 105

CHAPTER IX

FINANCE FOR SMALL INDUSTRIES

The phrase "whoever has the gold makes the rule" brings out the significance of the need of adequate finances for a small enterprise. In this chapter, various sources of funds for small industries have been discussed.

II. Financing of Small Industry by Commercial Banks

Following types of credit facilities are offered by commercial banks:

1. Cash Credit

Under this system, the banker specifies a limit called the 'cash credit limit' upto which the borrower can borrow against the security of tangible assets or guarantees. The credit is given in cash form. Though repayable on demand, cash credit limits are sanctioned for one year and reviewed and renewed thereafter, if considered necessary. Cash credit constitutes 29 percent of the total advances. The limit of cash credit is sanctioned after considering such things relating to the borrowing concern as production, sales, inventory levels, past utilisation of limits etc.

2. Overdraft

It is a facility allowed to current account holders on a temporary or permanent basis. The borrower is allowed to withdraw upto a certain limit over and above the credit balance in the current account. It constitutes 6 percent of the total outstanding advances.

3. Demand Loan

It is a term loan repayable within one year in instalments or lumpsum. It may be secured or clean. The loan amount is paid in lumpsum. No subsequent debits are made in it except interest and charges. All amounts credited are reduced from the amount of loan. Interest is generally levied on a quarterly basis on the outstanding debit balance. Security in this case is personal or in the form of shares/debentures or government securities or fixed deposits or immovable properties. It constitutes 4 percent of the total outstanding advances.

4. Term Loan

In contrast to a demand loan, the term loan is allowed for a fixed term which could be medium (1 to 7 years) or long (over 7 years) depending on the period of loan. It is given primlarily for financing fixed assets or working capital needs. Of the total outstandings, 21 percent are financed through it.

5. Bills Purchased (DIP)

It is a facility allowed for movement of goods. Bills may be clean or documentary. Documentary bills are accompanied by railway receipts, lorry receipt, bill of lading or airway bill etc. The bank holds the documents as security against advances for delivery to the drawee upon payment. However, clean bill facility is given only to trusted parties.

6. Bills Discounted (D/A)

This facility is allowed against usance bills arising out of trade tranactions and maturing after a given time or after sight or after the date of the bill. It could be clean or documentary. Documents are delivered to the drawee on acceptance and payment is collected on maturity date.

Formalities for Obtaining Bank Credit for a New Unit

1. Making of application for credit facilities in the prescribed form.
2. Submission of project report and projected financial statements (not necessary for loans upto Rs. 25000).
3. Provisional Registration with DIC/Director of Industries or licence from DGTD.
4. Submission of documents relating to the status or constitution of the borrower such as partnership deed and registration with Registrar of firms or declaration of sole proprietorship or Memorandum and Articles of Association, Certificate of Incorporation and Board resolution for borrowing in case of a joint stock company.
5. Approval/Registration/No Objection Certificate from concerned government authorities.
6. Approved building plans, if applicable.
7. Quotations for major machinery, equipment etc.
8. Bio-data of promoters, guarantors with assets and liabilities particulars.
9. Financial Statements of sister/associate concerns, if any.

10. Documents concerning progress made in the implementation of the project e.g. power connection, advances to machinery suppliers.
11. Market feasibility report, if any.
12. Bank Account particulars.
13. Source of margin money.
14. Appraisal Note and sanction letter of SFC/SIDC.

The formalities in case of renewal enhancement of credit limits are :

1. Application for credit facilities.
2. Latest financial statements [Balance Sheet, Trading and Profit and Loss Account]
3. Particulars of assets and liabilities of promoters and guarantors.
4. Sales Tax, Income Tax, Excise Duty particulars.
5. Quotations .
6. Permanent registration with DIC/DOI.
7. Capacity assessment, sanctioned quota for scarce raw materials.
8. Repayment record of loans raised from SFC/SIDC.
9. Major pending orders/queries.
10. Justification for additional limits applied; special achievements, explanation on adverse features etc.

Procedure of Appraising Credit Proposal by Bank

1. Preliminary scrutiny and discussion with the party to ascertain eligibility and suitability.
2. Opening of bank accounts.
3. Visit to the unit by Manager/Technical Officers.
4. Required Clearances/consents from the appropriate government authorities.
5. In-depth scrutiny of the following :
   (i) Promoters' background, managerial competence, creditworthiness, integrity etc.
   (ii) Technical feasibility–machinery, manufacturing process, skilled labour, location, infrastructure.
   (iii) Economic feasibility–scope and demand of products, marketing arrangements.
   (iv) Financial feasibility and profitability–cost of project, sources of finance, profits, cash flow, break-even point, debt- service coverage ratio.

6. Sanction at branch level or Recommendation to higher authorities, spelling out limits for separate credit facilities, terms and conditions for security, guarantee, margin, interest rátes, gestation period, repayment terms, other formalities, if any.

Disbursement and Follow up :

1. Documentation as per terms of sanction letter.
2. Specific Release as far as possible.
3. Ensuring end utilisation through
   (a) Periodic visits to the unit.
   (b) Keeping a watch over the transaction in the accounts, adherence to projections made, industry level development.
   (c) Submission of periodical statements by the party.
   (d) Timely submission of application/financial statements for renewal/ enhancement of working capital limits.

Credit Facilities Offered for Different Purposes

S. No.	Purpose of credit	Nature of bank credit	Security	Margin
1.	For acquiring land and building	Term Loan	Equitable or Registered Mortgage Cash margin FDR	$25 - 33\frac{1}{3}\%$ 10 – 20 %
2.	For purchase of Plant andMachinery, Tools, Furniture, Fixtures, Vehicles [Fixed assets]	Letter of Credit (Imports), Term Loan, Deferred Payment Guarantee (IDBI)	Hypothecation of assets out of Term Loan /Def. Payment Guarantee	$25 - 33\frac{1}{3}\%$
3.	For purchasing and hoding stocks of raw materials components, stores.	L/C (Imprt) Cash-Credt, Acceptance of usance bill	Cash margin Pledge/Hyp. of Stocks – do –	10 — 20 % 20 — 30 % Ni
4.	Against stocks of semi-finished/finished goods	Cash Credit Overdraft	Pledge/Hyp. of stocks	25 — 40 %
5.	For finor financing inlantsales Receivables	Cash Credit/OD	Pledge of Book RR/TR	30 — 40 %
		Documentary Bills Purchase D/P		0 — 10 %
		Documentary bills discount/purchase (D/A)	Clean	0 — 10 %
		Govt. Supply bills. of bookdebts	Clean	10 — 20 %

S. No.	Purpose of credit	Nature of bank credit	Security	Margin
6.	For execution of export orders	Packing Credit	Export Trust-Receipt Hype of stocks Deposit of Irrevo. L/C	10 — 25 % L/C or firm Order value
7.	For financing export sales receivables (post shipment export finance)	Foreign Documentary Bill (FDBP) Foreign usance bills discount	Bills of lading or Airway bill	0 — 10 %
8.	For total requirement of fixed assets	Composite TL	Hypo of machines/ stocks	Nil upto Rs 25000 10 - 25 %
9.	For guaranteeing repayment of third party loans performance obligations	Bank Guarantee	Cash Margin	—

Note : The above is only indicative of the usual type of facilities for SSI units. Margins are flexible.

Assistance By Other Agencies

I. National Small Industries Corporation (NSIC)

NSIC porvides industrial finance by way of supply of machines on hire purchase to small units. The corporation takes upon itself the entire purchase responsibility starting from locating competent suppliers to delivery of machines. The role of the person starting a small industry or of an entrepreneur is to make an application with necessary documents, pay the earnest money when an offer is made to him and execute the hire purchase agreement. The machines are delivered at his door step. Thereafter, he is expected to make efficient utilisation of the machines and pay NSIC hire purchase instalments in time. On the payment of last instalment, the property in the machine is transferred to the entrepreneur. No single application for machinery and equipment valued at less than Rs 5000/- is be accepted. Women entrepreneurs are accorded special terms. Applications are considered for indigenous machines upto Rs. 1 lakh / 2 lakh in value by the branch office of NSIC and above Rs. 1 lakh / 2 lakh by the Regional Offices. The terms of grant of assistance are summarised below :

1. Minimum quantum of assistance Rs 25000
2. Application Fee : Rs 100 for assitance upto

Rs. 2 lakhs and Rs. 250 beyond Rs. 2 lakhs

3. Earnest money : 30 %
4. Interest : 16 %with rebate of 2 % for timely payment
5. Service charge : 2 %

Tiny units and those started in backward areas or by technocrats, SC/ST, physically handicapped persons, ex-defence personnel in backward areas and women entrepreneurs are offered soft terms of lending.

The Corporation does not demand any security or collateral for assistance upto Rs. 6.00 lakhs.

II. The Industrial Development Bank of India (IDBI)

Established in 1964 it is required to perform *inter alia* the function of coordinating in conformity with national priorities, the activities of institutions engaged in financing, promoting and developing industry. Following is the gist of its activities.

A. Constitution of Small Industries Development Fund

IDBI is responsible for establishing SIDF in May 20, 1986. In addition to ensuring continuous flow of financial and non- financial assistance to small-scale sector, it also provides focal point for coordinating the activities of various organisations engaged in promoting growth of this sector. Following five categories of assistance are provided by IDBI through SIDF :

(i) Refinance assistance

It covers 'term loans' channellised through institutional network consisting of state level institutions such as SFCs/SIDCs ; commercial banks, cooperative banks and regional rural banks. Refinance is provided to the full extent of loan to SFCs/SIDCs and banks. IDBI has stipulated ceilings on the rates to be charged by the primary lenders so that benefits of concessional rates of interest are passed on to the ultimate borrower. The period of repayment is fixed by the lending institution after taking into account the profitability and debt servicing capacity of the assisted unit subjcct to a maximum period of 10 years.

Concessions under refinance scheme

a. In case of small units, a debt equity ratio upto 3 : 1 is permitted except for projects involving seed/special capital assistance where a ratio of 2 : 1 is applicable.

b. No margin is insisted in respect of composite loans and loans to physically handicapped (upto Rs. 50,000). Loans upto 50,000 to SC/ST entrepreneurs are refinanced without any margin. Loans to single/two vechicle owners and SRTO (i.e. those who own upto 6 vehicles) are refinanced at 15 percent margin.

c. Rebate of 0.5 percent in interest rate is allowed to small industries which obtain ISI mark for all their products.

d. Assistance to single / two vehicles operators is provided at concessional rate of interest of 12.5 percent. Interest on refinance is 9 percent.

e. No commitment charge is levied on undrawn sanctioned refinance for a period of 12 months from date of sanction in case of small units.

f. Central/State Investment Subsidy to projects coming up in specified backward areas is treated as equity for the purpose of debt equity ratio.

(ii) Special Incentives to Tiny Sector and Economically Backward Classes', Artisans, and Village and Cottage Industries

To augment flow of credit to village and cottage industries, IDBI has extended its Automatic Refinance Scheme to cover composite loans upto Rs. 50,000 sanctioned to artisans and village and cottage industries by SFC/SIDC/bank etc. The assistance may be utilised for equipment finance or working capital or both.

(iii) Integrated Term Loan Scheme

It covers loans upto Rs. 5 lakhs provided by SFC/SIDC to new small scale industries. This is inclusive of working capital upto Rs 2.5 lakh. The lending institution can seek assistance under Automatic Refinance Scheme. The repayment schedule in respect of working capital component in however to be submitted separately as in normal Refinance Scheme.

Loans upto Rs. 50,000 to SC/ST entrepreneurs are extended irrespective of location without insisting on promoter's contribution. Assistance for Quality Control Facilities is granted upto Rs 7.5 lakh to enable them to set up in-house quality testing facilities.

Ex-servicemen including widows of ex-servicemen and disabled persons are provided assistance in collaboration with Director General of Resettlement to set up SSI units. They are provided equity support to the extent of Rs. 1,80,000 per project (Rs 90,000 each from IDBI and DGCR) for starting SSI including transport and other service industries besides normal loans. Projects costing upto Rs. 12 lakh would be eligible for assistance under the scheme. The minimum promoter's contribution would be 10 percent of project cost. A nominal interest rate of 1 percent p.a. is chargeable on the equity type of assistance. The debt equity ratio would be 3 : 1. Repayment would be spread over 10 years including initial moratorium of 5 years. In case of transport, the repayment period would be 5 years including grace period of 3 years. Projects costing upto Rs. 50,000 will be covered under Composite Loan Scheme and usual norms of promoter's contribution, debt equity, security etc. will not be insisted on.

IV. Refinance Scheme for Rehabilitation of Sick Units

The units assisted by banks/SFCs/SIDCs and classified as sick are eligible for assistance under this scheme. ASSI unit is classified as sick if :—

(a) it has incurred cash loss during the previous accounting year and is likely to incur cash loss in current accounting year and has an erosion on account of cumulative cash losses to the extent of 50 percent or more of its net worth and/or;

(b) it has continuously defaulted in meeting four consecutive quarterly instalments of interest or two half yearly instalments of principal on term loans and there are persistent irregularities in the operation of its working capital limits.

Both the above-mentioned conditions must be satisfied in case of SSI unit. But it is sufficient if either condition is satisfied in the case of tiny and decentralised unit.

Rehabilitation assistance might cover *inter alia* margin money for additional working capital, payment of statutory liabilities, cash losses during nursing, over due instalments apart from minimum capital expenditure required for restarting the units towards a viable level.

V. Refinance for Modernisation

It is provided to help small units to adopt improved/updated technology and methods of production with a view to achieving higher production and improvements in the quality of the product. The eligible unit must have been in existence for at least 5 years except in case of industries involving fast changing technology. Loans upto Rs. 7.5 lakhs will be covered under ARS and proposals bigger than this would need certificate from Technical Consultancy Organisation of the State/SISI that the scheme would lead to modernisation besides one or more of the following :

(a) Upgradation of process, technology and product.
(b) Export- oriented/Import substitution
(c) Energy saving.
(d) Anti-pollution measures.
(e) Conservation/substitution of scarce raw materials and other inputs including recycling/recovery of wastes and by products.
(f) Improvement in capacity utilisation within the existing capacity through increase in productivity and de-bottlenecking.
(g) Improvements in material handling.

(b) Bills Rediscounting Scheme

IDBI re-discounts bills/promissory notes arising out of sale of indigenous machinery to purchaser. IDBI sanctions special rediscounting limits to banks for exclusive utilisation by small sector. This facility is available for purchase of machinery for expansion, diversification and modernisation. To avail it, the small unit need not submit the bills arising out of sale/purchase of machinery. An advance or down payment of 15 percent is usually insisted upon under the scheme with a reduced norm of 10 percent for commercial vechicles and textile machines.

The discount/rediscount for small sector are as follows :

	Rediscount (%)	Discount (%)
(i) Unexpired usance bills between 6 and 36 months	9.75	11.00
(ii) Over 36 months	9.25	10.50

Extent of Refinance to Institution

Category	*Extent of refinance (%)*
A. Units Financed by SFCs/SIDCs/SCBs and RRBs.	
1. Under Automatic Refinance Scheme (ARS)	
(a) Composite loans, loans to physically handicapped & SC/ST entrepreneurs upto to 50,000	100
(b) Loans upto Rs 7.5 lakhs to SSI units and SRTOs.	100
(c) Loans upto Rs. 7.5 lakhs to women entrepreneurs	100
2. Under Normal Refinance Scheme (NRS)	
(a) Loans upto Rs. 7.5 lakhs for quality control facilities	100
(b) SRTOs having national permit	100
(c) Loans (including for rehabilitation and modernisation purposes) to units located in—	
(i) 'A' Category backward districts	90
(ii) Others	85
3. Relief Refinance Facility	100
4. Integrated Term Loan Scheme (extended by SFCs and smaller SIDCs only)	100
5. Foreign Currency Refinance Scheme (extended by SIDCs/SIICs only)	100
6. Equipment Refinance Scheme (extended by SFCs/SIDCs only)	75
7. Scheme for Assistance to Ex-Servicemen (extended by SFCs & smaller SIDCs only)	
(i) Loans upto Rs. 50,000	100
(ii) Loans above Rs. 50,000	as at 2 (c) above
B. Units Financed by Commercial Banks Under all the schemes indicated at 1 to 3 above (except those covered by 1 (a) & 2 (a) where 100 per cent refinance is extended)	75

Refinace Interest Rate Structure

	Ceiling rate chargeable by primary lenders (% p.a.)	*IDBI's rate for primary lender (% p. a.)*
1	*2*	*3*
1. Basic lending rate	14.0	10.5
2. Concessional rates for		
(a) Composite loans upto Rs. 50,000 per units to artisans and industrial units in tiny cottage and village sectors.		
(i) in backward areas	10.0	6.5
(ii) in non-backward areas	12.0	8.5
(b) Loans upto Rs. 50,000 to units set up by SC/ST and by physically handicapped entrepreneurs	10.0	6.5
(c) Small-scale unit		
(i) in backward areas	1.25	9.0
(ii) in non-backward areas		
(a) upto the extent of first Rs. 25 lakhs loan	13.5	10.0
(b) above Rs. 25 lakhs loan	14.0	10.5
(d) Modernisation assistance	11.5	9.0
(e) Rehabilitation assistance	11.5	9.0
(f) Relief Refinance facility		
(i) Composite loans, loans to physically handicapped & SC/ST entrepreneurs upto Rs. 50,000	5.5	4.5
(ii) Other SSI units (upto Rs. 5 lakhs)	9.5	8.5
(g) Manufacture of or installation of renewable energy/energy saving systems	12.5	9.0
(h) Industrial estates	12.5	9.0
(i) Women entrepreneurs	12.5	9.0
(j) Quality Control facilities	11.5	9.0
(k) Integrated Term-Loan Scheme	12.5	9.0
(l) Ex-servicemen Scheme		

	Ceiling rate chargeable by primary lenders (% p.a.)	*IDBI's rate for primary lender (% p. a.)*
1	*2*	*3*
(i) Terms loans for units		
(a) In backward areas	12.5	9.0
(b) in non-backward areas	13.5	10.0
(ii) Term loans for acquiring transport vehicles	12.5	9.0
3. Loans to SRTOs		
(i) with one/two vechicles	12.5	9.0
(ii) with more than 2 but less than 6 vechicles	15.0	11.5
4. Equipment Refinance Scheme	15.0	11.0
5. Foreign Currency Refinance Scheme (SIDCs/SIICs)		
(i) Floating rate loans	1.5 % over LIBOR	0.5 % over LIBOR
(ii) Fixed rate loans		
US $	10.0	9.0
DM	9.5	8.5

Repayment Period under the Refinance Scheme

Category	*Repayment Period*
1	*2*
(a) Composite Loan Scheme	Normally 3 to 10 years with initial moratorium of 12 to 18 months (for both principal and interest)
(b) Loans under ARS	
(i) to SRTOs	5 years (moratorium of 6 months)
(ii) to SSIs assisted by Commerical Banks	7 years (moratorium of 12 months)
(iii) to SSIs assisted by SFCs/SIDCs	8-1/2 years (including moratorium of 18 months)
(c) Modernisation assistance	Flexible
(d) Rehabiliation assistance	Flexible
(e) Relief Refinance assistance	Flexible
(f) Women Entrepreneurs	10 years with an initial moratorium of 2 years.

Category	*Repayment Period*
1	*2*
(g) Quality Control facilities	8 years including initial moratorium of 3 years
(h) Integrated Term-Loan Scheme	
(i) Term loan component	10 years with initial grace period 18 months
(ii) Working Capital Component	5 years including a grace period of 36 months
(i) Ex-Servicemen Scheme	
(i) Term loans	10 yeaars with usual grace period
(ii) Transport loans	5 years including moratorium of 6 months
(j) Equipment Refinance Scheme	2 to 5 years (including moratorium of 6 to 12 months)

Promoters' Contribution

Category	*Minimum promoters contribution (% of projects cost)*
1. (a) Composite loans, loans to artisans, village/cottage industries and tiny units	Nil
(b) Loans upto Rs. 50,000 to SC/ST entrepreneurs	Nil
(c) Loans upto Rs. 50,000 to physically handicapped entrepreneurs	Nil
(d) Loans for financing quality control facilities by SSI units upto Rs. 7.5 lakhs	Nil
2. Projects set up in	
(a) 'A' Category backward district/regions	12.5
(b) 'B' Category backward districts/regions	17.5
(c) 'C' Category backward districts/regions	20
3. Projects set up by Women entrepreneurs, other than in 'A' Category backward districts	15
4. Projects promoted by technician entrepreneurs	17.5

Category	Minimum promoter's contribution (% of projects cost)
5. Equipment Refinance Scheme	20
6. Integrated Term-Loan Scheme	As at (2) above
7. Road transport operators holding national permits	Nil
8. SRTOs owning upto 6 vehicles	15
9. Modernisation assistance	
10. Rehabilitation assistance	Flexible
11. Relief Refinance facility	no fixed norms
12. Scheme for Assistance to Ex-Servicemen	10
13. Other than those indicated above	22.5

C. Special Capital/Seed Capital Scheme

(i) Special Capital Scheme of SFCs/SIDCs.

To provide equity type of assistance on soft terms to small entrepreneur to enable them to set up projects in small and tiny sectors, SFCs/SIDCs raise a special class of share capital from State Government and IDBI. It is designed to bridge the gap between minimum contribution of the promoter and/or equity stipulated for the proposal and the amount actually brought in the assistance is limited upto upto 20% of the project cost subject to maximum of Rs. 4 lakhs per proposal. The amount of assistance is estimated on the basis of debt equity ratio of 2 : 1.

(ii) Seed Capital Scheme of IDBI

It seeks to help entrepreneurs who lack resources to set up an SSI project. The scheme is operated through SFCs/SIDCs. Seed capital upto Rs. 15 lakhs is given in the form of interest free soft loan to proprietory and partnership firms, making sub-given scription upto 1 percent of the cumulative redeemable preference shares in the case of private limited companies, and 1 percent of equity or cumulative redeemable preference shares or both in case of public companies with a provision of suitable enhancement of interest rate depending on financial position and profitability of the company. Soft loan repayment is spread over a period of 10 years with a moratorium of 5 years.

(D) Assistance to National Small Industries Corporation (NSCI) for the Supply of Machinery on Hire Purchase Basis.

(E) Assistance to Small Industries Developoment Corporations of the States.

SIDCs which are the main agencies at state level providing extensive service to SSI sector in the field of supply of raw material, marketing, sale of machinery on hire purchase basis, setting up industrial estates etc. are given assistance in the form of subscription to ad hoc bonds/privately placed debentures repayable over a period of 10 years including grace period of 2 years at a concessional rate of 11 percent per annum. For the purpose of assistance, SSIDCs are deemed to be an industrial concern as defined in the IDBI Act.

F. Export Finance

In this field IDBI has three schemes namely :

(a) refinancing of medium-term export credit granted by approved banks,

(b) direct credit to exporters;

(c) overseas buyers' credit.

III. Credit Guarantee Scheme

For Small Scale Industries is designed to protect lending institutions against possible lossses from granting credit facilities to the small scale units. The guarantee extends to 75 percent of the amount in default or the amount guaranteed whichever is less. The credit institution has to pay a nominal guarantee commission to the guarantee organisation.

3. Assistance By State Financial Corporations (SFCs)

Constituted with the object of providing term finance to both small and medium units, they provide the following kinds of assistance :

(a) Assistance to educated unemployed and young technicians.

(b) Assistance to technocrats under the Technician Assistance Scheme.

(c) Seed capital assistance to help otherwise viable projects wherein capital is provided in the form of subscription to shares etc on a nominal service charge.

(d) Development Finance Schemes for the development of prototypes or processes by the proposed or existing units.

4. Industrial Credit and Investment Corporation

Sponsored by the world Bank and established in 1955, its object is to render financial assistance to medium and small scale industries through subscriptions and underwriting of shares/debentures, guaranteeing loans obtained from other institutions and granting long-term and medium-term loans.

Some Non-Traditional Methods of Financing

1. *Leasing* : Rather than tie-up massive amounts in capital equipment, plant and machinery etc, many small businesses opt for leasing on hire purchase. Instead of a lumpsum one-time payment, the costs are repaid over a few years. In India the lease financing is gradually gaining popularity. In the area of new technology, renting of equipment is preferred in foreign countries. The firm can try out a new piece of equipment before deciding whether to commit cash for it. Leasing is however different from renting. Leasing is a form of purchase although equipment belongs to the leasing company with commitment to make regular payment over a set period. Renting involves payment for use and there is no responsibility for repair if the machine breaks down.

2. *Factoring* : Problem with all business is that outflow of money from the business is much higher than the trickle of inflow form debtors. This risk can be taken care of by the ''factor'' who undertakes to collect debts and advances. In olden days, factoring resembled money lending. The factor would buy sale invoices (debts) and given 75 percent of their value immediately. He would then collect debts charging interest on money advanced and pay the rest of the money collected after deducting interest. Even the present day factor earns his money this way besides undertaking to underwrite bad debts he is unable to collect. The factor has incentive to perform efficiently and to collect debts since uncollected debts become his financial burden. Certain precautions however are necessary. Getting back the money is splendid provided factor is not achieving this miracle by using strong arm tactics. Since factor gives money against 'sales completed', he has no interest in borrower's survival and might even encourage small business to borrow beyond capacity.

Common Problems in Raising Finances

1. Risk of losing capital :

It may be due to several reasons, namely :

(a) Lack of competitive advantage.

(b) Difficulty in monitoring investment.

(c) Litigation.

(d) Initial problems arising from unlimited variables such as unknown product acceptance, untested product capability.

2. Low profits and low Return on Investment.

3. Failure of company to follow up the investors so that they are not adequately motivated to invest in the firm.

4. Lack of business experience.

Investment is a kind of confidence reposed in the entrepreneur, not the firm. The first aspect looked into by the investors is the experience and reputation of management. Undoubtedly, weak management born of inexperience is the primary factor in accounting for low profits.The elements considered by a prospective investor are : Whether management has good grasp of key factors for success in the business and whether management is honest or creative. In case the businessman is inexperienced, investors would be reluctant to invest.

5. Inadequate exposure to sources of venture capital.

CHAPTER X

LEGAL REQUIREMENTS CONCERNING BUSINESS

Modern business is characterised by the applicability of a large number of laws to it. Much of it is due to a change in the outlook of government towards business. Although it is well nigh impossible for a businessman to have expert knowledge of all the laws applicable to his business yet he must have enlightened awareness about them. He could obtain expert and professional advice in case of difficulty. Below is given a summary of the different laws of which a businessman should be aware:

I. THE FACTORIES ACT, 1948.

The object of the Act is to protect the workers against industrial and occupational hazards. It endeavours to secure for the workers conditions conducive to their health.

The scope of this Act is quite wide and covers all aspects relating to factories namely : approval ; licensing and registration ; inspecting authorities ; health, safety, welfare, working hours, employment of adults and young children ; annual leaves, and penalties for violation.

The broad scheme of the Act is described below :

1. **Meaning of "Factory"**

Section 2(m) defines a factory as any premises including its precincts wherein (i) a manufacturing process is carried on and (ii) the specified number of workers (10 in case manufacturing is carried on with the aid of power, and 20 if carried on without power) are working therein on any day of the preceding twelve months.

'Mines' governed by Indian Mines Act or mobile unit of armed forces or a railway running shed or hotel restaurant or eating place etc are not included in the term 'factory'.

2. The term **'worker'** is defined in section 2 (l) to mean 'any person employed directly or through an agency and whether for or without remuneration either in the manufacturing process or in some work

connected with or indcidental thereto.

3. Section 6 of the Act provides that before a site is used as factory, previous permission in writing of the State Government or the Chief Inspector must be obtained.
4. **Provisions for the health, safety and welfare of workers**

I. HEALTH OF WORKERS

Section 11 to 20 deal with the health of workers and contain to the following provisions :

(a) Cleanliness

Every factory must be kept clean and free from effluvia arising from any drain, privy or other nuisance.

(b) **Disposal of wastes and effluents** so as to render them innocuous.

(c) Ventilation and temperature

Effective arrangements must be made to secure and maintain in every work-room (i) adequate ventilation and (ii) such temperature as will secure reasonable conditions of comfort and prevent injury to workers.

(d) Dust & Fume

Where the manufacturing process is liable to give dust or fume, steps must be taken to prevent its inhalation and accumulation in any work-room.

(e) Artificial humidification

Regulation relating to the method to be used for artificial humidifications as prescribed by the state government must be observed.

(f) Overcrowding

To prevent overcrowding, there must be 500 cubic feet of space for every worker in a workroom.

(g) Lighting

In every part of the factory where worker are working or passing, sufficient lighting—natural, artificial or both shall be maintained

(h) **Drinking water**

Adequate arrangement for drinking water is to be made and where the number of workers is more than 250, cool drinking water shall be provided.

(i) **Latrines and urinals** with separate accommodation for male and female workers.

(j) **Spitoons** are to be provided at convenient places.

II. SAFETY OF WORKERS (SECTIONS 21—41)

(a) **Fencing of machinery**

The dangerous parts of all such machines as moving parts of prime movers, fly wheels, electric generators rotary converters etc shall be securely fenced.

(b) **Work on or near moving machines**

Work on moving machinery shall be carried out only by specially trained adult male worker wearing light fitting clothes and whose name has been recorded in a register.

(c) **Young persons** shall not be made to work on a dangerous machine unless fully instructed or sufficiently trained or placed under the supervision of an-experienced person.

(d) Provision and **maintenance of striking gear or other devices** for cutting off power.

(e) **Casing of new machinery**

All power driven machinery shall be encased or otherwise effectively guarded.

(f) Prohibition of **employment of women and children near cotton openers.**

(g) Hoists and lifts.

In every factory, hoists and lifts are to be of good mechanical construction, sound material and adequate strength and thoroughly examined by a competent person every six months.

Similar provision has been made with respect to **lifting machines, chairs, ropes and lifting tackles.**

(h) **Revolving machinery**

Where grinding is carried on in a factory, maximum safe working peripheral speed of grindstone shall be notified by means of a notice.

(i) In case of **pressure plants** safe working pressure is not to be exceeded.

(j) **Floors, Stairs and Means of Access**

All these shall be of sound construction and properly kept and maintained.

(k) **Pits, pumps or openings in floors** are to be securely covered or fenced.

(l) Provisions have also been made for **'protection of eyes'** and for taking precautions against **'dangerous fumes'**, 'explosive or inflammable dust, gas etc; and also in case of fire.

(m) **Obligation to appoint safety officers**

Safety officers shall be appointed if the factory employs 1000 or more workers or if the state government so prescribes.

The owner of a small industry is also advised to keep in mind the provisions relating to hazardous processes introduced by the Amendment Act, 1987.*

III. WELFARE OF WORKER (SECS. 42 — 50)

A worker would be entitled to the following facilities :—

(a) Washing facilities ; (b) Facilities for storing and drying clothing; (c) Facilities for sitting, (d); First-aid appliances; (e) Canteen (where 250 workers are employed); (f) Shelters, rest-rooms and lunch-rooms ; (g) Creches (if 30 or more women are employed); (h) Appointment of welfare officers in factory employing 500 or more workers.

IV. HOURS OF WORK (SECS. 51 — 54)

Maximum working hours for adult worker per week shall be 48. The daily hours of work shall be restricted to 9. There is to be **rest interval** of half an hour after 5 hours. The period of work cannot be **spread over** more than $10\frac{1}{2}$ hours.

There is a provision for holiday on the first day of the week (or other substituted day which is duly notified). Compensatory holiday must be given where the worker is deprived of his weekly holiday. Where a worker works for more than 9 hours in any day or more than 48 hours in a week, he will be entitled to double the ordinary rate of wages. There is a prohibition on double employment.

Employment of Children

Section 67 of the Act forbids the employment of a child (i.e. person below 14 years of age) in a factory. Though 'non-adult worker' who has completed 14th years but not 15th years and an 'adolescent' who has

---

* Chapter IV-A (SS. 41-A to 41-H)

completed 15th year but not 18th year may be permitted to work in a factory provided he has a certificate of fitness from a certifying surgeon and carries a token giving reference to that certificate while at work. But a person who has not completed 17th year of age shall not be allowed to work in a factory during night.

Working hours for a child shall be $4\frac{1}{2}$ spread over 5 hours. Moreover the period of work of children shall be limited to two shifts which shall not overlap. There is a further obligation to maintain a 'Register of Child-Workers'.

As already indicated, there is a general prohibition on the employment of children on moving machinery or dangerous machinery or for pressing cotton in a cotton opener.

There are comprehensive rules for 'annual leave with wages'.

2. The Employment of Children Act, 1938

The Act further prohibits employment of children below 15 years of age in any occupation (a) connected with transport of passengers, goods or mails by railway; or (b) connected with a port authority.

As regards a child who has completed 15th year but not 17 years, the working hours are to be so fixed that he is allowed a rest of 12 hours including at least seven consecutive hours between 10 p.m. and 7 a.m.

A child below 14 years is not to be employed in : bidi-making, carpet weaving, cement manufacturing, cloth printing, dyeing and weaving, match-manufacturing, explosives & fireworks, mica-cuttting, soap manufacture, tanning, wool cleaning etc.

3. The Employees' State Insurance Act, 1948

The principal object of this Act is to secure certain benefits to employees and their dependants. These benefits are available in the event of sickness, maternity and employment injury. The benefits are given in the form of (a) periodical payment and/or (b) medical treatment.

Coverage of the Act

The Act covers all persons employed for wages in or in connection with the work of factory or establishment irrespective whether they are manual, supervisory or salaried provided their remuneration does not exceed Rs. 1600 p.m.

The Act does not apply to : (a) Seasonal factories; (b) Factories or establishments under the control of the Government ; (c) A worker whose wages exceed the limit stipulated by the government ; (d) Factories working with the aid of power but employing less than ten persons ; (e) Factories working without the aid of power but employing less than twenty persons ; (f) Mines subject to the Mines Act, 1952; (g) Railway running sheds.

Benefits under the Act

(1) **Medical Benefit** : Medical treatment and attendance are provided for the insured person as well as his dependants at the State Insurance Dispensaries.

(2) **Sickness Benefit** : Under it, periodical payments are made to the person who is in receipt of free medical aid.

(3) **Maternity Benefit** : It consists of periodical payments in case of confinement of an insured employee woman. The benefit is payable for a period of 12 weeks of which not more than 6 shall precede the expected date of confinement.

(4) **Dependants' Benefits** : These are periodical payments to the dependants of an insured employee who has died as a result of injury sustained in the course of employment.

(5) **Disablement Benefit** : If an insured person is injured in the course of his work and disabled-permanently or temporarily he will get cash payments on a periodic basis.

Contributions

The scheme being contributory in nature, both the employers and employees have to pay their contributions at the rates prescribed in the Act. An employee whose average daily wage during the period is below Rs. 6 shall not be liable for the payment of contribution.

Conditions for Receipt of Sickness or Disablement Benefit

A person in receipt of sickness or disablement benefit (except that granted on permanent disablement) is required to observe the following conditions :

(i) To remain under medical treatment at a dispensary, hospital, clinic provided in the Act.

(ii) To carry out the instructions given by the medical officer .

(iii) Not to do anything which might retard or prejudice the chances of recovery.

(iv) Not to leave the area where medical treatment is given without the permission of the medical officer.

(v) To allow himself to be examined by any duly appointed medical officer or other person authorised by the Corporation.

Penalties have been prescribed for the following :—

(i) Failure to pay contribution,

(ii) Deduction or attempt to deduct employer's contribution from the wages of an employee.

(iii) Reduction in the wage or any privilege or benefits admissible to an employee.

(iv) Dismissal, discharge, reduction or otherwise punishing an employee.

(v) Failure to submit any return required by the regulations or making of a false return.

(vi) Obstructing any officer of ESIC in the discharge of duties etc.

The Employees' Provident Fund and Misc. Provisions Act, 1952.

The Act is a piece of welfare legislation designed to provide security for old age to the industrial workers. Under the Act, the employees and employers are required to contribute sums to the Provident Fund for the benefit of employees.

Application of the Act

The Act is applicable—

(a) to every establishment which is a factory engaged in any industry specified in Schedule I in which twenty or more persons are employed; and

(b) to any other establishment which the central Government may by notification in the Gazette, specify.

The Act could be made applicable by the Central Provident Fund Commissioner if an application in this behalf is made to him or there is a mutual agreement between the employer and majority of employees.

Contribution

The contribution to be made by the employer and employee has been fixed @8.33 percent of basic wages, dearness allowance* and retaining allowance if any.

---

* According to Explanation 1 to Sec. 6, 'dearness allowance' is deemed to include the cash value of any food concession allowed to the employee.

5. The Industrial Employment (Standing Orders) Act, 1946

The object of the Act is to require employers to define the conditions of employment and to make the said conditions known to the workmen. The matters regarding which provisions have to be made in the standing orders have been given in the Schedule attached to the Act. The standing orders after being certified by the apporpriate authority will constitute statutory terms of employment between the industiral establishment and its employees. The Act is applicable to every industrial establishment employing 100 or more workmen. The following matters are required to be specified in the standing orders :

(a) Classification of workmen (permanent, temporary, probationer etc.)
(b) Manner of intimating to workmen periods and hour of work, holidays, pay days and wage rates.
(c) Shift working.
(d) Attendance and late coming.
(e) Procedure to be followed while applying for leave and holidays, and the authority to whom application is to be made.
(f) Requirement to enter premises by certain gates and liability to search.
(g) Closing and reopening of sections of the industrial establishment, termporary stoppages of work and rights of employer and workmen arising thereform.
(h) Suspension or dismissal for misconduct and acts which constitute omission.
(i) Termination of employment and the notice thereof to be given by the employer and workmen.
(j) Means of redress for workmen against unfair treatment or wrongful exactions made by the employer.

The draft standing orders are required to be submitted to the certifying officer within six months of the date of application of this Act to the establishment.

6. The Industrial Disputes Act, 1947

Broad object of the Act is to make provision for the investigation and settlement of industries disputes, and to :

(a) promote measures for securing goods relations between employers & workmen;
(b) inquire into any matter connected with or relevant to an industrial dispute;

(c) promote the settlement of industrial disputes;
(d) refer individual disputes to grievance settlement authority;
(e) prevent illegal strikes and lockouts;
(f) prevent unfair labour and practices;
(g) provide for the payment of wages from date of award till final decision in court.

By an amendment in 1982, it has been made obligatory for an employer to set up a 'Grievance Settlement Authority' in an industrial establishment in which fifty or more workmen have/had been employed in the preceding twelve months. It shall have the responsibility to settle industrial disputes connected with an individual workman.

The employer has been made liable to pay compensation in the event of lay off*, retrenchment,**, transfer of undertakings and closing down of undertakings.

7. The Workmen's Compensation Act, 1923

The Act aims at securing the payment of compensation by employers for injuries sustained by an employee in an accident which has occurred either in the course of or out of employment. Thus the Act makes the employer liable to pay compensation if :—

(a) a personal injury has been caused to the workman;
(b) the injury has been caused by an accident ;
(c) the accident has arisen out of and in tthe course of employment ; and
(d) the injury has resulted either in the death of the workman or in total or partial disablement for more than 3 days.

The employer is also liable to pay compensation for occupational diseases contracted by a workman. Schedule III of the Act gives a comprehensive list of occupational diseases peculiar to certain occupations.

Compensation is payable for : (i) death, (ii) permanent total disablement, (iii) permanent partial disablement and (iv) temporary disablement—whether total or partial.

Part II of Schedule I to the Act gives a long list of injuries deemed to result in permanent partial disablement along with percentage of loss of earning capacity which is deemed to result in each case.

The employer is *not* liable to pay compensation in the following cases:

---

* Refer to Sections 25 (C) of I.D. Act. 1947.
** Sec. 25 (F). Ibid.

(i) In respect of an injury which does not result in the total or partial disablement of the workman for a period not exceeding three days.

(ii) If, at the time of accident, the workman was under the influence of drink or drugs.

(iii) If the workman is guilty of wilful disobedience of an order given or rule expressly framed for securing the safety of workman.

(iv) If the workman is guilty of removing or disregarding any safety guard or other device which has been provided for his safety.

(v) If the injured workman has instituted a civil suit for damages in respect of the injury against the employer.

(vi) If the accident causing death or injury did not arise out of and in the course of employment.

8. The Trade Unions Act, 1926

A trade union is an association formed primarily for the purpose of regulating the relations between workmen and employers or between workmen and workmen or between employers & employees. The Act prescribes the regulations for registration of trade unions and then define the law relating to registered trade unions. The basic object is to protect trade unions from civil or criminal prosecution on the ground of conspiracy so that these could carry on their legitimate activities. In specific, the Act lays down (i) the rights and liabilities of registered trade unions; (ii) the objects for which general funds of registered trade union may be spent; (iii) constitution of a separate fund for political purpose.

The Act assumes significance for a small businessman in the event of a trade dispute. He will be required to negotiate with the recognised trade union for the purpose of settlement of dispute.

9. The Payment of Wages Act, 1936

The object of the Act is to secure to workers the payment of wages in a particular form and at regular intervals without any unauthorised deductions. The Act mainly deals with the responsibility for payment of wages, the fixation of wage period, the time for payment of wages and most importantly the deductions that can be made from the payment of wages.

Applicability

The provisions of the Act are applicable to persons employed in a factory or industrial or other establishment or in a railway—whether directly or indirectly through a sub contractor. The Act does not apply to persons whose wages exceed Rs. 1600 p.m.

Responsibility for Payment

The Responsibility for payment of wages has been vested with the employer although the following persons shall also be so liable :

(a) manager in the case of factories,

(b) person responsible to the employer for the supervision and control of the industrial or other establishment in the case of industrial or other establishment,

(c) persons nominated by the railway administration in the case of railways.

Time for payment : In the case of establishments and undertakings which employ less than 100 persons, wages shall be paid before the expiry of the seventh day and in all other establishments, wages shall be paid before the expiry of tenth day, after the last day of the wage period in respect of which the wages are payable. The wages of a person whose services have been terminated shall be paid on the next day after such termination. The payment must be made on a working day.

Permissible Deductions: Only following deductions can be made from the wages of an employee : (a) fines, (b) absence from duty, (c) damage/loss of goods or of money entrusted to employee, (d) housing accommodation provided by the employer, (f) any amenity or service supplied by the employer, (f) recovery of advances or adjustment of over-payment, (g) recovery of loans, (h) income tax, (i) contribution to and repayment of advances from any provident fund, (j) payment to cooperative society or scheme of insurance maintained by the Indian Post Office, (k) deduction made with written authorisation of employee for payment of premium on his life insurance policy or purchase of securities.

The total amount of deductions shall not exceed 75% of the wages where deductions are made for payment to cooperative societies and in any other case 50% of the wages.

Rules for imposition of fine : Fines can be imposed in respect of approved list of acts and omissions. the list must be exhibited at or near the main entrance of the factory or at the prescribed places in the case of railway. Before imposing fine, the employee shall be given an opportunity of showing cause. The total amount of fine shall not exceed an amount equal to half-an-anna in the rupee of the wages payable to him in respect of that wage period. No fine shall be imposed on a person below the age of 15 years.

All fines and amounts realised on account of such fines shall be recorded in a register.

Similar rules have been made with regard to deductions for absence from duty, damage and loss, recovery of advances, payment to cooperative societies etc.

10. The Minimum Wages Act, 1948

The object of the Act is to provide for fixing minimum rates of wages in certain employments mentioned in the schedule attached to the Act. The employer is required to pay wages at the prescribed rates without any deduction except those as may be authorised.

11. The Employment Exchanges (Compulsory Notification of Vacancies) Act, 1959.

By virtue of this Act, employers in private or public sector establishments are required to notify to the employment exchanges all vacancies other then those in the unskilled categories or of less than three months or in the domestic service or the vacancies proposed to be filled through promotion. The employers are also required to file returns relating to staff strength at regular intervals.

12. The Apprentices Act, 1961

It is important for the owner of an enterprise to ascertain whether the provisions of Apprentices Act have been made applicable to it. In that case he will have to discharge the following types of obligations :

1. To provide the apprentice training in his trade in accordance with the legal provisions.
2. To appoint a qualified person to give training to the apprentice.
3. To pay to every apprentice during apprenticeship training a stipend at not less than the prescribed minimum rate.
4. To pay compensation to the apprentice in accordance with the provisions of the Workmen's Compensation Act if personal injury is caused out of and in the course of his training.
5. To maintain records of the progress of training of each apprentice.

13. The Indian Boilers Act, 1923

Where the manufacturing process necessitates the use of a boiler, the provisions of Boilers Act, 1923 must be observed. Firstly, a permit is needed for its use. To obtain this permission, boiler must be registered by applying to the Inspector. Secondly, the transfer of boiler from one state to another needs to be reported to the prescribed authority. Thirdly, the boiler cannot be operated at more than the maximum pressure recorded in the certificate. Lastly, the boiler must be put in-charge of a person holding a certificate of competency.

14. The Payment of Bonus Act, 1965

This Act creates a statutory obligation on the employers to pay bonus to the employees. The Act applies to : (i) a factory as defined in Section 2 (m) of the Factories Act, 1948; and (ii) every other establishment in which 20 or more persons are employed on any day during an accounting year. However, the government is empowered to extend the Act to any establishment employing less than 20 but not less than 10 persons by giving two months notice.

Every employee who has worked for not less than thirty working days in an accounting year shall be eligible for bonus. The bonus depends on the calculation of available surplus as per the prescribed procedure. The Act has also stipulated the minimum and maximum amount of bonus.

15. The Payment of Gratuity Act, 1972

Gratuity is a payment in recognition of the long and meritorious services rendered by an employee. The payment is made at the time o retirement. The payment of gratuity is regulated by the Gratuity Act. The Act is applicable to : (i) every factory, mine, oilfield, plantation, port, railway company; (ii) every shop or establishment in which 10 or more persons are/were employed on any day of the preceding twelve months. All employees in such establishments drawing remuneration upto Rs. 2500 p.m. are eligible for gratuity provided they have rendered continuous service of not less than five years except in case of termination of employment by death or disablement. The gratuity is payable at the rate of fifteen days' wages as last drawn for every completed year of service or part thereof in excess of six months.

Gratuity is not liable to attachment in execution of any decree or order of any civil, revenue or criminal court.

16. There is also the obligation to register under the Central Sales Tax Act, and/or State Sales Tax Law as and where applicable.

CHAPTER XI

TAXATION BENEFITS TO SMALL INDUSTRY

The taxation laws of the country are geared towards the promotion of small industries. A knowledge of such benefits or concessions is essential for a small entrepreneur. Below is given a description of such taxation benefits as are available under the Income Tax Act, 1961. For a further clarification, the entrepreneur is advised to persue some standard text on 'Taxation Laws' or better consult a professional tax advisor.

1. Depreciation

Under Section 32 of the I.T. Act, 1961, a deduction as per the prescribed rates and conditions in respect of depreciation of a block of assets such as buildings, machinery, plant and furniture owned by the assessee and use by him for his business or profession in the previous year.

The conditions for claiming depreciation benefit are as follows :-

(i) It is available only in respect of buildings, machinery plant and furniture.

(ii) The asset must be owned by the assessee.

(iii) The asset must be used for assessee's own business or profession in the previous year.

(iv) The prescribed particulars must be furnished to the I.T.O. as required under Section 34 (1).

The term 'plant' is defined in section 43 (3) to include 'ships, vehicles, books, scientific apparatus and surgical equipments'.

From assessment year 1988-89, depreciation is allowed in respect of **block of assets*** calculated at the specified percentage as given in Appendix-1 to I.T. Rules on the written down value of such block of assets.

From assessment year 1991-92 in the case of a company, deprecia-

---

* Block of assets means a group of assets in respect of which the same percentage of depreciation is allowed [Sec. 2 (11)] of I.T. Act, 1961]

tion will' be limited to 7590 of the amount calculated at the specified percentages on the written down value of block of assets.

Following points need special attention in this context.

1. Where actual cost of plant & machinery does not exceed Rs. 5000, the whole of it shall be allowed as deduction in respect of the previous year in which it is first put to use by the assessee for his business or profession.
2. Where new machinery and plant is installed during the previous year for the production of any article or thing and such production (or manufacturing) is done by using any technology or know-how developed or invented in laboratory of the government/public sector company/university/duly recognised institution, then such plant and machinery shall be treated as part of the block of assets qualifying for depreciation @50% of written down value subject to following conditions :
   (a) the right to use such technology etc. has been acquired from the owner of the laboratory or from any person who has derived the right from such owner;
   (b) the return filed by the assessee for the year of installation is accompanied by a certificate from the prescribed authority that such technology is develped etc. in such laboratory; and
   (c) the machinery or plant is not used for the manufacture of any low-priority article as listed in Eleventh Schedule.

There is also a provision for the "Set-off and Carry Forward of Unadjusted depreciation" to subsequent years.

2. Investment Allowance and Investment Deposit Account [Sec. 32-A and 32-AB]

Deduction on account of investment allowance was withdrawn from Ist April, 1987 though it was revived and allowed in respect of specific assets acquired from Ist April 1988 (Assessment Year 1989-90). Investment Allowance has again been withdrawn from Ist April 1990 (i.e. Assessment Year 1991-92)

Accordingly, plant and machinery installed in a small-scale industrial undertaking will be eligible for deduction @20% of the actual cost of the asset.

A higher investment allowance @35% of thé actual cost is allowed in case of certain assets installed before 1st April 1987 [e.g. plant and machinery developed through indigenous technology in government owned laboratory etc. or equipment for the control of pollution/protection of environment].

Conditions for claiming investment allowance :

(i) Assessee must submit particulars of the plant and machinery acquired by him.

(ii) 75% of the investment allowance to be actually allowed in a previous year must be debited to Profit and Loss A/c and credited to 'Investment Allowance Reserve Account'.

(iii) The investment allowance will be deducted from the taxable profits or rthe previous year in which the concerned asset has been acquired and installed or if it has been used in the immediately succeeding previous year, then in that succeeding previous year.

(iv) Within 10 years from the expiry of the previous year in which the plant and machinery was installed, the amount standing to the credit of investment allowance reserve must be utilised for the acquisition of a plant and machinery etc.

(v) Till the acquisition of new asset as aforesaid, the reserve is not to be used for distribution of dividend or for remittance outside India as profits or creation of any asset outside India.

(iv) The transfer of such asset is forbidden before the expiry of eight years from the end of previous year in which it was acquired/installed. This prohibition does not apply where the transfer is made to : (a) government/local authority/statutory corporation/government company or (b) it is in connection with any scheme of amalgamation or succession.

No investment allowance is allowed if deduction is claimed under section 32-AB.

INVESTMENT DEPOSIT ACCOUNT [SECTION 32-AB]

Investment Deposit Account was substituted in place of Investment Allowance. However, the facility has been withdrawn from 1st April 1990 [i.e. Assessment Year 1991-92]. The amount of deduction will be *lesser* of the following :

(a) the amount deposited in the Development Bank or utilised in the prescribed manner; or

(b) 20% of the profits of the business/profession.

The deduction is allowed before setting off any loss carried forward from an earlier previous years and Sec.-72.

3. Expenditure On Scientific Research. (Sec. 35)

Following expenditure incurred on scientific research is allowed as deduction :

(a) Any revenue expenditure on scientific research related to the business of the assessee in the previous year.

(b) Any sum paid to scientific research association or university, college, institution or to a public company.

(c) Any expenditure of capital nature on scientific research related to the business carried on by the assessee subject to the provision of Sec. 35 (2)

Unabsorbed capital expenditure on scientific research can be carried forward for adjustment against profits of the subsequent years without any time limit.

4. Expenditure on Acquisition of Patents and Copyrights (Sec. 35-A)

Where a patent or copyright is used for a business whose profits are taxable, the expenditure on its acquisition is deductive in 14 equal instalments beginning with the previous year in which the expenditure was incurred, or where the expenditure was incurred before the commencement of business, the previous year in which the business was commenced.

5. Expenditure on Know-How (Sec. 35 AB)

Any expenditure on acquiring know-how for the purpose of business is allowed to be deducted in *six annual instalments* beginning form the previous year of acquisition.

Where technical know-how has been developed in a university, laboratory or institution, the expenditure will be deductible in three equal instalments beginning from the year of acquisition.

6. Amortisation of Certain Preliminary Expenses (Sec. 35-D)

An Indian company or a resident assessee is allowed to write off the preliminary and development expenses incurred by it in connection with the setting up of a new industrial unit or extension of an existing industrial unit. Such writing off is allowed against profits in ten equal annual instalments beginning with the previous year in which new unit commences production or extension of existing unit is completed. Example of such expenditure are : preparation of feasibility or project report, conducting of market survey, engineering services, legal charges etc.

The qualifying limit of deductible expenditure is 2.5% of the actual cost of fixed assets or of capital employed in the business of the assessee (in the case of a company only).

7. Section 36 allows the following deduction from gross receipt of a business :
   (i) Insurance premium paid on stock and stores used in the manufacture of products.
   (ii) Premium for employees' health insurance.
   (iii) Bonus or commission to employees.
   (iv) Interest on borrowed capital.
   (v) Contribution to provident or other funds at prescribed rates.
   (vi) Bad Debts.

8. General deductions in respect of expenditure not covered under Sectors 30 to 36 is allowed by Section 37 provided :

(a) It is not in the nature of capital expenditure.
(b) It is not in the nature of personal expenses of the assessee.
(c) It is laid out wholly and exclusively for the purpose of business or profession of the assessee.

DEDUCTIONS FROM GROSS TOTAL INCOME

Assessee is allowed deduction from gross total income of certain payments made by him as well as of certain incomes received by him during the previous year. Some important items of such kind are described below :

(i) Profits of newly established industrial undertakings or approved hotels set up in any backward area. [Sec. 80 HH]

20% of the profits of such undertakings étc. are allowed to be deducted for 10 years beginning with the year of commencement of manufacture or production. However, the deduction is not available to those undertakings etc. which begin to manufacture or start functioning after 31st March, 1990.

(ii) Small Scale industries in rural area [80-HHA]

20% of the profits of newly established small-scale industrial undertaking are allowed to be deducted for 10 years from the year of commencement of manufacture provided :

(a) It is not formed by splitting or reconstruction of a business already in existence.

(b) It is not formed by transfer to it of any building, plant or machinery already used for any purpose.

(c) Its accounts are audited by a chartered accountant.

(d) If the goods held by the undertaking are transferred to any other business carried on by the assessee *vice versa* and the consideration obtained is less than the market value of goods on the date of transfer then for the purpose of deduction, the profits will be computed as if such transfer has been made at the market value.

(e) It does not claim simultaneous deduction under section 80 HH.

(iii) Inter-corporate dividend [Sec. 80-M]

A domestic company whose gross income includes any income by way of dividends from another domestic company, it is allowed deduction upto the maximum amount of dividend distributed by such company on or before the due date * out of its income.

(iv) Royality from foreign sources [Sec. 80-O]

50% of the royalty received by an Indian company from foreign enterprise is exempt provided :

(a) the relevant contract is approved by Chief Commissioner or the Director General.

(b) the income is received in convertible foreign exchange in India and is brought in India in accordance with any law regulating dealings in foreign exchange.

(v) Profits from business of publication of books [Sec.80 QQ]

With effect from 1992-93, 20% of the profits of an assessee from the business of publication of books are liable to be deducted from the gross income. The deduction will be available for a total period of five assessment years beginning with the assessment year 1992-93.

(vi) Profits of industrial undertakings (Sec. 80-1A)

Section 80-1A which has replaced Sec.80-I w.e.f. assessment year 1991-92 allows deduction of profits and gains from an industrial undertaking or ship or hotel, or repair to ocean going vessels etc. at prescribed rates for a total of ten assessment years. The conditions for claiming this benefit in the case of industrial undertakings are as follows:

(a) It is not formed by splitting up or reconstruction of any

---

* It means the date for furnishing the return u/s 139 (1)

business already in existence.

(b) It is not formed by transfer to the new business of any machinery or plant previously used for any purpose.

(c) It produces or manufactures articles or things or operates cold storage plant in any part of India and has begun production on manufacture after 31st March, 1991.

(d) It employs ten or more workers in a manufacturing process carried on with the aid of power or twenty or more workers in a manufacturing process carried on without the aid of power.

CARRY FORWARD AND SET OFF OF ACCUMULATED LOSSES AND UNADJUSTED DEPRECIATION IN CERTAIN CASES OF AMGALGAMATION [Sec. 72-A]

In the following cases, the accumulated losses and unadjusted depreciation of the amalgamating company will be deemed to be the loss and depreciation of the amalgamated company in respect of the previous year in which amalgamation took place.

(i) The amalgamating company owns an industrial undertaking or a shipping unit.

(ii) The amalgamating company had accumulated loss on the last day of the previous year in which amalgamation took place and such loss was being carried forward.

(iii) The amalgamating company was not immediately before such amalgamation financially viable by reason of liabilities losses and other relevant factors.

(iv) The amalgamation was in public interest.

The object of such amalgamation would be to help in the rehabilitation and revival of the business of the amalgamated company.

Conditions which amalgamated company must fulfil to claim set off of accumulated losses and unadjusted depreciation:

(a) Business of the amalgamating company is carried on by the amalgamated company during the previous year in which set off is claimed. Where the said business is modified or recognised for the purpose of efficiency or economy, it must have been approved by the Central Government.

(b) The amalgamated company must submit alongwith the income-tax return for the relevent year, a certificate from the specified authority to the effect that adequate steps have been taken by that company for rehabilitation or revival of the business of the amalgamating company.

Benefits under this section can be availed only after amalgamation has taken place. The carry forward is allowed for a maximum of *eight* years immediately succeeding the assessment year in which amalgamation was effected.

CHAPTER XII

PROFIT BUDGETING, PROFIT PLANNING AND COST CONTROL

A budget is essentially a projected profit and loss account relating to next 12 months of trading activity. It is based an certain assumptions. But it reflects basically the management plans for the future after proper identification of its objective following a detailed analysis of available resources and the operational constraints.

In small firms, the budget system would generally involve the following :

1. Operational Budget

It quantifies the planned trading activity interms of sales, cost of sales, overheads and the profits.

2. Capital Expenditure Budget

It lists the capital expenditure in the budgeting period. The expenditure is financed from profit and is therefore not included in the operating budget. However, acquisition of capital items has an important bearing on cash flow and it must, therefore, be included in the cash budget.

3. Cash Budget

It is a cash flow forecast identifying the implication of operating and capital expenditure budget and available cash resources. It shows the liquidity position of business.

4. Management Information

For the attainment of targetted objectives, it is important that company's performance is regularly measured and compared with original budget. Though such an approach is no guarantee of success yet it will make failure less likely.

Budgeting control aids decision making and facilitates control of expenditure. It motivates the management team as they visualise budget figures as targets to achieve. Budget serve as important delegatory tool in the armoury of small business. Budgetary control informs the entreprenuer as to where he is headed for and where he currently stands.

VARIOUS TYPES OF BUDGETS

The various types of budgets to be prepared in small business are :

1. The Sales Budget

It forecasts sales for say next 6 to 12 months Ideally, the forecast should be made in unit terms and converted into monetary terms. Following exercise can help in the preparation of sales budget.

(a) *Analysis of past trends* : Historical performance is useful guide to future. Analysis of individual items of various products may reflect important trends which may affect future sales. Seasonality, if applicable, should be taken care of :-

(b) *Trends in market place :* It is important to ascertain whether market is expanding or contracting, whether competition is increasing and what would be the effect of price increases on demand.

(c) Forward order books to get an idea of anticipated sales in the short run.

(d) Reports of the sales staff who are in regular touch with customers.

(e) Reports from major customers.

2. Cost of Sales Budget

To establish monthly cost of material necessary into support budgeted sales, the number of units to be sold each month should be multiplied by unit cost. If this is not possible, it would be correct to base material cost on historical material usage relationship duly allowing for any factor that may cause this relationship to change. Budgeting in this area should take into account such factors as change in stocklevel, manufacturing lead time. Wages pertaining to manufacturing should be included in the budget.

3. Overhead Budget

Historical information derived from previous financial statements can provide useful guidance as to trends but it should consider the known changes in overhead structure in coming months and cost escalations.

With the help of these budgets, the firm will be able to calculate the level of profit to be earned during a particular trading period.

BUDGETING FOR CASH

Business success is an admixture of two factors namely : (i) profitability and (ii) liquidity.

Commonest reason for the demise of any business is its inability to meet its commitments as and when they fall due. Whatever the reason for this unfortunate state of affairs, illiquidity or insolvency is the inevitable outcome of shortage of cash. Hence the necessity to formulate a cash budget.

A cash flow forecast i.e. cash budget is based on well defined assumptions and actuals may not tally with the original projections. Discrepancies arise because cash plan is formulated from various budgets relating to sales, cost of sales, overheads, profits etc. which are themselves based on assumptions and the views of the management as to future.

A cash budget should enable the firm to answer the following questions :

(1) Possibility of fructifying the plan with available cash resources.
(2) Effect of planned capital expenditure on cash position.
(3) Time when funds would be needed further.

Preparation of cash budget is relatively simple provided various operating and capital expenditure budgets are available. Without these important documents, a cash budget is likely to have several inaccuracies. A cash budget is therefore a restatement in cash terms of original budget taking into account the timing differential and excluding non-cash items of revenue and expenditure.

The process of preparation of cash budget is outlined below :

(1) Preparation of operating budget and capital expenditure budget. These are prepared in monetary terms on a month by month basis. It will require the projection of sales on a monthly basis, planning of the raw material purchases so as to achieve production cycle, consideration of the stock holding policy of the company etc. Similarly, direct labour will have to be assessed.

The cash forecast will interpret these budgets in terms of receipts and payments of cash.

(2) Production of cash flow forecast relating to the following :
   (i) Sales;
   (ii) Purchase;
   (iii) Direct Labour;
   (iv) Overheads;
   (v) Capital and other expenditure.

At this stage, business will have various schedules of cash receipts and payments which should be compiled into a single document. The monthly cash inflows and outflows should be calculated and related to cash book balance on a monthly basis. It would provide a plan of cash requirements of the company for a predetermined period and facilitates planning and control.

PROFIT PLANNING

Profit is the motivating force in a business. It is a measure of success of a business. Profit may be described as the amount left over for the business owner after the goods or materials have been paid and the bills met. Thus, it is business owner's pay off.

Profits should not however be left to chance. These must be planned and not simply hoped for. A firms profit potential may be evaluated with the help of the following :

1. Breakeven analysis, and
2. Marginal Income analysis.

1. Breakeven Analysis

It is a tool in evaluating the effect of cost structure on profitability. For instance, two firms may not earn similar profits despite having same production and sales volume. It is because of the difference in their cost structure.

Breakeven analysis is the determination of the cost-volume profit relationship. Cost and profit vary with the volume of sales. For the purpose of this analysis, costs are classified as follows :

(a) Fixed cost

It is that part of the total cost that does not vary with the change in volume. These are the costs that are needed to maintain the essential skeleton of the business. These must be incurred even if the firm is temporarily shut down for lack of business. Its examples are : rent, depreciation, salary of the owner, intest etc.

(b) Variable costs

It is that part of the total cost that varies in direct proportion to volume such as materials, direct wages, interest on floating debt etc.

(c) Semi-variable cost

It is the grey area between fixed and variable so that some costs increase with increases in volume but not in direct proportion. These are stand-by costs. For practical purposes, these are considered as fixed. However, the costs that vary in volume in a steep fashion above the minimum level of operation such as advertising, are considered variable.

The significance of breakeven chart for purposes of profit planning is that it clearly shows that above the breakeven point, the firm can make increasingly greater profits. In other words, above the level of sales at which the company breaks even, its rate of profit increases faster than the rate of increase in sales. Conversely, the company suffers increasingly greater losses with decreases in sales. The breakeven chart graphically illustrates to the small business owner the importance of maintaining a high level of production and sales for minimization of losses or the maximization of profits. It also enables the owner to determine changes in breakeven volume and rate of profit resulting from (i) a change in the cost e.g.; a cost reduction programme, or (ii) change in price or product mix.

2. Marginal Income Analysis

In making this analysis, it is the incremental cost associated with a particular plan or alternative course of action that is important not the conventional concepts of average or total cost. Where a small business owner operating at half the capacity is required to choose between two orders A and B, he should compare only the added income and costs associated with each other in order to determine the net effect on profit.

SECTORAL DEPLOYMENT OF BANK CREDIT

Incremental cost may be fixed as well as variable. Let us illustrate. Suppose, the execution of order A requires the firm to obtain special tools which could be used only on that cost, the added cost is regarded as fixed programmed cost which would be charged against the income produced by that order. On the other hand, if the plant was already working at full capacity and the company decides to execute both the orders A and B at overtime, the overtime labour cost would be the variable programmed cost. The incremental cost analysis is of special significance when a plant has large amount of excess capacity.

COST CONTROL

Just as firms in a given industry differ in terms of cost structure, they may also differ in their operating efficiency. Many of the small firms can increase their profits by careful planning and control of operating expenses. Only the fixed (passive) costs i.e. those remaining unaffected by volume changes during the budget period are non-controllable.

In modern business, control is always exercised in relation to some goal. It requires the determination of objectives prescription of standards, and prompt current reporting for comparisons with standards and prompt executive action to bring performance in tune with the plans. The standards may be in the form of time, output, production, employment or other operating aspects of business.

Control of expenditure in any case is the most significant. Expense budgeting, like cash and capital budgeting is a valuable management aid. In the context of expense budget, the object is to achieve certain volume of business at minimum cost. The expense budget is therefore a must for every business. In launching a new enterprise; it helps decide whether the venture be undertaken. To an established business, it means the difference between success and failure.

Profit Limiting Factors

I. Internal Factors

These arise from firm's operations and result in reduction of profits. These are :

(a) Managements reluctance to change so that they are more interested in maintaining the status quo.

(b) Firms focus on building up its reputation than profits as to assume the leadership status.

(c) Preference for liquidity so as to have a current sound financial position.

II. External Factors

(a) Obsession with image building so that firm wants to project itself as charging "fair" prices.

(b) To put entry barriers for new firms, an existing monopoly firm may prefer lower profits.

(c) To limit demands of labour unions.

(d) To avoid the charge of restrictive trade practice under the MRTPA, 1969.

CHAPTER XIII

WORKING CAPITAL MANAGEMENT

Working Capital Management or Current Assets Management is one of the most important aspects of overall financial management in an enterprise. It is basically concerned with the management of current assets, current liablities and the inter-relationship between them.

MEANING OF WORKING CAPITAL

Working Capital is "the amount of funds needed by an enterprise to finance its day-to-day operations". It is that part of the total capital which is employed in short-term operations such as raw materials, semi-processed products, sundry debtors, short-term investments.

Because of its variable nature, the working capital is also referred to as circulating capital. It may be pointed out that the total working capital is composed of two parts namely: (i) Regular and (ii) Variable. Regular working capital is required for permanent investment in any business for holding certain minimum quantity of raw material, finished goods or cash. Such investment is the irreducible minimum and remains permanently sunk in business. The remaining portion of the working capital is variable. The variable portion first gets tied up in raw materials which are then converted into finished goods. On the sale of goods, it gets converted into account receivables or cash and the circle is then completed. It is depicted in the following figure.

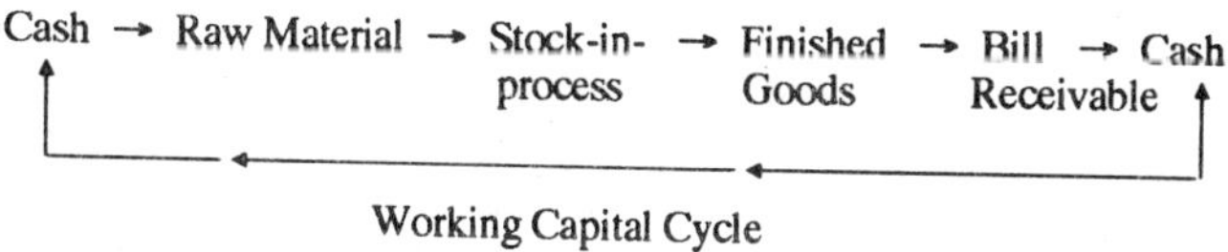

Working Capital Cycle

The term working capital is usually used in two different senses namely:

1. Gross Working Capital
2. Net Working Capital

1. Gross Working Capital

It represents the total value of current assets. In other words, it is the sum total of net working capital and current liabilities. It is a quantitative concept showing the total amount available for financing the current assets. It cannot reveal the true financial position of the company. For instance, every increase in borrowings will increase the gross working capital but the net working capital will remain the same.

2. Net Working Capital

It represents the excess of current assets over current liabilities. "Current Assets" include cash, debtors, stock, bills receivable. "Current liabilities include bills payable, accounts payable, expenses payable. It indicates the liquidity position of an enterprise i.e. the soundness or otherwise of the current financial position. The ratio of 2:1 between current liabilities and current assets is considered sound. The concept of net working capital is a qualitative concept indicating firm's capacity to meet operating expenses and current liabilities. Net working capital is increased only when there is an increase in current assets without corresponding increase in current liability.

Thus, Net working Capital=Current Assets-Current liabilities.

SIGNIFICANCE (NEED) OF WORKING CAPITAL

1. Any business is characterised by :
   (a) Conversion of cash into inventory, (b) Conversion of inventory into receivables, and (c) Conversion of receivables into cash.
   These events constitute operating cycle of a business. If all these events could happen simultaneously, there would not arise any need for working capital. Since cash inflows and cash outflows do not match, an organisation needs necessary cash or liquidity to be able to meet its obligations. Thus adequate working capital is essential for the smooth operation of any business concern.

2. Sound working capital management results in the maximisation of productivity and profits. It requires the maintenance of proper balance between working and fixed capital so as to maintain both profitability and solvency. Proper management synchronises cash receipts and cash outlays.

3. For a small concern, efficient working capital management is still more essential to ensure purchase of inputs at competitive prices and timely payment to factors of production. It may be noted that shorter the gap between spending of money on production of goods and the recovery

of money through rapid sales turnover, the better shall be the quality of working capital management.

FACTORS AFFECTING WORKING CAPITAL REQUIREMENTS

In the case of a small enterprise, the various factors affecting its working capital requirements could be the following :

1. Size of the unit and the volume of business.
2. Nature of production process i.e. lengthier the duration of production, higher shall be the working capital needs and vice-versa.
3. Proportion of raw materials to total cost.
4. Terms of purchase and sale e.g. sales are on cash terms, lesser working capital will be sufficient.
5. Turnover of Inventories: If inventories are large and their turnover is slow, larger working capital would be needed.
6. Labour intensive vs. capital intensive, the former requiring higher amounts of working capital.
7. Cash requirements will have direct impact on working capital quantium.
8. Availability of good and dependable banking facilities reduces working capital requirements.
9. Seasonal requirements may push up the amount of working capital needed.
10. Contingencies: If the demand and prices for small concerns products are subject to wide fluctuations, contingency provision will have to be made for arranging higher amounts of working capital.

DETERMINATION OF WORKING CAPITAL NEEDS

Working capital requirements of a small enterprise vary from unit to unit and in accordance with the differences on the nature of the enterprise. Broadly speaking, working capital should be adequate to meet operating expenses like raw materials, labour, factory and other overheads etc. Operating expenses can be ascertained from the final accounts of the firm. But the working caapital requirements need not be equal to the level of expenses. Operating cycle is of primary significance in every case. For instance, if in a given industrial/commercial unit, the operating cycle is of 3 months, its working capital requirement would be $\frac{1}{4}$ of the annual operating expenses.

Therefore:

$$\text{Total Working Capital Requirement} = \frac{\text{Total Operating expenses in the previous year}}{\text{Number of operating cycles in the year}}$$

Adjustment in the figures of operating expenses must be made in accordance with the changes in price level.

The Puri Committee has suggested a scientific and systematic way of assessing working capital requirements. Banks are using the format suggested by Puri Committee. These formats are given below :

Assessment of Working Capital Requirements upto Rs 25,000

Name of the Bank		*Interview-cum-Appraisal form*
	Figures for last years in case of existing units Rs.	Next year in the case of existing and new units Rs.
1. **Average Monthly sales**	√	√-----------(A)
2. **Monthly Expenses :**		
(i) Raw Materials/ Spares/Stores.		
(ii) Wager and Salaries.		
(iii) Drawing for sustenance of propritor/partners.		
(iv) Other expen ses R.Q. Rent	√	√-----------(B)
Monthly Expense (A-B).	√	√-----------(C)

Working Capital Required

(i) Minimum stock of raw-materials required. -----------days of production

(ii) Production time for converting raw materials into finished products. --------days

(iii) Stocking period for finished goods. --------days

(iv) Normal credit given on sales. --------days

Total length of operating cycle [Total of (i) to (iv)] ----days (D)

Raw Materials and Expenses $= \dfrac{B \times D}{30} =$ .... (Rs.)

required for this period*

Less Amount that can be contributed by applicant. .... (Rs.)

Amount required as working capital loan from the bank. Rs.

---

* Total expense on Raw Materials and Labour Total time taken for converting raw material into cash.

Assessment of Working Capital Requirements
(for advances between 25000 and Rs.2 Lakh).

Name of the unit..................

Anticipated monthly sales	Rs. ------------
Cost of production per month	Rs. ------------
Cost of raw materials per month	Rs. ------------

Item	Stocking/payment peroid.	Working capital required.	Margin. % value	Permis-sible limit
1.	Imported raw materials		--------- months.	
2.	Indigenous raw material		--------- months.	
3.	Stock-in-process		--------- months.	
4.	Finished goods		--------- months.	
5.	Sundry Debtors		--------- months.	
6.	Expenses		--------- months.	
	Total			

Total Working Capital required. --------------- Rs — [A]

Less:- (i) Liquid surplus in Balance Sheet as on------------ Rs.—

(ii) Credit on purchases (months) Rs. —

(iii) Limit recommended Rs. —

Rs — ------------ [B]

DEFICIT [A–B] ------------ [C]

Notes : 1. In the column of 'Working Capital Required', state the value of receivables at cost. Under the column of 'Permissible Limit', give the value thereof at the sales value less margin.

2. For item (3) and (4), the basis of calculation would be the cost of production.

3. Deficit, if any, in the Balance Sheet is to be added to working Capital Requirements.

TANDON COMMITTEE RECOMMENDATIONS REGARDING WORKING CAPITAL

Deficit in working capital may have to be filled up through bank credit. The small business owner should, therefore, acquaint himself with the norms on which bank credit is made available. These norms have been prescribed on the basis of recommendataions of Shri P.L.Tandon , Chairman of Punjab National Bank. This Study group was appointed by the RBI in July 1974.

Terms of Reference of Tandon Committee

1. To suggest guidelines to be followed by commercial banks for supervision of end use of funds and to keep a watch on the safety of advances and to suggest the type of operational data and other information that may be obtained by banks periodically from the borrower, and by the RBI from the lending banks.
2. To make recommendations for obtaining periodical forecasts from borrowers of :
   (a) business ;
   (b) production plans; and
   (c) credit needs.
3. To make suggestions for prescribing inventory norms for different industries both in the private and public sectors and to indicate broad criteria for deviating from these forms.
4. To suggest criteria regarding satisfactory capital structure and a sound financial base in relation to borrowings.
5. To make recommendations regarding the sources for financing the minimum working capital requirements.
6. To make recommendations as to whether the existing pattern of financing working capital requirements by cash credit/overdraft etc. requires to be modified. If so, to suggest suitable modification, and.
7. To make recommendations on any other related matter.

The reference had become essential to tackle the evils connected with the prevalent credit system. The various evils and appropriate tasks are mentioned below :

1. To decide about the *norms of inventory* so that the sanctioned credit is not in excess of actual requirements. Earlier the banks had been following a *security oriented approach* which favoured wealthy parties alone.
2. To suggest *new approach to lending* so that evils of *double financing* could be minimised. Previously, parties used to take loans even against goods purchased on credit.
3. To suggest a *new style of credit* which may discourage entrepreneurs from getting higher limits sanctioned than actually required. By eliminating this evil, banks could plan their credit distribution more effectively.
4. To suggest a new style of INFORMATION SYSTEM OR FOLLOW UP OF CREDIT to make the borrowers more disciplined in

financial affairs. It would enable the bankers to obtain quick knowledge about financial changes in borrowers position thereby ensuring better end-use of funds.

The study group submitted its report in August 1975. Committee's suggestions regarding the above-mentioned four areas are described below.

TANDON COMMITTEE RECOMMENDATIONS

1. Inventory Norms

The study group suggested inventory norms for 15 major industries covering about one-half of total industrial finance of commercial banks. The industries covered were : cotton and synthetic textiles, man-made fibre, jute textiles, rubber products, fertilizers, pharmaceuticals, dyes and dye-stuff, basic industrial chemicals, vegetable oil, paper, cement, engineering (automobiles), engineering ancillaries etc.

The suggested norms for inventories and receivables, are depicted in the following table.

Suggested Norms for Inventory and Receivables

Industry	Raw Materials (Including stores and other items used in the manufacturing process)	Stock–in–process	Finished Goods	Receive--able Bill and purchased dis counted
1. Cotton and Synthetic Textiles	Cotton 2 (Bombay, and Ahmedabad areas) 3 Eastern Area-Bihar, Orissa West Bengal and Assam) $2\frac{1}{2}$ other than above area	$\frac{3}{4}$ [Composite Textile Mills]	→ $2\frac{1}{4}$	←
2. Man made fibre	$1\frac{1}{2}$	$\frac{1}{2}$ [other mills]	→ $1\frac{3}{4}$	←
3. Jute Textile	$2\frac{1}{2}$	$\frac{1}{4}$	1 for domestic sales $1\frac{1}{2}$ for exports	
4. Rubber products	2	$\frac{1}{4}$	→ $1\frac{3}{4}$	←

5. Fertilisers	$\frac{3}{4}$(units near refinery)		1 where stock are in plantoite	
(a) For nitro-enous Plant	$1\frac{1}{2}$ 1 untis away from refinery)	Negliible	$1\frac{1}{2}$ where stock are in upcountry area	$1\frac{1}{4}$
(b) For phos-phate plant	2 (units in port area) 3 (units away from post area	Negligible	1 where stock are at plant site $1\frac{1}{4}$ where stock are in upcountry areas	$1\frac{1}{4}$
6. Pharmac-entcals	$2\frac{3}{4}$	$\frac{1}{2}$	2	$1\frac{1}{4}$
7. Dyes and dyestuff	$2\frac{1}{4}$	1	$\frac{3}{4}$	$2\frac{1}{4}$
8. Basic indust-rial chemicals	$2\frac{3}{4}$	$\frac{1}{2}$	1	$1\frac{3}{4}$
9. Double orig nated	1	Negligible	→ $\frac{3}{4}$	←
10. per	2.6 [Bamboo and wood to be built in stages from Nov. to May]]	Negligible	1 (for controlled sales) $\frac{1}{4}$ (for free sales)	$\frac{3}{4}$
11. Cement	$2\frac{1}{4}$ Gypsum $1\frac{1}{4}$ Limestone $\frac{3}{4}$ Coal $1\frac{1}{4}$ Packing material	$\frac{1}{2}$	→ 1	←
12. Engineering utomobiles & Accessories	$2\frac{1}{2}$	$\frac{3}{4}$	$2\frac{1}{2}$	←
13. Engg. (Cons-umer Durables)	2	$\frac{3}{4}$	→ $2\frac{1}{4}$	←
14. Engg. [An-cillaries] other than Automo-bile & Compo-nent Suppliers	2	$\frac{3}{4}$	→ $2\frac{1}{2}$	←
15. Engg. machin-ery Manufac turers and other Capital Equipment Suppliers	$2\frac{3}{4}$	$1\frac{3}{4}$	→ $3\frac{1}{2}$	←

RBI has asked the commercial banks to adopt the above norms in respect of all industrial borrowers including small-scale industries enjoying total limits in excess of Rs 10 lakh. Industries like railways, boilers, steel plants, mining machinery etc. have been left out from the purview due to their small number, variation in requirements from item to item making generalisations difficult, and because their production cycle run into years. The norms prescribed by the Tandon Committee represent the miximum level of holding inventory and receivables in each industry. The object of prescribing inventory norms is to make borrowers more disciplined.

Deviation from Norms

The prescribed norms are not inflexible. Deviations are permitted in following cases:

1. (a) power cuts, strikes and other unavoidable interruptions in production process.
   (b) transport delays or bottlenecks.
   (c) bunched receipts of raw materials including imports.
   (d) accumulation of finished goods due to non-availability of shipping space, disruption in sales etc.
   (e) build up of stocks due to buyer's failure to take delivery.
2. Sometimes due to *special circumstances*, a unit may request a bank to permit a higher inventory hold up. If the bank is convinced, it could grant a higher limit subject to the following regulations :
   (a) When the limit sought is above Rs. 50 lakhs, reference may be made to RBI and its permission obtained.
   (b) As regards limits between Rs. 25 lakhs and Rs. 50 lakhs, the concerned bank may decide on its own provided information of this decision is given to RBI.
3. In case of *cotton and jute industries* where stock holding is regulated respectively by the Textile Commissioner and Jute Commissioner, bank must make adjustments in the norms accordingly.
4. In case of sick units, demand for higher inventory may not be justifiable except when obsolete stocks have not been disposed of.
5. In case of *export contracts*, deviation could be permitted only where an escalation clause is not incorporated in the contracts. Bank should see that stocks are used for declared purpose only.
6. In case of imported raw materials, deviation is permitted only when import content is very high and the import is being made under the 'Actual user licence'.

Interchangeability of norms not permissible

It may be noted that separate norms have been prescribed in respect of raw materials, stock-in-process, finished goods, bills receivables etc. Borrowers have to comply with each of them separately and interchangeability between one another is not allowed.

2. New Approach to Lending

(I) Working Capital Gap and Bank Finance

According to Tandon Committee, the bankers's main role is to supplement the borrower's resources in carrying a reasonable level of current assets in accordance with the norms. The working capital may be met by the bank as follows :

(i) Bank may work out the working capital gap i.e. current assets minus current liabilities excluding bank borrowings. It may finance maximum of 75 percent of the gap, the balance coming out of borrower's long-term funds namely owned funds and term borrowings.

(ii) Borrower has to provide for a minimum of 25 percent of the total current assets out of long-term funds i.e. owned fund plus term borrowings. A certain level of credit for purchases and other current liabilities will be available and the bank will provide the balance. The total current liabilities inclusive of bank borrowings shall not exceed 75 percent of the current assets.

(iii) The same as in (ii) above except the core currents on the theory that core assets should be financed out of long-term funds.

The above-mentioned three alternatives are illustrated below :

Illustration :

Given is the borrower's financial position as at the end of the next year :

Current Liabilities	Rs.	Current Assets *	Rs.
Creditors for purchases	100	Raw Material	200
Other current liabilities	50	Stock-in-process	20
	150	Finished Goods	90
Bank borrowings including bills discounted	200	Receivables including bill discounted with bank	50
		Other current assets	10
	350		370

* As per suggested norms, whichever is lower in relation to projected production for the year.

First Method		Second Method		Third Method	
Total current assets	370	Total current assets	370	Total current assets	370
Less current liabilities other than bank borrowing	150	25 % of this from long-term sources	92	Less current liabilities from long-term resources	95
Working capital gap	220		278	Real current assets	275
25 percent of the above from long-term sources	55	Less current liabilities other than bank borrowing	150	25 % of the above from long-term sources	69
Maximum bank borrowing possible	156		128		256
		Working capital gap	220	Less current liabilities other than bank borrowings	150
		Maximum bank borrowing permissible	128		56
				Working capital gap	220
				Maximum bank borrowings permissible	56
Excess borrowing	35	Excess borrowing	72	Excess borrowing	104
Current Ratio	1.17 : 1	Current Ratio	1.33 : 1	Current Ratio	1.79 :1

If net working capital (i.e excess of current assets over current liabilities) exceeds 25 percent of working capital (in the First Method), or 25% of total current assets/real current (in the Second or Third Method), the contribution of long -term sources shall ordinarily be to the extent of already existing net working capital.

In the First Method, the bank would finance upto maximum of 75 percent of working capital gap of Rs. 220 and borrower would have to contribute Rs. 55 out of his long-term funds i.e. owned funds plus long-term borrowings. This method gives current ratio of 1:1.

In the Second Method, borrower would finance a minimum of 25 percent of total current assets (i.e. Rs. 92) through long-term funds. The gap of Rs. 128 (Rs. 278—150) would be provided by bank. This will give a current ratio of 1 . 3: 1.

The Third Method would mean further reduction in bank borrowings and strengthening of current ratio. It is an ideal method since it is the largest multiplier of bank finance. To avoid hardship, beginning be made with the first method and then switch over to Second and Third Method. The limit of 75 percent may be proper for setting up of projects in backward areas or restructuring of companies with a weak financial base. Once borrower reaches a stable position, there may be no need to provide bank credit on the same scale.

II. Aligning credit with priority industries

Credit should be provided in consonance with national priorities of industries as laid down by monetary authorities. Relatively low credit be given to low priority industries.

III. Reasonable relationship between equity and total term loans

(i.e. from financial institutions and banks) must be maintained.

IV. Additional Credit

Where a borrower who has already excess borrowing needs additional credit, following points be taken into consideration:

(a) If additional credit is needed on a regular basis, borrower should bring matching contribution under relevant method of lending e.g. from retained earnings or by raising additional equity, issuing debentures and so on.

(b) If borrower cannot raise requisite funds immediately, bank may sanction term loan provided his cash generation capacity is sufficiently good to take care of amortization of existing term obligation including proposed additional loan within a short period.

(c) When additional fund is needed for a short period and cannot be met from existing credit arrangement, additional credit may be granted without insisting on matching contribution.

3. Style of Credit

(A) Bifurcation of the credit limit

Rather than availing the entire permissible limit in the form of cash credit, bank should bifurcate the limit into two parts:

(i) Loan Content: It would comprise of the minimum level of borrowing which the borrower expects to use throughout the year.

(ii) Cash Credit to take care of the fluctuating requirements.

(B) Rate of Interest

- As the loan will carry interest throughout the year, it will compel borrowers to plan their requirements correctly to ensure that very little portion remains unutilised. The banks can plan and diversify their credit.

The demand cash credit is charged a slightly higher rate of interest than the loan compoment.

Where term loan is sanctioned to fill the gap in owner's contribution (i.e. 25%), rate of interest thereon shall be higher than cash credit i.e. $1\frac{1}{2}$ percent higher than loan component.

4. Information System

To check the unplanned use of credit facility, the study group recommended the introduction of quarterly budgeting reporting system. To help the bank assess the borrower's fund requirements, the following be asked to be submitted :

(a) an operating statement;
(b) a finds flow statement for the next year; and
(c) a projected Balance Sheet as at the end of next year.

The next year's statement shall contain plan of action relating to the following :

(a) expansion or diversification of business activity;
(b) investment of funds in other business;
(c) raising of additional credit from various sources;
(d) change in dividend policy;
(e) payment of certain long-term liabilities;
(f) any proposed change in management/ownership.

The quarterly review system has been proposed as the new information system. The object is to enable the bank to assess proper end-use of credit and detect any incipient sickness. The quarterly information system will apply to borrowers enjoying total credit limits of Rs.1 crore or more. Permissible drawings for the next quarter will be equal to drawings of the previous year + the deficit or surplus in the quarter. Within the overall permissible level of drawings, the day-to-day operations on the account will be regulated on the basis of drawing power as per the monthly stock statements. Quarterly statements need not be audited but audited statement will have to be submitted within 3 months of the close of financial year.

Review of Cash Credit System by Chore Committee

Chore Committee was appointed by the RBI in 1979 to review the cash credit system and to make suitable recommendations. It submitted the following recommendations in December 1980.

1. Cash credit system cannot be replaced totally. Rather the need is to

streamline it. The banks should undertake periodical annual review of all borrowing accounts enjoying working capital credit limit of Rs. 10 lakhs and over.

2. Need to strictly enforce the submission of quarterly statements in respect of borrowers having working capital limit of Rs. 50 lakhs and over.
3. Bifurcation of cash credit into core loan portion and variable cash credit portion has not been put into practice to a significant degree. Need is *to fix the core portion at a fairly high level say 80 to 85 percent of the total cash credit.* Moreover, core idea is not applicable to seasonal industries like tea, sugar, coffee. Therefore bifurcation system be withdrawn in future. Where cash credit accounts have already been bifurcated, steps be taken to abolish differential in interest rate.
4. Banks should fix *separate credit limits for peak level and normal non-peak level* in case of agro-based industries like tea, coffee, sugar and also consumer industries like those producing fans, fridges etc.
5. *Drawal of funds* be regulated through quarterly statements. Drawal in excess or below the fixed limit should be considered an irregularity indicating defective planning. If quarterly statement is not filed within prescribed time limit, banks may charge penal interest of one percent per annum on total outstanding for the period in default. Bank should caution the borrower that if the default continues, the account may be frozen with prior notice.
6. *Ad hoc or temporary limits* in excess of the sanctioned limits should be discouraged except in case of unforeseen circumstances. Banks should charage one percent p.a. over normal rate on those limits except in justified cases.
7. *Enhancement of borrower's contribution*

With effect from 1st January, 1981, banks must adopt Second Method of lending recommended by Tandon Committee. Accordingly, borrower's own contribution to meet working capital requirements will be at least 25 percent of total current assets.

8. *Encouragement for bill finance*

Steps be taken to convert all cash credit limits into bill limits wherever possible.

Thus Chore Committee has introduced more rigidity in sanctioning credit limits. On the banks's part, it will entail additional work in the form of fixation of peak and non-peak levels, penal interest, freezing limits and so on.

Ingredients of Working Capital Management in a Small Enterprise

1. Budget the material requirements and devising a proper system of control.
2. Ensure that production goes on uninterrupted so that there is minimum blockage of working capital in the production process.
3. Expeditiously despatch the finished goods to realise cash fast.
4. Follow the bills for early realisation of cash.
5. In the field of cash management, clearly identify the quantum of really surplus cash which could be utilised to meet financial obligations.
6. Ensure proper management of working capital sources so that there is no costly fund raising. There must be a judicious blending of different resources so that sufficient funds are raised at the cheapest cost.

CHAPTER XIV

MANAGEMENT STRATEGIES FOR SMALL BUSINESS (PLANNING)

Studies have revealed the inadvisability of transferring management skills appropriate to a large form to a small firm. It is because of the difference in the nature of these businesses. Moreover, management of activities is different from acting as an employee. The question of devising appropriate management strategies is particularly significant in the case of a small firm where distinction between owner and employee is quite hazy and blurred. The management responsibility of a small business owner require him to perform various management functions described below:

PLANNING

Planning in small business is often entirely overlooked or carried out in a haphazard manner. Substantial number of business failures are attributable to inadequate planning, and lack of experience and managerial competence.

Barriers to planning in case of small firm

(i) The misconception that small firms are relatively simple

Many entrepreneurs base their decision on intuition, rule of thumb, and past experience. Small size of their firm makes them to consider that planning is something meant only for large firms.

(ii) Nature of small enterprise

The entrepreneurs have a personal involvement in business and take personal responsibility for solving all types of problems.

(iii) Desire to maintain secrecy

Small business is born of a desire to keep the secrets with the entrepreneur himself. He may not like to lose them to any outsider who he may have to contact for the purpose of planning.

(iv) Short range perspective of problems

Small business owners tend to take a short range view of problems and seldom develop a long range orientation.

(v) Inadequate planning skill

Small business owners are generally good salesmen or engineers but lack requisite planning skills. Consequently critical planning function tends to get neglected.

(vi) Lack of staff support

Small units lack specialist staff which could collect critical information for formulating a plan. For want of information, planning is unthinkable.

Guidelines for developing effective planning

Guidelines for developing a formal planning system for use by a small business entrepreneur are given below:

1. Understand the barriers to a small business planning.
2. Start with a simpler approach and expand it as the firm's planning experience improves. Initially, formulate a planning-oriented checklist covering strategic factors.
3. Evince a deep commitment to planning and instil the same among subordinates. Involve executives in making a diagnosis of internal weaknesses, external opportunities and threat.
4. Design a planning system suited to specific requirements of the entrepreneur's business rather than implanting some other firm's planning system.
5. Undertake a thorough reappraisal of current managerial practices and decision-making processes before ontŕoducing formal comprehensive planning.
6. Pay adequate attention to existing organizational structure.
7. Make planning a regular feature and use it as a basis of control.

Meaning of planning

Planning is the process of setting the objectives of the firm and then choosing a course of action to move from where it is to where it wants to be at some future time. It is a basic function which enables managers to lay the foundation for other functions. It must cover both long range (covering a period of five years) and short range plans (covering a period of a year or less). Most small business managers spend the bulk of their time on short range planning.

Nature of systematic planning

1. **It is a rational process.** It involves:
   (a) development and especification of a balanced set of organizational objective;

(b) assessment of internal resources (resource analysis) besides an analysis of external environment.

(c) competition analysis i.e. competitive strength of the enterprise vis-a-vis its competitors.

2. Planning is the creation of integrated structure of plans

Planning should be done with reference to different time perspectives or functional areas and all of them must be well integrated. For small enterprises, the time span of long range plans should preferably be three years. The time span of medium and short range plans should extend to two and one year respectively.

3. Planning is a way of life, a kind of philosophy

The managers must have a deep commitment to planning and be ever ready to explore future opportunities and risks. A mental orientation to formal planning should be preferred over intuition.

4. Planning involves political process of negotiation, compromise and strategy formulation

Recognising the existence of inter-relationships between people working in the organisation, the enterprise must incorporate debates, discussions, resolution of differences; consensual decision-making is indispensable for encouraging the staff to work for achieving organisational goals. If inter-personal inter-relationships are competently handled, planning becomes a much smoother and easier exercise.

Advantages of planning

1. It eliminates negative consequences of uncertainty and change.
2. It focusses attention on objectives and provides direction to decision-making.
3. It ensures efficiency in operation.
4. It facilitates control by allowing comparison between actual achievement and established standards.
5. It introduces an element of flexibility in decision-making.

PLANNING PROCESS

Irrespective whether enterprise is large or small, systematic planning involves the following steps :

I. Resource Analysis

It consists of an evaluation of firm's strengths and limitations as well as an awareness of available resources and their utilization.

Comprehensive Planning Format (as developed by Roger A. Golde) covering different facets of business is contained in the following table.

Table showing strategic factors of planning.*

Strategic Factors	Degree of satisfaction with present level of competence					Remedial Action to Improve Competence
	1	2	3	4	5	
• **General Management** • Clearly established objectives. • Ability to attract competent personnel for management positions. • Ability to communicate policies to employees. • Ability to provide effective leadership and to motivate employees. • Management Information System • Use of quantitative tools and techniques in decision-making • Effective organisational structure. • Effective overall cooperation. • Ability to perceive new needs for company's products/services. **Finance** • Ability to raise short-term capital. • Ability to raise long-term capital: . Debt . Equity • Ability to achieve satisfactory ROI. • Effective cost control. • Ability to reduce costs. • Ability to finance new product development. **Marketing** • Ability to gather needed information about markets.						

* **Source :** Adapted from Steiner George A. *Strategie Factors in Business Success.* Financial Executive Research Foundation, N.Y. 1969, p. 4-5.

• Ability to establish a wide customer base.						
• Effective sales organisation.						
• Effective distribution system.						
• Imaginative advertising and sales promotion.						
• Reduced warranty costs. Improved product/service.						
• Development of new markets for existing products.						
Products						
• Improvement of present products.						
• Improved rate of new product development.						
• Improved product quality.						
• Expansion of existing product line.						
• Improvement of product line selection.						
• Effective subcontracting of manufacturing.						
• Engineering and Production						
• Location of production facilities.						
• Plant layout.						
• Technical efficiency of production facilities.						
• Product quality and control. Possibilities for cost reduction.						
• Ability to achieve economies of scale.						
• Flexibility in using production facilities for different products.						
• Product Engineering.						
• Automation of production facilities.						
Personnel						
• Ability to attract qualified employees.						
• Effective personnel relations with employees						
• Effective use of incentives to motivate employee performance. • Financial incentives • Non-financial incentives						
• Relations with labour unions.						
• Ability to level peaks and valleys of employment requirements.						
• Employee turnover.						
• Absenteeism.						
• Employee Morale.						

The scale used in the above table may be interpreted as follows:

1. Not meeting the requirements at all.
2. Not very satisfactory.
3. A little better not good enough.
4. Average, just about passing.
5. Quite satisfactory.

II Situation Audit. It would cover the following :—

(a) Determination and analysis of objectives of the organization as well as its basic strategies. It would be still better if the objectives are stated in the form of specific sub-objectives as illustrated below:

Long range objective.	**Sub-objective**	Sub-sub objective.
To achieve 20% ROI by the end of fifth year	1. Raise gross profit to Rs- in 5 years 2. Upgradation of work force	(a) Reduce overhead (b) Sell obsolete machinery. (c) Reduce advertisement expenditure. (a) Institute management training programmes (b) Replace the unskilled through discharge.

The degree of clarity with which objectives and subobjectives are identified by the entrepreneurs, shall depend the effectiveness of his planning effort.

(b) Analysis of current sales with reference to sales volume by product and sales to key-customers and customer segment. The past sales trends must be analysed to make appropriate strategy changes. Suppose the analysis reveals that 70% (say) of the sale revenue is generated by one-third of the products. The entrepreneur could consider a contraction of the product line.

(c) *Appraisal of resources* covering physical facilities, financial position, managerial capabilities, performance, products etc. In making such an appraisal, ratios derived from balance sheet and profit and loss statement could be of considerable help. Of particular use are ratios pertaining to firm's profitability, operating expenses, gross margin and use of financial resources, as revealed by turnover ratios* — the higher the turnover,

* For instance, Asset turnover Sales/Assets, Inventory Turnover i.e. Sales/Average Inventor; Accounts Receivable Turnover i.e. Total Credit Sales/Average Account Receivable, etc.

the more efficient the use of available capital. The actual ratios* to be used would depend on the specific requirements of each business.

(d) *Environmental analysis* i.e. evaluation of external conditions such as economic developments, government regulations, technological changes etc.

(e) *Competition analysis* i.e. comparative analysis of firm's strengths and weaknesses in relation to major competitors.

(f) *Development of non-financial ratios:* With a view to ascertain the inefficiencies or weaknesses, small business should develop some non-financial ratios of the following kind:
It is calculated as follows :
Potential maximum utilization of machines.

   (i) *Production capacity utilization ratio:* It is helpful in production and investment .

   (ii) *Personnel turnover ratio* : It reveals the rate of change of personnel. A high ratio indicates negative impact on productivity. It equals:

$$= \frac{\text{Separations over a given period}}{\text{Average number of employees}}$$

To involve the personnel in planning, a standardized format given below could be provided for use by them:

FORM IDENTIFYING FIRM'S STRENGTHS AND WEAKNESSES

Planning Issue......................
Identified as : Weakness. ☐ Strength. ☐ Threat. ☐ Opportunity.
Statement of the issue..
Observations are based on...

III. Development of Plan Based on Situation Audit.

The future course of action to be adopted can be determined by undergoing the following process :

(a) Establishment of plan priorities.

---

* Refer to, Sanzo, Richard. **Ratio Analysis for Small Business.** Small Business Administration, Washington.

(b) Alternatives for averting the threats and exploiting the opportunities.
(c) Selection of specific course of action for each planning issue.
(d) Grouping of plans into 'action programmes' for different functional areas.
(e) Time scheduling i.e. the timing of future action.

IV. Formalization of plans

The information secured through the aforementioned exercise is formalised in the shape of working documents covering various time horizons and functional areas. Written formalization facilitates the communication of plans to those responsible for its execution. It also works as the basis of control. Two major advantages of such formalization are:

(a) Specification of organizational objectives in the form of sales volume, growth of earnings, market share etc.
(b) Formulation of appropriate strategies.

V. Implementation of plans bearing in mind that :

(a) It is not necessary to give equal weightage to all planning areas. Instead, the significance to be given to a planning area will depend on firm's nature of business, resource analysis etc.
(b) The time horizon of planning should be related to the degree of certainty with which future changes can be anticipated.
(c) The planning exercise should be made a regular and continuous feature.

VI. Plan review/revision and replanning

The firm should not consider formalized plans as sacrosanct. Realistic plans need periodic review and revision on account of the impact of unforeseen events. It would help both in the updating of plans and their maintenance as effective vehicles.

2. Organisation

The term 'organisation' has different meanings depending on the context in which it is used. Firstly, it means the organisation itself. Secondly, it may refer to the group of people who are members of a formalized structure and cooperate in the achievement of organizational objectives. Thirdly, it is used to characterize the process of developing and maintaining a system of working relations amongst people of an enterprise and of dividing the work that has to be done. In this sense it is "a formalized intentional structure of roles or positions." It may however be defined more precisely as "the process of identifying jobs that must be performed, defining authority and responsibility of employees, and establishing authority relationships between employees so that objectives developed in the planning function are attained"

PRINCIPLES OF GOOD ORGANISATION

Good organisations have some common traits. A small organisation can adopt these as guidelines in organising the enterprise. The principles are discussed below :

1. Human use of human resources*

A good organisation should integrate requirements of work with the aspirations and capabilities of its people for satisfactory interpersonal relations.

2. Division of work

The activities to be performed must be divided into meaningful tasks. Each task should fit individual capabilities and skills so that there is perfect matching of demands made by a task and employee capabilities.

3. Appropriate departmentalization of activities

Similar tasks should be grouped into same departments. The criteria for departmentation are : functions (marketing, finance, accounts); product line (electrical, instruments, engineering); customers (industrials, households); geographical area (region); production process etc.

4. Unity of command

Each employee should report and be accountable to a single superior. Orders and directions should come from a single boss. Division of accountability reduces organization's effectiveness as well as employee morale.

5. Balance of authority and responsibility

The authority given to an individual should be commensurate with

---

* Mc Gregor Douglas. *The Human Side of Enterprise.* Mc Graw Hill, New York 1960.

the responsibility. It should neither be less nor more. Whereas lesser authority would make the employee ineffective, an overdose of authority could make him tyrannical.

6. Specification of Authority and Responsibility for every Position

Every position should have clearly defined responsibilities and requisite authority. Such specification should be done in the shape of statements called 'Job Descriptions'. These provide details of required tasks, reporting relationships, interaction between different positions. A perusal of this statement can provide the employee a clear understanding of what is expected of him and resources at his disposal.

7. Proper Delegation

Management should concentrate only on the most significant tasks delegating the rest to the people at lower levels. Adoption of exception principle in delegation would ensure greater effectiveness of the organization.

8. Proper Span of Control

'Span' signifies the number of subordinates that a manager can manage effectively. It depends on the nature of task assigned and competence of subordinates. The span of control has a direct bearing on the number of levels in an organization which in turn determines the length of firm's line of communication. The management should pay attention to the following in desigining the span of control :

(a) Characteristics of the task to be performed.
(b) Ability of the superior to supervise a given number of subordinates.
(c) The capabilities of employees.
(d) The required degree of coordination.

Generally, small enterprises tend to have a broader span since they cannot afford the cost of additional organizational layers. But such a situation is inherently dangerous because of heavy work load, lack of planning, weaker control and reduced work efficiency.

9. Flexibility

Organisational structure should be conceived as a dynamic structure responding to changing external and internal conditions. It necessitates a periodic review of the structure to ascertain whether it is responding to changed environments.

PROCESS OF ORGANISING

Following is the process of organisation.

1. Activity analysis

It consists of the determination of specific activities necessary to achieve organizational objectives. It requires determination of the following :

(a) Major functions involved in achieving organizational objectives.
(b) Various sub functions in each major function.
(c) Volume of work generated by each major function and its sub-functions
(d) The number of positions necessary to perform the activities.

This analysis would show the range of tasks to be performed in the enterprise and organisation of tasks into specialised units so that these could be assigned to individual employees according to their capabilities. This is illustrated below :

Activity Analysis in XYZ firm.

Major functions	Sub-functions
1. Merchandizing	(i) Buying
	(ii) Selling
	(iii) Budgeting
2. Publicity	(i) Advertising
	(ii) Hoardings
	(iii) Sales promotion
3. General Administration	(i) Staff Management
	(ii) Customer Dealing personnel
	(iii) Receipt & Inspection of materials
	(iv) Delivery
	(v) Maintenance of records
4. Finance	(i) Cash management
	(ii) Credit and its collection
	(iii) Accounting
5. Personnel	(i) Employment
	(ii) Training
	(iii) Compensation
	(iv) Employee Welfare

2. Departmentalization and designing of an appropriate organizational structure

As mentioned earlier, departmentation could be done on different basis like functions, products, services etc. The functional approach suits smaller organisations. The departments are then integrated into a formal organizational structure which can be displayed in the form of an organizational chart. This chart displays the major positions in an enterprise, their hierarchical order, and formal reporting relationships among them.

Forms of organization :—

There are three types of formal organisations in use :

(i) Line organisation, (ii) Line and staff organisation, and (iii) Matrix organisation.

Line structure is the most suitable for small enterprises. This is shown below :

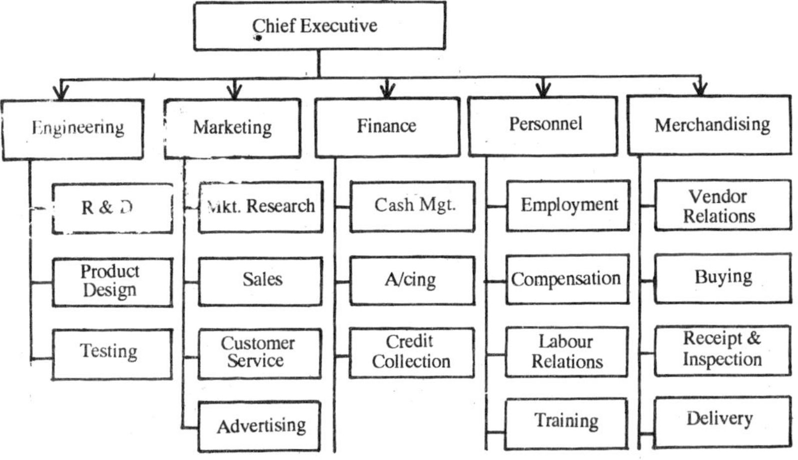

Line Organisation

I. Line organisation

Herein, a straight line of command exists from the highest to the lowest position. Each subordinate is liable to only one superior. The area of responsibility of each employee is clearly defined. Advantages of this type of organisation are : (a) simplicity, (b) clear definition of reponsibilities, (c) comparative ease of changing it and fitting new positions in the existing structure.

II. Line and staff organisation

The need of this type of organisation arises as the enterprise grows. The management begins to experience difficulties in dealing with specialised technical details. Experts are therefore inducted in staff positions. They advise line managers and operative personnel. However, the final authority for making decisions and issuing orders rests with line official.

The following figure depicts this type of organisation.

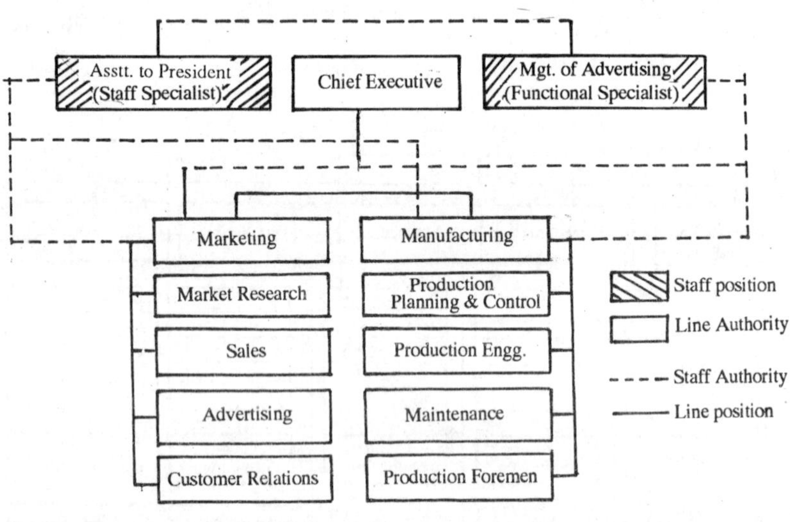

Fig. Line and Staff Organisation

This organisational structure facilitates the use of experts without increasing the number of decision-making centres in the organisation. But a combining of line and staff leads to problems of misunderstanding and internal personal conflict. Since line people hold authority, they feel shy of seeking staff advice. Staff advice is considered to be an encroachment on line authority. This form of organization can be adopted when the small firm has grown in size and begins to operate in a dynamic environment.

III. Matrix organization or Project organization

It combines functional and project responsibilities. The company may assign special project to a project manager who uses relatively stable functional organization for project execution. In other words, the project manager depends on the cooperation of functional departments for carrying out project work. The task of project execution is entrusted to the project manager whereas departmental managers remain responsible for technical activities and the quality of work.

Small firms can utilize this form of organization in the following circumstances :

(a) If several projects are being carried out simultaneously.
(b) If the project is a unique one.
(c) If each project is technically complex requiring high degree of coordination among different technical specialists.

The principal advantage of matrix organisation is that it focusses the attention of management on completion of specific projects.

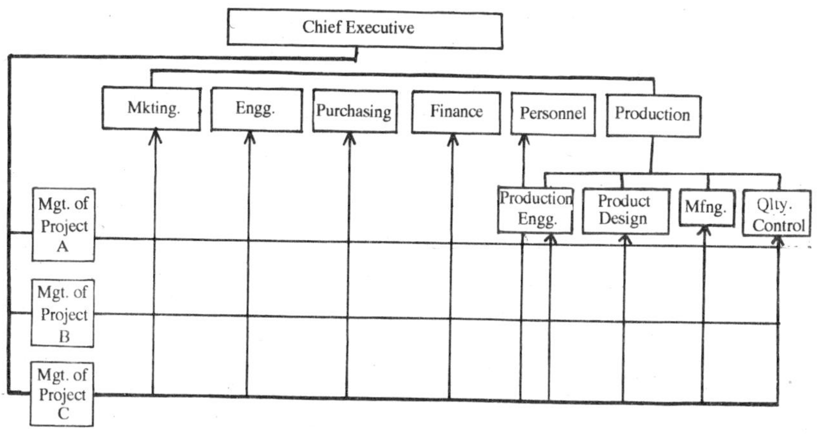

Fig. 3 Matrix Organisation

3. Job Assignments and manning the organisation

It consists of assigning specific positions and activities to individual employees or simple selection of persons to fill each position. For proper matching of job requirements and individual capabilities, it is better to build up job descriptions and job specifications for each position. 'Job description' comprises a definition of the functions, responsibilities, authority and accountability of the person in a particular position. On the other hand, '*job specification*' states the personal qualities capabilities and skill requirements for satisfactory execution of the functions specified in job description. It is done by indicating requisite educational background, experience, aptitude for placement in a given position. Both job description and job specification play their respective useful roles in recruitment, development and evaluation of employees.

PROBLEMS IN ORGANISING

Following are the probable problems in organising small business :

1. Overcentralization i.e. Lack of Sufficient Delegation

No organisation is either totally centralized or decentralized rather there exist different degrees of admixture of both in reality. Centralization is the retention of authority at the top whereas decentralization refers to a greater degree of delegation at lower levels. Small business entrepreneurs/executives can make better contribution to firm's success if they focus on strategic planning, control and leadership rather than on routine matters. A greater degree of decentralisation can be achieved by adopting the principles advocated by Koontz O'Donnell.* These are : (a) Define, assign and delegate authority in the light of results expected; (b) Select the person on the basis of job to be done; (c) Maintain open lines of communication; (d) Establish proper control; (e) Reward effective delegation and successful assumption of authority.

2. Inadequate specification of job responsibilities and organizational relationships

Specification of responsibilities and interrelationship among different positions can be done through job description and organisational charts. In their absence, employees cannot determine with definiteness as to what is expected of them. Failure to clarify job responsibilities is a common pitfall in small firms and can lead to intra organizational conflict, shifting of responsibility and costly inefficiencies.

3. Imbalance between authority and responsibility

Non-accomplishment by employee may sometimes be due to lack

---

* Koontz, Harold and O'Donnell, Cyrell. **Principles of Management : An Analysis of Management Functions.** 5th Ed., McGraw Hill, N.Y. (1979), 351, 53

of appropriate authority. On the contrary, in certain situations, the employees might have more authority than warranted by responsibilities. Parity between these two is possible only through Management by Objectives programme or periodic performance review system.

4. Organisational inflexibility

A good organisation must have the capacity to adapt to change in internal and external environment. Small firms normally suffer from inflexibility due to following reasons :

(a) Shortage of time and specialisation.
(b) Internal resistance to change.
(c) Low management turnover.
(d) Hesitancy on the owner's part.

These problems can be overcome through periodical review of organisational structure.

5. Overlooking informal organizational relationships

Occurrence of informal groups in any organisation is a reality. Their presence has both negative and positive effects. The informal organization may sabotage the formal organization by adopting such practices as work-restriction, idle chatter, gossiping and other counter-productive activities. The small entrepreneur should ascertain their existence and the role played by them. If they are found to be disruptive, the leader of the informal group should be identified and taken into confidence for changing the attitudes of his peers. Efforts should be devoted to bring about synergic interaction between formal and informal organisations for the overall benefit of the company.

3. Staffing

This forms the subject-matter of a separate chapter in this book.

4. Leading

It is the process of influencing employees towards the accomplishment of organisational goals. Undoubtedly, quality and style of leadership is a major factor in shaping the success of business. According to McGregor, the style of leadership would be determined by a person's method of perception of others. To explain a person's perceptions, he put forward two extreme theories described below :

Theory X—Its Assumptions

(i) Average human being has inherent dislike for work and will avoid it.

(ii) Due to this reason, people need to be coerced, controlled, directed, threatened with punishment etc to coax them to work towards organisational goals.

(iii) Average human being prefers to be directed and wants to avoid responsibility.

(iv) Average human being has little ambition and wants security.

Those who follow this theory like to be autocratic managers and strive for control. They do not delegate and provide few outlets for employee creativity. Close supervision, pressure tactics and reprimand are the tools relied upon by them.

Theory Y—Its Assumptions

(i) Expenditure of physical and mental energy is as natural as play and rest.

(ii) Instead of external control and threat of punishment, people will exercise self-direction and self-control.

(iii) Commitment to objectives depends on the rewards associated with their achievement.

(iv) Average individual learns under proper conditions not only to accept but also to seek responsibility.

(v) The capacity to exercise relatively high degree of imagination, ingenuity and creativity in solving organizational problems is widely, not narrowly, distributed in the population.

(vi) Under conditions of modern industrial life, the intellectual potentialities of the average human being are only partially utilised.

Those who advocate this theory practise 'participative leadership'. They encourage employees to share in decision-making. Their attempt is to build up an organisation that recognises the value of an individual. They not only seek ideas and suggestions from subordinates but also try to make constructive use of them. Communication flows freely in this type of organisation. It stresses extensive use of teamwork.

Theory Z—Its Assumptions

It is a contingency theory based on the assumption that no single leadership is best for all occasions. Employee efficiency may be increased by the use of autocratic or participative leadership depending on circumstances.

5. Controlling

It is the process of measuring current operations to determine whether actual performance conforms to objectives and plans. It provides continuous feedback to the managers on the progress of the company towards goal attainment. The process of controlling is described below :

(i) Establishing standards of performance:

Standards indicate the expected performance level. It links planning with control. Various types of control standards are illustrated below :

(A) Production : Quality, Quantity, Cost, Machine.

(B) Marketing : Sales, Volume, Sale expenditure, Advertising expenditure.

(C) Personnel Management : Labour Relations, Labour turnover, Absenteeism Safety.

(D) Finance : Capital expenditure, Inventories, Flow of Capital, Liquidity.

(ii) Comparison of performance with the standards.

(iii) Noting down deviations, if any, and its analysis.

(iv) Taking corrective action so that future performance is directed towards the established standards.

6. Communication

It is the inter personal process of transmitting information between two or more people so that understanding is created between them.

The success of small business depends on developing a communication system related to business operations. An effective communication system provides the employees an opportunity to become involved in company matters as well as afford the managers an insight into employee attitudes towards the company. In small business, most of the communication occurs face to face because of direct contact between employers and employees.

PROCESS OF COMMUNICATION

The process of communication is depicted in the following figure :

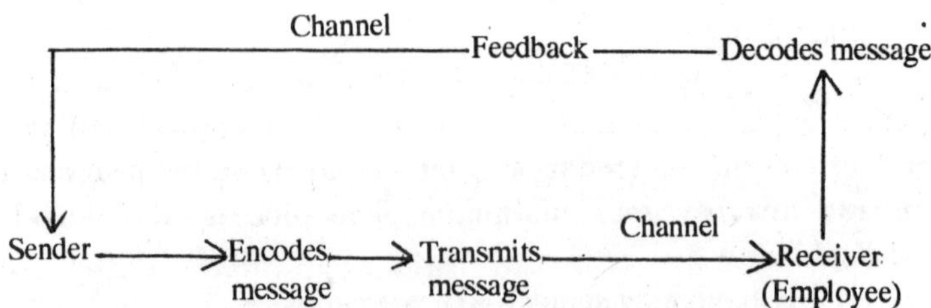

Fig. 4. Process of Communication

Communication passes through the following phases :

(i) Need for sending message.

(ii) Encoding of message. The message may be verbal, written, non- verbal (gestures) or a combination of all.

(iii) Transmission of message.

(iv) Channel: The message is sent through a channel to the receiver.

(v) Decoding of message by the receiver who gets the message.

(vi) Feedback by the receiver to indicate that he has understood the message.

BARRIERS TO EFFECTIVE COMMUNICATION

1. Psychological Barriers

There is breakdown of communication due to distortion of information and problems arising from interpersonal relationships. These are :

(a) Filteration i.e. passing on only positive information to the boss/entrepreneur.

(b) Selective perception i.e. hearing what one wants to hear instead of what is actually being said.

(c) Credibility gap i.e. lack of trust between sender and receiver.

2. Semantic Barriers

These arise because words have different meanings to different people. A single word may have multiple meanings. For instance the word round' has 50 different meanings as per Webster's New Collegiate Dictionary. Where an entrepreneur uses a word that has multiple meanings, it shall be ensured that right meaning goes home.

3. Use of Unfamiliar terms particularly technical words or a special language (called 'jargon').
4. **Communication Overload** i.e. conveying too much information so that receiver is unable to separate important from the unimportant. It causes a blockage. Too much information is as detrimental as too little.
5. **Physical Distractions** which interfere with the effective conveyance of message. For instance, ringing of telephone, traffic noise, noise of machines etc.
6. **Absence of feedback** i.e. when receiver does not respond to show whether he understands or not.

GUIDELINES FOR EFFECTIVE COMMUNICATION

1. Encouraging employees to express their ideas and opinions.
2. Listening carefully to ideas, suggestions and complaints.
3. Keeping employees well-informed of all changes affecting them.
4. Updating awareness on how employees are feeling and thinking.
5. Encouraging two-way communication.
6. Recognising good work and expressing appreciation for jobs well-done.
7. Communicating messages accurately, completely and clearly.
8. Explaining the 'why' of decisions.
9. Striving to create an atmosphere of trust and confidence by reporting facts to employees.

TIME MANAGEMENT

For an entrepreneur, the time is really valuable. Small business owner-managers can reap substantial improvements in their as well as company's performance through more efficient use of time. Time management is a systematic analysis of how the owners and employees use their work hours. Time use analysis can reveal the type of activities on which a person spends his time and the consequent ability to spend it on more critical, high priority matters. By identifying high priority activities and eliminating activities of less importance, the goal of investing owner- manager's time on quality rather than on quantity is highlighted.

FUNDAMENTAL GUIDELINES FOR ACHIEVING EFFECTIVE TIME MANAGEMENT

1. Observing time expenditure

At least for two weeks, keep a record of how each hour of day is spent. Include each activity, howsoever minute like making of phone calls, commutation, reading of paper, tea break etc. At the end of the first week, one would have a clear idea how much time is spent on each activity.

2. Establishing a work-cum time schedule

It will provide a time frame to be filled up with business responsibilities.

3. Make a list of all the responsibilities and how much time each requires. Make provision for personal responsibilities. These tasks for which one does not have the time but wants to do should be noted at the last.

4. Set priorities

Make a realistic assessment of all the tasks and the number of hours available. Eliminate the activities that can be delegated. Note which activities are taking more time than necessary and explore ways to be more efficient e.g. keeping phone conversation short.

5. Delegate responsibilities

Since priorities have been worked out, the less important tasks should be assigned to subordinates.

6. Organise your day

Each day list the tasks to be accomplished in an order of priority Plan how and when various tasks shall be accomplished. List only what is feasible and realistic for the day. Reduce the amount of time wasted between tasks.

7. Evaluate the system

Evaluate the priorities and responsibilities from time to time. As the business grows, demands on time will change. Be aware of the way the time is spent and of the need to be more efficient.

CHAPTER XV

MANAGEMENT OF PERSONNEL IN SMALL BUSINESS

RECRUITMENT, SELECTION AND TRAINING

Talented employees are the key-assets of the company. The problem with small business entrepreneur is that it cannot afford the luxury of a full time specialist in personnel area. The entrepreneur himself is generally a novice and tends to look after this aspect rather haphazardly. Either the owner personally takes care of the personnel function or delegates it to an employee who performs it alongwith his main job. The general tendency is to hire the first person who comes the way and accepts the lowest salary. Their basic thrust is on marketing, regarded as primary to existence. No wonder one day such entrepreneurs discover themselves surrounded by semi-qualified and incompetent people unable to meet the challenges facing a growing enterprise. Therefore, small entrepreneur should do well clearly define the kind of personnel with whom to build the enterprise. Objectivity and courage are essential to taking such a course of action. The idea should be to have competent, progressive and compatible staff. Not only should there be a well-designated personnel policy, it must also ensure replacement of dead-wood after company has grown efficiently.

1. Defining Job Requirements

The pre-requisite to efficient selection is the systematic defining of requirements of each task. The identification process has three phases:

(a) Conducting job analysis,

(b) Developing job descriptions, and

(c) Preparing job specifications

(i) Job Analysis

It is the process of investigation and collection of pertinent information about each task in terms of skill, abilities, duties and responsibilities. It covers: **(a) Job** Title, (b) Department to which it relates, and

(c) Line of supervision, (d) Description of job including major and minor duties; (e) Relationship with other jobs i.e. promotional avenues, transfer, possibilities, experience required etc., (f) Unique job characteristics (location, physical setting), (g) Type of material and equipment used, (h) Educational qualifications, (i) Experience, (j) Mental and Manual dexterity, (k) Physical requirements (l) working conditions.

(ii) Job Description

It consists of a written statement of the major and minor duties involved in each task along with a description of responsibilities, work conditions and task requirements e.g. hazards, time involvement etc. The job description, therefore, focusses on what, why,when and how tasks are to be performed.

(iii) Job Specification

It describes the salient features of the person expected to fit in the job. It enumerates qualities, knowledge, skills and abilities an individual should possess to perform satisfactorily alongwith such other characteristics as planning, leadership and decision-making abilities, experience, education etc. It provides a standard against which to measure how well an applicant matches the job.

2. Recruitment—Engaging the Employee

It is the translation of job specifications into actual recruitment of the employee by exploring main sources of supply. The major sources of supply could be:

(a) Current employees or references i.e. asking friends and acquaintances to provide a good person.

(b) Newspaper advertisement specifying the requirements of the position to attract individual with appropriate qualification. The small firm could emphasise the unique advantages offered by it e.g. opportunity for growth, comraderie, wide scope for individual contribution etc.

(c) Drop—In Applicants i.e individuals who occasionally drop in to inquire if any job is available. It is better to take down some information relating to them.

(d) Unsolicited applications i.e. those who may have applied in anticipation of vacancy. Maintenance of record of them could be advantageous

(e) Technical journals to look up to candidates with specific technical qualifications and background.
(f) Universities, Colleges and technical institutes.
(g) Employment Agencies—public and private.
(h) Former employees who may have voluntarily quit.

3. Selection and Hiring the Right Candidate

It involves a number of activities which may be performed either by the owner-manager himself or with the assistance of specialists. Following is the process of selection.

(i) Application Blank

It contains a written record of candidates qualifications, name, experience, references etc. From a perusal of this record, a broad idea can be formed about the applicant's potential. The format of the application blank is given.

Personal : Name
Address.
Date of birth.
Phone No.

Educational : High School — College — Special Training — with year and institutions attended

Reference : Names of persons preferably former supervisors

Name	Address and Phone	Position
....	....	....

Personal Comment : Why the candidate consider himself suitable for the position.

Work Experience : List of period of employment starting with the most recent employment

Organisation	Period Worked	Nature of Work

Applicant's Signature

(ii) Personal Interview

The purpose of this interview is to ascertain technical competence of the candidate and his capacity to meet the requirements of the position. The fundamental mistakes committed in interviewing are:

(a) not spending enough time analysing the requirements of the job to be filled;
(b) failing to ask right questions to test strengths and weaknesses of the candidate;
(c) relying too much on gut reaction instead of making an objective analysis.

(iii) Checking References

References listed by the applicant should be cross-checked through telephone and preferably through a written letter.

Letter for cross checking the reference

Mr......... is being considered for a position as........ and has given us permission to contact you for a confidential reference. We would appreciate your answers to the following questions:

(a) What was applicant's assignment ?
(b) How did the applicant perform ?
(c) Does the applicant get along well with people ?
(d) Do you have any reservation in recommending him ?
(e) Would you rehire the applicant if opportunity arises ?
(f) Additional comments (about interests, potentialities)

(iv) Employment Tests

Though not a sole criterion of selection, these tests are making the employee selection more efficient. These are :—

(a) *Aptitude Test* to measure mechanical, clerical, manual dexterity and other potential talent.
(b) *Achievement Tests* to measure performance (skill proficiency).
(c) *Intelligence Test* to measure general mental abilities e.g. verbal ability, reasoning, comprehension etc.
(d) *Personality Test* to select managers

Whatever tests are used, these must be valid (i.e. there must be a relation between test scores and performance on job) and reliability (i.e. consistency)

(v) Final Interview

It is designed to form final impression based on earlier assessments and particularly to ascertain interpersonal competence (capability to go along well with others), whether he has autocratic/democratic disposition, cooperativeness, rigidity/flexibility. The interviewer should do well to adopt a balanced approach. He should guard against 'Halo Effect' i.e. forming rational judgement on the basis of first impression. What happens is that the interviewer forms a favourable or unfavourable impression of the applicant very early and searches for confirmation.* To guard against it, the interviewer should withhold judgement until after the interview.

(vi) Physical Examination to determine whether the prospect meets health standards demanded by the job.

ORIENTATION

The new employee should be provided thorough orientation regarding company policies and specific nature of the job. It markedly reduces apprehension during the first few days of the employee. He should be introduced to colleagues, explained as to how the job fits into overall goals of the company, the operations and conditions of employment. Some employers have 'Employee Handbooks' containing written information about salient aspects of company e.g. company's expectations of employees, pay-policies, working conditions, fringe benefits etc.

4. Wage and Salaray Administration

Principal object of a compensation plan is to motivate employees to achieve higher levels of performance. Following are the elements of wage and salary administration.

(i) Wage and salary level.
(ii) Wage and salary structure.
(iii) Individual wage determination.
(iv) Method of payment.
(v) Individual compensation or fringe benefits.
(vi) Management Control.

A small entrepreneur cannot afford to engage a specialist for performing wage and salary administration. It is mainly performed by the entrepreneur himself. With the growth of the business of the firm, specialist may however be added in order to maintain its competitive thrust.

---

* Webster Edward C. *Decision-making in the Employment Interview.* Industrial Relation Centre, McGill University, Montreal. (1964) 112-114.

(i) Wage and Salary Levels and Structure

The wages should be established by reference to the following:

(a) Prevalent wage levels in the industry.

(b) Compliance with minimum wages laws and other enactments governing compensation.

(c) Standards and values of the entrepreneur.

(d) Consent of the trade union.

By adhering to the above, a small firm can hire and retain productive work force.

(ii) Wage Determination and Method of Payment

Determination of compensation for each position is the second step in salary administration. More responsible and more difficult a job, higher should be the pay-packet. Also establish a range of compensation for each position. The wage structure must be such that the staff has the motivation to work for vertical movement. The incentives and fringe benefits associated with each position should also be settled. To attract qualified, hardworking and loyal staff, small firms may introduce special awards.

Benefits to be offered to managers pose special problem. The popular forms of benefits given to them include: stock option, profit-sharing, use of company vehicle, club membership, reserved parking etc.

Small firm should use its limited resources carefully and devise a productive salary administration. Broad objectives of a good salary programme include: maintenance of competitiveness, capacity to attract managers of superior calibre, rewarding superior performance and motivating the staff to achieve higher production levels. Two more ingredients of efficient compensation plan are:—

(a) It should link reward and performance.

(b) It should ensure payment of reward as soon as after achievement.

Compensation plans suitable for small business are : (i) Straight salary; (ii) Hourly wage-to reward employees whose work is difficult to measure or where employer has no control over output; (iii) Piece Rate; (iv) Commission based on sales; (v) Combination of salary and commission.

5. Training and Development

Objectives of training:

(i) To improve job performance.

(ii) To develop employees for new responsibilities.
(iii) To prepare employees for promotion.
(iv) To reduce accidents and wastage.
(v) To instruct in the operation of new equipment.
(vi) To ensure management succession.

Effective management succession requires prior planning. Seemingly simple matter has special problems in the case of small business particularly when it comes to its practical implementation. The entrepreneur is moulded in thinking in a groovy fashion. Moreover, training is not a one time job. It is a rather continuous process. Training seeks to upgrade an employee's knowledge to keep abreast of changes in competitive business environment and prepare for advancement to challenging opportunities.

Before initiating a training programme,the owner/manager should ascertain as to what training would induct change. Change herein implies the attainment of improved ability. The change should benefit both individual and organization. The change should occur in the following five areas:

(a) Knowledge

It rerfers to the storage of information by an individual for use in problem-solving and decision-making. Greater the amount of knowledge, better equipped shall be a person to accomplish a job.

(b) Attitude

It is a state of mind which creates an urge to work for personal and organizational growth.

(c) Ability

It is the proficiency in performance of a given task.

(d) Job performance

It measures how well the individual meets the requirements of a position.

(e) Operational results

These indicate how well the organization has been able to achieve its objectives and goals.

CONDITIONS FACILITATING TRAINING AND DEVELOPMENT IN A SMALL COMPANY

1. Existence of a board that insists on management succession programme and its follow up.
2. Steady growth of the company which stimulates the need to prepare staff for foreseeable changes.
3. Recognition of the need for training by the entrepreneur who devotes his time and energy towards it.
4. Freedom given by the entrepreneur to young executives to experiment with new ideas and to accept the risks connected therewith.
5. Degree of delegation of responsibilities.
6. Provision of training programmes on a continuous basis.

METHODS OF TRAINING

1. On-the-job Training

It is the most practical and often used technique in small business. Depending on the complexity of the task and experience level of the employee, the training may vary from few hours to several days. Training of this kind is given in three phases:

(a) **Demonstration** The job is demonstrated and each stage is thoroughly explained. It is done slowly so that the trainee could ask questions as well as provide feedback on his understanding of the work procedure.

(b) **Performance** i.e. the employee applies what he has learnt in the preceding stage.

(c) **Inspection of the work** of the employee to provide immediate reinforcement of correct method of performance.

The object of such training is to provide continuous training to update job skills as well as prepare the employees for promotion.

2. Apprenticeship Training is a form of training that combines both formal classroom learning and on-the-job experience particularly in technical cadres.

3. Job Rotation

It is particularly beneficial in the case of small companies wherein each employee has thorough understanding of different functions.

Employees are moved from job to job for few hours to few days. It helps employees combat the problem of monotony and boredom because of varied work experience.

4. Group Training Through Conference Method

Major advantage of this technique is that participants have opportunity to express their viewpoint and share their experiences through a discussion of common problem.

5. Heir Apparent Technique

In it, the entrepreneur identifies the person to be trained for management succession. He is encouraged to learn about every facet of company's functioning. He is rotated through various positions in the company and is given gradually increasing responsibility. Special emphasis is placed on attending company meetings, párticipate in discussion and decision-making. The entrepreneur coaches, trains and shares his experience with the heir. The entire company is informed about this grooming. Problems that it requires the heir to have high degree of interpersonal skills. Where the heir is young, it could cause personality clashes with older managers.

6. Off the Company Premises Training

It includes:

(a) University and Technical Colleges.
(b) Correspondence Courses.
(c) Training Films.

Evaluating Training Needs in Small Business

The evaluation of training needs by a small business can be done by asking the following:

1. What are the objectives of training ?
2. What do employees need to learn ?
3. How much will the programme cost ?
4. What type of training should be offered ?
5. What method of instruction should be used ?
6. What kind of physical facilities would be needed ?
7. What shall be the duration of training ?
8. Who will conduct the training ?
9. What special equipment would be required ?

10. Which employees should be deputed for training ?
11. How will effectiveness of programmes be measured ?

CONDITIONS THAT STIMULATE LEARNING

1. Behaviour of the Boss

Boss is the key figure in an organisation. Others tend to emulate him. Every meeting between the boss and subordinate presents a learning-teaching situation. If the boss favours training and development, the subordinates tend to become positively inclined to learn. Therefore, the boss should exhibit a tendency to value learning and training.

2. Behaviour of Informal Group

Informal group sets the behaviour norms for its individual members. It may either support or resist the introduction of any change. If the informal group supports training, the managers would find a motivated group inclined towards obtaining it.

3. Influence of Formal Organization

The organizational structure, policies, procedures, objectives etc. reflect and reinforce the behaviour which the formal organization prizes. For instance, if the company keeps the top management within the family or has rigid control, there would be little opportunity for growth. Learning is stimulated when there is openness, lack of constraints and climate of exploring new ideas and the objectives of the organisation support training and development.

4. Economical and Technological Influences

A rapidly growing company in an expanding technological field offers more opportunities for growth through training.

PERFORMANCE APPRAISAL

It is a form of counselling and coaching. It is used for detecting and correcting errors. It is the process by which owner gathers information about each employee's performance, effectiveness and communicates the same to the employee. It includes: (a) establishment of standards, (b) recording of performance (c) reviewing performance in accordance with standards, and (d) taking corrective action.

Purpose of Performance Appraisal

1. To evaluate performance over a specific time.
2. To motivate employees through performance feedback.
3. To evaluate individual employee's potential for growth and development.
4. To collect information for taking decisions concerning transfers, promotion, rewarding, termination etc.
5. To evaluate the effectiveness of training programme.

Limitations of Performance Appraisal

1. Limitation of Job Description

People are unique. The same job may be peftormed differently by different people. The same is true of conditions within the organisation. While framing position descriptions, the managers attempt to find some congruence between the job description and their knowledge of requirements. No wonder, the position descriptions may not be totally correct.

2. Inadequacy of Appraisal and Problem of Reliability

Many of the items that are included in appraisal such as initiative, quality of work, cooperation, adaptability etc. are subject to personal standards of the appraiser. Bias and prejudice are the common failings of every individual. Therefore, no evaluation can be considered as absolute. The limitations of appraisal arise from: impossibility of evaluation of certain traits with any degree of precision, manipulation of responses and lack of standardized appraisal procedure.

Due to these defects, ratings tend to vary widely and raise doubts about their reliability.

3. Impediments in Communication

Managers insist on fair criticism, based on performance appraisal. The employees, however, regard it as censure and tend to adopt a defensive mechanism against it. Therefore, there arise conflicts which make the goal of appraisal self-defeating.

4. Filure to Motivate

Appraisal procedures are not designed to provide motivational impact. The urge to change must come from within the individual. There is too long a gap between the act and its consequence and hence its failure to play any significant role in motivating the employees.

Guidelines For Conducting Performance Review

1. Decide the purpose of performance review—whether evaluation, criticism, training, coaching.
2. Inform the employees as to what is expected of them and how they are going to be evaluated.
3. Maintain records so as to back up any criticism/comment.
4. Make review a live exercise through employee participation.
5. Discuss the evaluation with each employee.
6. Be specific and constructive in criticism.

In small business, performance review should be kept as simple as possible.

EMPLOYEE MORALE

Morale is the attitude of the employee towards factors in the work environment such as job, pay, superiors etc. Since it is an attitude, it cannot be measured as can the profits. Therefore, indirect techniques are used to measure morale. One such technique is 'survey'. In it, the employees are asked to check how they feel about particular factors in the company. Questions could be in the form of true, false, multiple choice or scaled ranging from completely satisfactory to completely dissatisfactory.

Illustration

EMPLOYEE SAMPLE SURVEY

Listed below are 18 statements about your job and the company in which you are working. Please check each statement according to how you perceive them. You may Agree, Disagree or be uncertain (if you can't decide or you do not know).

	Statement	Agree	Disagree	Uncertain
1.	I have the opportunity to participate in decisions that affect me.	—	—	—
2.	Communications within the company keep me informed about company plans.	—	—	—
3.	My supervisor does not use unreasonable pressure to get employees			

	to meet work schedules.	—	—	—
4.	My job performance is evaluated fairly and constructively.	—	—	—
5.	I have considerable freedom to take initiative and exercise judgement on the job.	—	—	—
6.	I have job security as long as my job performance is satisfactory.	—	—	—
7.	Opportunities for promotion are based on ability and job performance.	—	—	—
8.	My pay is fair as compared to pay others receive.	—	—	—
9.	The company provides safe and satisfactory physical working conditions.	—	—	—
10.	My job is interesting and challenging.	—	—	—
11.	Grievances and discipline matters are handled fairly.	—	—	—
12.	My colleagues are friendly and cooperative.	—	—	—
13.	I receive recognition for doing goodwork.	—	—	—
14.	Supervisors and subordinates work together as a team.	—	—	—
15.	Standards of performance for my job are realistic.	—	—	—
16.	Fringe benefits are satisfactory.	—	—	—
17.	I derive personal satisfaction from doing my job well.	—	—	—
18.	I have a feeling of pride in working for the company.	—	—	—

Another method of collecting morale data is 'descriptive survey' wherein the employees are asked to provide written answers to questions.

Indicators of employee morale are as follows :

(i) High employee turnover ratio.

(ii) Higher number of accidents.

(iii) Lower productivity.

(iv) Higher incidents of absenteeism and tardiness.

(v) Increased number of defective output.

(vi) Increased number of grievances.

All these are negative indicators and adversely affect small companies. For instance, high turnover would lead to increased costs of recruitment, selection and training of employees.

DISCIPLINE

Disciplinary problems arise due to lack of knowledge, lack of interest and carelessness. The following acts call for disciplinary action:

1. *Disorderly conduct*: reporting for work under influence of liquor.
2. Dishonesty.
3. Obtaining employment by using false or misleading information.
4. Violation of safety precautions.
5. Gambling.
6. Excessive tardiness/absenteeism without reason.
7. Insubordination.
8. Wilful destruction of company property.

TYPES OF DISCIPLINE

1. Progressive Discipline

It consists of minimum disciplinary action for first offence. The degree of punishment increases for subsequent violations. It may be in the form of oral warning, reprimand; written warning stating consequences of future violation, disciplinary lay off, demotion, discharge etc.

It should have following ingredients:

(a) a forewarning;
(b) immediate action;
(c) consistent;
(d) impersonal administration.

2. Positive Discipline

It is the most effective type of discipline since it corrects and strengthens an individual. Guidelines in this behalf are :

(a) Disciplining should be done in private and never in front of fellow employees.
(b) Concentrate on mistakes than on individual.
(c) Listen to the employee so as to get complete facts and clarify misunderstanding.

(d) Explain not only that something is being done incorrectly but also on as to why employee should be doing it the other way.
(e) Solution should be equitable.
(f) There must be no favourites and privileged.
(g) Allow employees to express themselves against unreasonable rules or hazardous working conditions.
(h) Provide for appeal against decisions considered unfair.
(i) Consult employees while establishing rules.
(j) Recognise good performance, reliability and loyalty.

CHAPTER XVI

FINANCE RECORD KEEPING

Survival and success of a small firm depends on financial control. Proper financial record keeping is the pre-requisite of good financial control. Proper financial records mean having a simple recording system and accomplishing the necessary accounting job.

Basic Accounting Equation is: Asset=Liabilities+Capital (net worth). Or Assets—Liabilities=Capital. Assuming that A, a small businessman has cash worth Rs. 60,000, personal belongings worth Rs. 8000 besides Rs. 20,000 in the bank account. It means A has total assets worth Rs. 88,000. Suppose A's only debt is the last instalment of car amounting to Rs. 4000, A's accounting equation would be as follows :

88,000 (Assets)=4000 (Liabilities)+84,000 (Capital)

If A earns Rs. 5000, the equation would appear as follows :

Assets	=	Liabilities	+	Capital
88000	=	4000	+	84000
+ 5000	=			5000
93000				89000

In case A payout Rs. 2000, the accounting equation would appear as follows.

Assets	–	Liabilities	+	Cápital
93000		4000	+	89000
– 2000		–2000		
91,000		2000	+	89000

Recording of the effect of various changes in accounting equation is the basis for double entry book-keeping. The "double" in the equation means that :

(i) there must be equal minuses and pluses on one side of the equation; or

(ii) the same amount of minuses or pluses on both the sides of the equation.

In any case, the accounting equation must be in balance. For instance, purchase of shirt worth Rs. 200 would add to personal property but reduce, cash by the same amount. Similarly, the receipt of cash will mean increase of assets alongwith capital.

Income and Expense

To record what is earned by business and what is paid out by it, the income and expense are used rather than making adjustments in capital section. For instance, purchase of fruit for Rs. 100 and selling it for Rs. 120. The difference between the two could be adjusted to capital account. The difference will also be equal to difference in cash.

	Income	Expense	Cash
Sale of fruit	120	—	120
Purchasing of fruit	—	100	—100
	120	100	20

Increase of Rs. 20 in cash would mean increase of Rs. 20 in capital when adjusted to capital account. Consider the basic equation :

Assets =	Liabilities +	Capital
91000	2000	89000
+ 20		+ 20
91020	2000	+ 89020

Debts and Credits

In accounting, the terms 'debit' and 'credit' are used to denote increase or decrease in assets, liabilities and capital as well income and expense. Assets have debit balance. Liabilities and capital carry credit balance. In other words, increase in assets means 'debit entry' whereas decrease is denoted as credit. Conversely, increase in capital is called credit, and decrease a debit. Since income and expense are adjustments in capital account, increase in income is credit, and an expense and debit. These facts are depicted below :

Category	Transactions that increase the amount	Transactions that decrease the amount	Usual balance in the category
Asset	Debit	Credit	Debit
Liabilities	Credit	Debit	Credit
Capital	Credit	Debit	Credit
Income	Credit	Debit	Credit
Expense	Debit	Credit	Debit

In double entry, for every debit ('Dr.') there must be a corresponding credit (Cr) and vice versa.

SYSTEMS OF ACCOUNTING

There are two methods of accounting although the custom is to keep the accounts on an accrual basis.

(i) Cash Method of accounting

It records transactions as they occur. It is considered proper in terms of keeping accounting records but it distorts the financial picture when applied to a specific period.

(ii) Accrual Method of accounting

It records income and expense at the time they are earned or incurred regardless of when monetary transaction occurs.

To illustrate the difference, suppose a firm's financial year ends on 31st December. It has purchased some goods on December 29, 1991 and sends cheque to the vendor for the amount on January 5 , 1992. In case the firm uses accrual method, it will record the transaction in 1991 itself. The payment however will be made in the year 1992. When account is paid in 1992, it will lead to reduction of cash and liability.

On the other hand, if the firm uses cash method, it will not record the item until January 5, 1992 when there will be reduction of cash and an expense for the year.

It may be noted that accural method is more complex in terms of accounting records and statements but it gives more accurate picture of the financial state of affairs of the firm.

BOOKS OF ACCOUNTS

The principal books of account are (i) Journal and (ii) Ledger.

1. Journal

It is a book of prime entry so that as and when an entry takes place, it is entered in this book. Now-a-days, different type of journals (called subsidiary books) are used. These are as follows :

(a) Cash Book to record all cash and bank transactions.
(b) Petty cash book to record petty cash expenditure.
(c) Purchase book for recording credit purchases, and the Purchases Return Book.
(d) Sales Book for recording credit sales and Sales Returns.

The format of a journal is as follows :

Date	Particulars	L.F.	Dr. (Rs.)	Cr. (Rs.)

Notes :

1. Date is the date of transaction.
2. Particulars contain the detail of the account to be debited and credited alongwith a brief narration of the transaction.
3. Ledger Folio i.e. page of the ledger where particular account appears.

2. Ledger

It is a principal book used for posting transactions to various accounts in a summarised and classified form. For example, all purchase transactions are posted to purchase account. The small entrepreneur can obtain information relating to total purchases or sales from it. It has two sides : debit [L.H.S.*] and Credit [R.H.S.**]. Each side also has columns for date, particulars, folio, and amounts. Consider the following ruling :

Name of the account

Dr. Cr.

Date	Particulars	Folio	Amount (Rs.)	Date	Particulars	Folio	Amount (Rs.)

The debit side records the name of the account from which the benefit received and credit side records the name of the account to which the benefit is given. The word 'To' is affixed to the name of the account entered in the "Dr. side", and word "By" to the account entered in the "Cr. side".

Posting :

The process of transferring entries from Journal to Ledger is known as posting.

---

* Left Hand Side

** Right Hand side

Illustration : JOURNAL

Date	Particulars	L.F.	Dr.	Cr.
1992 Jan 1	X Account—— Dr To Sales Account (Being the credit sales of goods to X)		100	 100

LEDGER

X's Account

Dr. Cr.

Date	Particulars	Folio	Amount (Rs.)	Date	Particulars	Folio	Amount (Rs.)
1992 Jan 1	To Sales A/c		100				

SALES ACCOUNT

Date	Particulars	Folio	Amount (Rs.)	Date	Particulars	Folio	Amount (Rs.)
				1992 Jan 1	By X		100

It may be noted that two or more accounts should not be opened for the same person.

Balance of Ledger Account

The difference between total of debits and total of credits is called ''balance''. For instance, if debit total is bigger then the resultant would be ''debt balance'' or alternatively credit balance, To close the account, the debit balance is put on credit side to make both sides equal.

Proprietor own account is called 'Capital A/c'. Capital brought in by him is shown on the credit side and the amount withdrawn is shown on the debit side of Drawings Account. The drawings account is closed by transfer to capital account.

Cash Book

It records all cash transactions of a business. Receipts are entered on debit side and payments on credit side. The difference represents cash in hand. Since cash book is nothing but cash account in the ledger, there is no need to open cash account in ledger. The ruling of cash book is the same as ledger except that it has additional column for discount received and discount allowed.

ACCOUNTING STATEMENTS

Major accounting statements are : (i) Balance Sheet, (ii) Income Statements, (iii) Budget, and (iv) Cash Flow Statement.

I. Balance Sheet

It is a measure of value of a business at a time characterised by the equation :

Assets = Liabilities + Capital

The various components of Balance Sheet are discussed below :

(i) **Assets*** : These are usually divided in three categories :

(a) *Current Assets* are those which can be easily and quickly converted into liquid assets (cash). These include cash, account receivables, raw materials, finished goods, stock etc. Most of these undergo a change over relatively shorter period of time.

(b) *Fixed Assets* comprise of property that are not needed over short period and cannot be easily converted in cash. These are depreciated over long periods. These include land, buildings, machinery etc.

(c) *Intangible Assets* are those which have value but are not visible e.g. goodwill.

II. Liabilities are debts of business. These are calssified into :

(a) Current Liabilities i.e. debts due in less than one year e.g. Account Payable, Income Tax.

(b) Long Term Liabilities are those debts due more than one year from the date of balance sheet e.g. mortgage, long term loan.

(c) Capital is a measure of value of business to owner. It represents all assets minus liabilities.

Characteristics of Balance Sheet

1. Estimation

Except cash, almost all assets listed in balance sheet are estimates. For example, all receivables cannot be collected and an estimated amount is substituted for bad debts. Prices of inventories may change from time

* These represent the properties owned by an organisation.

to time. Prices of fixed assets are all estimates and are listed at cost. Depreciation is charged to them every year. Goodwill is a matter of subjective valuation.

Liabilities are accurate because they are specific debts incurred by the business. By subtracting accurate liabilities from estimated assets, one can obtain estimated capital. The only way to determine the exact value of a business would be to sell.

(ii) Balance Sheet measures value of business at one moment in time. For instance, inventory is an estimate only for the date of balance sheet.

Liabilities are being continuously incurred. Those included in the balance sheet represent only that day's amount.

The advantage of balance sheet lies in the fact that it measures changes in financial position of the enterprise. Computation of ratios with the help of Balance Sheet figures can help a firm recognise its financial weaknesses or strengths. For creditors, such an analysis is quite significant since it is from this that they can assess the repayment possibilities.

Income Statement [Profit and Loss Account]

It measures how business has performed over a given period. It shows all income minus all expenses.

Major components of income statement are income and expense.

(i) **Income :** It includes several heads such as sale, interest, dividend etc.

(ii) **Expense :** It is classified as follows :

(a) *Cost of Goods Sold* : In a trading firm, it comprises opening inventory plus all purchases for the period minus inventories at the end of the period.

(b) *Cost of Goods manufactured :* (in case of manufacturing firms) comprising of Direct Labour, Material and Overheads.

(c) *Operating Expenses are* those connected with the operations of the business.

(d) *General Expenses* i.e. indirect costs incurred in administration of business e.g. office expenditure, postage, telephone etc.

(e) *Other Expenses* i.e. the expenses that do not fit into any other expense category e.g. interest.

It may be pointed out that if any expense item is an estimate, the Profit and Loss Account will also be an estimate. Moreover, the income statement pertains to a specific period. The statement may be analysed to ascertain the success of operations of the business over a specific period.

BUDGET

A budget is an estimate of next year's income statement and is a major planning and control device for a small enterprise. It consists of (i) income, (ii) cost of goods, sold & manufactured, (iii) controllable expenses, and (iv) uncontrollable expense.

1. **Income :** It is ascertained by forecasting projected sales.
2. **Cost of Goods sold**

   On the basis of number of units estimated to be sold, the cost of goods sold or manufactured as well as controllable and uncontrollable expenditure are determined.
3. **Controllable Expenditure** are those over which the firm has some control e.g. advertisement, travel, entertainment.
4. **Uncontrollable Expenditure** are relatively fixed in operating a normal business e.g. postage, telephone, interest.

Budget has all the items that are there in the income statement except for the difference that all figures in it are estimates.

CASH FLOW STATEMENT

It is measure of change in cash position of the business. It projects all cash receipts less all cash disbursements. It tells as to what has occurred to cash or it is projected in future to determine future cash needs.

XYZ Company

PROJECTED CASH FLOW

	January'92 (Rs.)
Opening cash balance	9000
Cash Receipts :	
Cash sales	22000
cash from A/c receivables	8000
Total cash needs For the month	30000

Cash Disbursements :	
Cash payment	18000
Advertisement	2500
Insurance	500
Salaries & Commission	3000
Entertainment	150
Travel	200
Office Expenditure	1000
Postage	100
Telephone	450
Interest	250
Total cash disbursed	26150
Cash increase or decrease from operations	3850

Components of cash flow statement

It begins with cash in hand at the beginning and adds all cash receipts to the balance and subtracts all cash disbursements to arrive at cash in hand at the end of the month.

Cash Receipts include all funds that are received in the form of cash e.g. cash sales, cash received.

Cash Disbursements include all expenses, purchases and payments made in cash. It does not include depreciation or amounts relating to purchases on credit. The items included in it are advertisement, payments to vendors, insurance premium, salaries, office expenditure. Until payment is actually made, it would not be included in this category.

Significance of cash flow statement to a small entrepreneur lies in the fact that it identifies future problems as regards cash. It warns months in advance when there will be a cash shortage and by how much so that action could be planned well in advance. When it shows surplus funds, plans could be made to invest them in profitable avenues.

RATIOS

The accounting ratios are computed from items in the accounting statements. They are a measure of performance. Some of the ratios are enumerated below.

1. **Current Ratio** : It is a measure of firm's ability to meet debt obligations. It studies the relationship between current assets and current liabilities.

$$\text{Current Ratio} = \frac{\text{Current Assets}}{\text{Current Liabilities}}$$

ACID TEST RATIO OR QUICK RATIO

It measures firm's ability to meet current debts. It shows the relationship between liquid assets and current debt.

$$\text{Acid Test Ratio} = \frac{\text{Cash + Account Receivables + Marketable Securities}}{\text{Current Liabilities}}$$

DEBT TO NET WORTH RATIO

It shows creditor contribution relative to owner's contribution. It shows firm's ability to meet creditors' and owner's obligations in case of liquidation of the firm.

$$\text{Debt to Net Worth Ratio} = \frac{\text{Total Liabilities}}{\text{Tangible Net Worth}}$$

Tangible net worth = Tangible worth — Intangible assets

RATE OF RETURN ON ASSETS

It is a measure of profitability of the firm. It indicates the amount of assets necessary to produce the current level of profits.

$$\text{Rate of return on assets} = \frac{\text{Profit}}{\text{Total tangible assets}}$$

(i.e. Total Assets—Intangible Assets)

CHAPTER XVII

PURCHASING

As more than 50 percent of the sales revenue of a small firm is spent in purchasing materials and services, purchasing assumes special significance for it. The purchase bill is as high as 70 percent in the case of food business. Therefore, efficient purchasing is the prerequisite of higher profit earning by any business.

Purchasing is the process of buying the right quality of materials in the right time and right place and from the right vendor.

In the case of small business, it is the owner who usually takes the purchase decision as regards the items to be purchased, the size of purchase orders and the time and quality of purchase. As business grows, the purchasing function is delegated with specification of limitation on purchaser's authority e.g. the maximum amount of purchasing.

THE PURCHASE PROCESS

Good purchasing is an art and this skill must be adequately developed considering the fact that the purchase manager is responsible for spending more of the enterprise's money than anyone else. The significant aspects of purchase process are discussed below :

1. Right Quality

Quality refers to the suitability of the material for intended purpose. Quality requirements can be ascertained through value analysis.

Value Analysis is a systematic study of a component or product to determine whether any changes in parts or functions can be made that will provide the same value to users at less cost or greater 'value' at the same cost.

Quality specifications can be stated in terms of essential features such as shape, strength, size, colour, appearance etc. Value analysis may result in eliminating a part, substituting one part for another or change the design or material requirements.

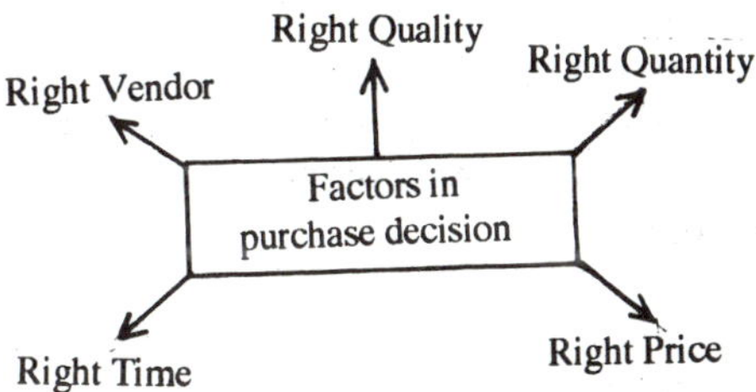

Fig. 1. The Purchase Process

2. Right Quantity

Whereas wholesale purchasing may lead to substantial savings in quantity discount yet it would involve high proportion of funds in merchandise inventory. There is also the likelihood of spoilage or obsolescence. Conversely small-lot buying leads to frequent reordering and higher per unit cost. In the meantime, the products may get out of stock. Therefore, the object of right quantity is to assure availability of adequate stock to minimise disruption in manufacturing or business activity. The right quantity can be determined by reference to the following :

(a) Amount of materials needed for production.
(b) Quantity of materials lost through damage or defects.
(c) Amount of materials in the inventory.
(d) Amount of average inventory carried.

3. Right Price

Best price need not be the lowest purchase price. Lower price may require compromising with quality. Therefore, best price may be described as 'lowest purchase price consistent with quality'.

4. Right Time

Timing of purchasing is crucial. Determination of 'lead time' for obtaining supplies i.e. the time lag between issue of purchase requisition and delivery of goods, is quite significant. The buyer and supplier's actions must be coordinated as regards the timing of purchase. For instance, if purchase order is placed too far in advance, the operating capital would be tied up in inventory. On the contrary, ordering without sufficient lead time may lead to delivery of material after the Peak period is over and the resultant accumulation of inventory. Proper timing of purchases therefore avoids the problem of excessive inventory or stock-out. The optimum inventory is a matter of judgement based on the knowledge of firm's operations, supplier's abilities, and industrial and economic conditions.

5. Right Source (i.e. Vendor)

Selection of vendor constitutes another factor affecting efficient purchasing. The vendor to be chosen must be able to meet quality, quantity, price and time specifications of small business owner.

Vendor Analysis

Best purchasing strategy is dependant on proper selection of the vendor. Vendor strongly influences firm's competitive position and marketing strategy. Following factors affect the evaluation of vendors.

(i) Dependability and Reliability

These are determined by reference to supplier's adherence of delivery schedules, consistency in quality, capacity and past record.

(ii) Services provided by the vendor i.e. capability of the vendor to provide repair and replacement of un-statisfactory/defective materials, capacity to provide technical advice, to give suggestions about how more efficiently to utilize materials, offer of quantity/cash discounts. A comparative analysis of concessions offered may be made so as to check which vendor is the best. Following points be considered in making the comparison.

- (a) Special help in solving merchandising problems.
- (b) Credit terms.
- (c) Quality, Delivery, Service.
- (d) Investment in inventory.
- (e) Special price concession other than quality discount.
- (f) Opportunity for prior selection of desirable merchandise.

(iii) Number of vendors

Ascertain whether a single or multiple supplier can best meet the needs of the firm. Problems with single supplier are : financial difficulties, inability to supply adequate quantity during rush/peak periods, lack of motivation to provide goods/services promptly since there are no competitors. For this reason, small business owners find it advantageous to split their purchases between two or more vendors and strive to develop close relations with them. It provides assured supply of merchandise as each vendor would make timely supplies and give dependable service.

(iv) Vendor location

Location of vendor is important due to heavy transportation costs which may push up the product cost and affect competitive capacity. With greater distance, there is greater chance of disruption of transport due to strike, weather, or other unforeseen events. It will necessitate the carrying of higher safety stock. Thus local vendors are more preferable on account of their ready accessibility and promptness.

(v) Terms of sale need careful considerable on account of substantial variations among different vendors.

(vi) Vendor representatives

They make regular calls and provide prompt and accurate price quotation, follow through the orders, expedite deliveries and handle complaints.

(vii) Other considerations include : ethical. standards, financial strength and management capabilities of suppliers.

PURCHASE POLICY

It should be addressed to the following :

(i) The person who will have the authority to make purchases on behalf of the company.
(ii) Categories of purchases that the authorised person may make.
(iii) Variety of vendors to ensure sufficient competition.
(iv) Careful review of prices in a non-competitive situation.
(v) Criteria for selection of vendors.
(vi) Purchases from customers (reciprocal purchasing)
(vii) Fairness, honesty, courtesy.
(viii) Confidentiality.
(x) Entertainment

Any deviation from the above must be approved in writing by the owner or the purchase manager.

PURCHASE PROCEDURE

The detailed action for completing a purchase is described below :

1. Initiating a Purchase Requisition

Purchases are initiated through purchase requisition which is a formal request to the purchasing department to order certain materials. It contains description of materials wanted, quantity and date by which required, place they are to be delivered and identification of the person making the request.

ABC CO. Ltd.
PURCHASE REQUISITION

Dated.................. No............

Purpose....................

Quantity	Description	Code No.	Delivery Required		Purchase Order		
			Date	Place	No.	Date	Supplier

Originating Department..................... Authorised by.....................

Fig 2 : Purchase Requisition

2. Evaluation and selection of vendors

Examination of different sources of supply consistent with the best of quality and lowest possible price is the second phase. Except for some special materials, there must be a number of vendors whose records are maintained in the company. The final selection is made after careful consideration of terms and delivery dates and the degree of reliability of the supplier.

3. Determination of price

Price could be ascertained from catalogues or settled through negotiations or competitive bidding. The latter method involves considerable time to write product specification and to secure price quotation, it is usually not used in small business.

4. Placing the order

It is a written authorisation to the supplier to supply a specified quantity and quality of material at a stipulated time and in accordance with the terms mentioned therein. The order may be in the following form:

ABC Co. Ltd.
---------(address)
PURCHASE ORDER

Supplier --------- Order No. ------
Date ----------
Requisition No. ------------
Date required ------------

Please supply the following in accordance with the instructions contained herein :

Description	Qnty. or Weight	Rate	Amount

Delivery at__________ __________Signature
Terms of Payment ____________ Purchase Manager

Fig. 3. Pruchase Order

5. Follow up

It is done to ensure that the vendor will be able to meet the delivery date.

6. Receipt and inspection of materials

Seller's invoice and original purchase order are compared in terms of quantity, terms, prices and description of materials so that they conform to specifications. Discrepancies should be promptly notified to the vendor and the invoice note be returned to him for necessary corrections. If material is rejected, the buyer must obtain authorisation from the seller for return and replacement.

7. Completion of purchase records and payment

Copies of purchase requisition, purchase orders, goods received note and invoices are sent to the accounting section for vouching and checking. If everything is in order, a voucher authorising payment is prepared and sent to cashier for payment.

ECONOMIC ORDER QUANTITY

It is a technique of enhancing purchase efficiency. It helps in the determination of the right quantity to order that would minimise the total variable costs in buying and maintaining merchandise in inventory. Purchase expenditure consists of the following :

(i) Purchase price, carriage inward, customs duties, octroi, insurance etc.

(ii) Procurement/ordering costs i.e. the cost of placing the order and receiving the supplies, handling of supplies etc.

(iii) Costs of carrying inventory i.e. storekeeping, insurance, interest on capital locked up in stores, risk of obsolescence, deterioration and wastage etc.

There is an inverse relationship between ordering cost and cost of carrying stock. Procurement costs decline with large sized order as fewer individual orders have to be placed. But if large quantities are ordered, the cost of carrying stock will go up. The problem is, therefore, to balance the cost of carrying inventory against the diminishing cost of ordering. The following formula has been evolved for fixing economic quantity :

$$EOQ = \sqrt{\frac{2A.B}{C.S}}$$

Where, EOQ = Economic Order Quantity

A = Annual Consumption
B = Buying cost per order
C = Cost per unit of material
S = Storage and carrying cost.

PURCHASE DISCOUNTS

Small business owners should strive to continuously search for and take advantage of all opportunities to reduce their cost of operation and consequently improve firm's operating efficiency. One such area of economising is "purchase discounts". Discounts represent a reduction in the purchase price of materials by the vendor. It would require the computation of the cost of money with the amount of discounts allowed. The following table shows the various types of discounts.

Table of Purchase Discounts

Type of Discount	Basis of allowing the discount
1. Cash Discount	Time of Payment
2. Quantity Discount	Size of Order
3. Trade Discount	Classification of buyer as : a) Manufacturer b) Wholesaler c) Industrial buyer d) Retailer
4. Seasonal Discount	Depends on selling season.

These are discussed below :—

1. Cash Discount

It is offered for prompt payment and to that extent the price is reduced.

2. Quantity Discounts

These are given on the basis that it is more economical to process fewer larger orders than many small orders. Before availing of these, the small business owner must compare the carrying cost of large inventory including risk of obsolescence, deterioration etc, with the savings made through quantity discounts.

The quantity discounts could be of two types :

(a) **Non-cumulative quantity discount :** It is given when quantity purchased in a single order exceeds a stipulated volume. Consider the following :

Size of order	Percentage of Discount
Under one dozen	Nil
1-2 doz.	1 %
3-4 doz	2 %
5-4 doz	4 %

(b) **Cumulative quantity discount :** In it, the discount is given if purchases exceed a specified quantity or amount over a pre determined period such as a month or year. For instance, 5 % discount if yearly pruchases exceed Rupees one lakh.

3. Trade Discount

These are given by manufacturers off the list price in some lines of business to certain categories of traders such as manufacturers, wholesalers etc. These are given regardless of the size of order. It is given on thc basis of marketing function performed for the manufacturer. For a higher discount is given to a wholesaler who sells to small buyers as compared to the discount offered to the industrial buyer who buys directly from the manufacturer.

4. Seasonal Discounts

These are offered by the suppliers during off-season such as refrigerators during winter. These are given to motivate buyers to place orders during slack season so that the manufacturer could continue with his manufacturing activity. But before availing them, the small owner should take into account all aspects of purchases e.g. possibility of changes in style, overbuying, high inventory, chances of spoilage etc.

5. **Promotional Discounts** are given to buyers for performing special promotional activities on behalf of the seller e.g. advertising, offering free merchandise.

CHAPTER XVIII

INVENTORY CONTROL

Major inventory costs are incurred in the following forms:

(i) **Storage Facilities** i.e the cost of storing the merchandise. These are in the forms of land, building, rental costs etc.

(ii) **Spoilage and obsolescence** : Perishable items in the inventory are prone to some form of spoilage. Some other goods are subject to obsolescence due to change in fashion, introduction of better products etc.

(iii) **Insurance of inventory:** Large the value of stocks, larger shall be the size of premium.

(iv) **Handling:** Handling involves costs in the form of manpower, equipment and damaged goods.

(v) **Interest on funds** invested in inventory.

The incurring of above-mentioned costs is essential for having adequate inventory control. Higher the quantum of inventory, higher shall bee the increase in these costs. Laxity in control may lead to additional losses. For instance, piling up of stocks may lead to non-discovery of ertain equipments. It also encourages pilferage. Inadequacy or absence of inventory records may creatr problems in making insurance claims. Sometimes, a business may lose money from loss of inventories without even knowing it.

Two principal advantages of inventory control are:

1. Maintenance of sufficient inventory is basic to customer retention. Non-availability or delayed availability of desired goods is likely to put away the customers. The focus of a small firm must be to balance inventory costs and customer relations.
2. For designing adequate inventory control system, and ascertaining a reorder point, small firm must maintain proper inventory records.

VARIOUS INVENTORY CONTROL SYSTEMS

There are three broad types of inventory control systems :

1. Perpetual Inventory System

Small firms use bin tags or bin cards which are attached to the appropriate bins. Receipts and withdrawal of items are noted on the tag as and when they are effected. The information carried on this card are : (i) name of the item, (ii) code number, and (iii) reorder point. Every time additional items are received from vendors, their number is recorded and added to the balance. Issue of items is similarly recorded and subtracted from the balance. A glance at the bin will reveal the amount of inventory ate hand of that item.

SPECIMEN BIN CARD

Item : Green Giant English Peas
Reorder point : 100 cans Order : 400 cans Stock Control

In		Out		Balance
Date	Amount	Date	Amount	
21/3/92	400			80
				480
		1/4/92	60	420
		4/4/92	40	380

The system is ideal for firms having small number of items in the inventory or a small number of transactions.

Specialised Perpetual Inventory System

(i) Sale Ticket Control

In it, sales tickets are completed each time merchandise is sold. Such information as the department, number of items sold, type of items sold, unit price, total price are entered in it. The ticket is then used for posting to the card.

(ii) Floor Sample Control

This system is used in furniture, refrigerators or other electrical items vending organisations. Method consists of having pads with consecutive numbers printed on each page say 1 to 100. Each item will have one of the pad pages pasted onto it. Suppose 25 items of a product are received. Pads 1 to 25 shall be attached to them. Once these items have been sold off these numbers are removed. By having a look at the remaining numbers, the amount of stock left can be ascertained.

(iii) Visual Control System

This is based on business owner's experience. Over the years, the small business owner becomes aware of his inventory requirements. This is a usual method of stock control in small enterprises. A daily visual examination allows the owner to know-howmuch should be ordered. But it is not very effective. It is suitable for these firms that have stable sales, large numbers of each item in stock and where merchandise is segregated in shelves. Inability to determine shortage is the major handicap of this system.

2. Periodic and Partial Control System

The firms which find it difficult to introduce perpetual inventory due to inventory volume adopt periodic or partial control system in conjunction with visual system. In it, purchase and re-order level are recorded at reordering time. A variation of this method is to take complete inventory count at specific periods.

Revolving Perpetual Inventory

Some firms adopt a perpetual stock taking system for expensive items and periodic for low value merchandise. Some firms may apply perpetual inventory to a part of the merchandise on a rotating basis. For instance, record may be kept of all gift items sold and purchased during a month. At the end of the month, a physical inventory count may be taken. By adding purchase to initial inventory and deducting the closing inventory, the sales figures for the month can be determined. Advantages of revolving perpetual inventory are as follows :

(i) It can identify reorder points more accurately.
(ii) A more accurate determination of optimum order size becomes possible.
(iii) It can spot slow-moving items.
(iv) A greater control is exercised on items susceptible to theft.
(v) It helps in identifying stocks that have greater loss of merchandise.

PHYSICAL VERIFICATION

Despite the existence of an inventory system, it is necessary to undertake physical verification of stock so as to detect mistakes and shortages. There are two methods of performing inventory counts.

1. Regular count once a year (say).

2. **Periodic counting.** A comparison is made between the list of items in stock with those that should be in stock. One person verifies the number in stock and another tallies it. Deviations or discrepancies are instantly noted.

SLOW MOVING ITEM

Efficent stock control should enable identification of slow moving items. The methods of dealing with them are as follows:

(i) Elinination of the item from the inventory after determining its contribution to profit relative to cost of keeping it in stock.

However elimination cannot be done indiscriminately. Sometimes it may affect customer relations particularly when the firm is building up the image of having everything in stock. Many of the slow-moving items are a part of this image building exercise.

(ii) Another method is to mark down the merchandise to cleara the stocks.

SHELF SPACE ANALYSIS

Few firms attempt to ascertain whether they are making an optimum use of the available shelf space. It is of considerable significance to know the amount of store space required to sell a specific item. A technique adopted for this purpose is the shelf space analysis. It is used to measure the profitability of each item in terms of turnover, profit per item and the amount of selling space required to sell the product.

Consider the following:

1. Per unit costs of an item × Percentage mark up = Gross profit per unit.
2. Gross profit per unit × Number of units sold during a period = Total gross profit for the period.
3. Total gross profit÷ shelf space occupied in square inches = Gross profit per square inch for the period.

Thus, to perform shelf analysis, firstly find out the space occupied by an item. Then find out the average number of units sold per month (i.e. initial inventory plus purchases minus closing inventory and dividing it by 12). Thereafter, average cost of unit plus mark up is computed to determine average gross profit per unit sold. The average number of items sold per month times the per unit gross profit shall give the profit per month.

Illustration

Item :	Watches
Cost per unit	Rs. 200
Markup percentage	50%
Grossprofit per unit =	100
Number of units sold	× 5
Gross profit	Rs. 500

Illustration:

Shelf space occupied = 15 × 20"

Total shelf space accupied = 300 sq. inch

Gross profit per sq. inch

of shelf space per month =Rs. 500 + 300= Rs. 1.67

A comparison between various items would reveal the most profitable item in terms of gross profit produced relative to selling area.

CHAPTER XIX

PRICING–METHODS & POLICY

Meaning of 'Pricing'

Pricing is the art of translating into quantitative terms the value of a product to customers at a point of time. The notion of value is subjective and flexible. The same product may have different values to different customers or it may have different values for the same customer over a time. Salient ingredients of pricing are :

(i) Pricing covers the total marketing offering. It includes item and mode of payment, distribution methods, currency used etc.

(ii) Not only 'goods' but the services too have a price.

(iii) Price is of significance to all types of organisations.

Pricing is thus different from 'price' which connotes the exchange value of a product or service. Price is the amount of money required to purchase an item.

Pricing Policy and its Objectives

Price policy begins with the clarification of basic objectives or pricing. Pricing objective stems from company's overall goals and aims. Pricing objectives are discussed below :

1. Profitability Objectives

(a) *Profit maximisation :*

According to Classical Theory, the aim of business is to maximise profits. Profit is a function of two variables viz. sales revenue and cost of production. It is postulated that price should be increased upto a point where it causes a disproportionate decrease in the number of units sold. For instance, if a five percent increase in profits results in 3% reduction in the firm's revenue, it adds to the revenue. On the other hand, if 5% increase leads to 6% reduction in sales revenue, the total revenue would be reduced. This is called 'marginal analysis'. It identifies the point of profit maximisation where addition to total revenue is just balanced by an increase in total cost.

(b) Target Rate of Return to gain a specific profit level so as to gauge its performance. The rate however would depend on actual market conditions.

2, Sales Volume Objectives

(a) *Maximisation of sales revenue*

It postulates that maximisation of sales revenue can be attained through high sales volume. To attain it, a minimum acceptable profit is established and then sales are sought to be increased to a point where profit begins to decline below the minimum level.

(b) *Maximisation of customer volume*

To achieve rapid penetration, a firm may offer an unusually low price. It may dramatically increase the number of customer.

3. Other objectives

(a) Social and ethical objectives wherein pricing depends on the ability to pay, e.g., the prices charged by doctors.

(b) Status quo objectives i.e. where the firm doesnot want to change the situation if it is favourable.

(c) Prestige objective i.e. where a firm sets relatively high prices so as to maintain its high quality image.

(d) To discourage entry of new firms.

In actual practice, a firm may pursue more than one objective at the same time.

Pricing Considerations

Following are the considerations in the pricing of the product.

1. Impact of price and output on revenue and cost.
2. Output level that can contribute maximum towards overheads and profit.
3. Possibility of price adjustments to changes in cost and demand conditions.
4. Finding out long-run and short-run implications of any price change.
5. Consideration of rival's pricing strategies and reactions.
6. Elasticity of demand and revenue.
7. Coordination of pricing policy with overall policy of the firm.
8. Impact of price changes on entry of new firms.
9. Consideration of goodwill vis-a-vis price changes.

10. Impact of pricing on various individuals such as buyers, rival firms, potential rivals, middlemen and the government.

THE PRICING PROCESS

According to Oxenfeldt, pricing involves a series of successive decisions mentioned below :

(i) Identification of the target group

It consists of the identification of that segment of the market which will be most suitable for the product under consideration. It involves a determination of consumer income groups, their tastes, complementarity of firm's product with existing products, competitiveness etc.

(ii) Deciding about the image to be created

Different firms have different kinds of images in their mind. Some try to give the impression of being economical, others of high quality, high price, while some others as innovators. Pricing is done in consonance with the kind of image to be portrayed.

(iii) Selection of appropriate sales strategy

For instance where the firm decides to increase prices, the sales strategy shall be to focus on its quality aspects. Where prices have been lowered the sales strategy would overplay the price aspect.

(iv) Selection of pricing policy conducive to the needs and conditions of the firm

For instance, where the firm follows a price leader, price has to be fixed keeping in mind the leaders bench mark.

(v) Choosing a pricing strategy

Pricing must be done in accordance with firm's capabilities and corporate goals e.g. lower pricing may be done either to penetrate the market or to discourage the entry of rivals.

(vi) Setting specific prices

It is within the framework of pricing policy and pricing strategy that a firm fixes the prices of its products.

PRICING PRACTICES

1. Full-cost or Cost-plus pricing

Full cost pricing is that level of price which covers total costs including the overheads besides a predetermined mark up. This method is adopted in following situations.

(a) When the enterprise is entering a new technological area and long term costs cannot be accurately predicted. The aim is to recover full cost plus a reasonable profit.

(b) Where the customer has no choice but to accept it i.e. where price leadership exists.

The method is simple and easy to understand. It leads us to prompt cost calculations. But it encourages inefficiency and overlooks competitive forces.

2. Marginal (or Direct) cost pricing

In it the price of the product is based on incremental cost of production. It is adopted in following cases:

(a) In public utility services where social returns are more important than generation of profit,

(b) When there is cut-throat competition,

(c) Where firm has unutilised capacity e.g. where a transport vehicle is empty, it is advisable to carry additional traffic even at reduced rate.

(d) To introduce the product into new markets.

Marginal cost pricing is a short-term measure. Though it has important advantages, indiscriminate reliance upon this technique can be dangerous.

3. Going-Rate Pricing

The firm simply examines the general pricing structure in the industry and then accordingly fixes the prices of its own product. This policy is prevalent in industries characterized by price leadership. But such an arrangement may not always work since firms do not have complete control over costs.

4. Loss Leaders

This should not be considered to lead to losses. Actually, it is a policy which aims at increasing profits. Sometimes, a firm manufacturing or selling multiple products may charge relatively low price on some popular products with the hope that customers who come for this product will also buy other products. Thus 'loss leader'connotes that the price charged is lower than what could have been otherwise charged. The basic idea is that profit sacrificed will be made good by profits on other products. This is widely used in retailing business.

5. Stay-Out Pricing

Sometimes, a firm may start with a high price and when unable to sell, it may keep on lowering the price until it succeeds in selling the targeted quota. It enables the firm to ascertain the maximum price it can charge.

6. Programme Pricing

In it, price is related to supply price. The firm adds a mark up over the supply price which may be the wholesale price or godown price. It is quite popular in case of retail and wholesale trade.

7. Price Lining

Herein price of one product out of total range of products is fixed. Price of the rest of the products is determined from their relationship with that commodity e.g. a shoe firm may fix price of a particular size and fix prices of the rest on the basis of differences in size.

8. Odd Number and Round Number Pricing

The price is fixed in a manner which gives the impression of its being low. For instance, price of a product may be fixed at Rs. 109.90 rather than Rs. 110 to create a favourable impact on consumers. This has impact on sales. On the contrary, some firms round up their price to next higher rupee so that accounts are easily maintained.

9. Trade Association Pricing

To avoid uncertainties of pricing decision and downward pressure on prices which competition exerts, firms may make formal agreements to maintain prices at uniform level. Since these types of agreements are illegal, the firms make implied agreements.

10. Customary Pricing

In case of certain commodities, prices get fixed because these have prevailed over a long period of time e.g. price of a cup of tea is customarily fixed. Changes in cost of production leads to either quality changes or smaller quantity per cup. It is only when costs change appreciably that the customary price changes.

11. Price Leadership

Sometimes an industry may be dominated by one or more big firms. In such a situation, small firms may not like to enter price war with big firms. They may therefore follow the price lead given by the big firm(s). For instance Cadbury may be accepted as a price leader in chocolate industry. In fact, price leadership is a way of coexistence. Generally pricing under this pattern does not fluctuate much.

12. Cyclical Pricing

When pricing by a firm is based on general economic situation, it is called cyclical pricing. During depression the firm reduces prices in order to continue in the market whereas during boom the prices are hooked up to take benefit of rising prices. These price adjustments are made notwithstanding that the cost of production has remained unchanged.

13. Administered Prices

These are statutorily fixed prices after taking into account the cost and stipulated profit. The object is to regulate the prices of essential commodities and to provide goods and services at affordable prices. Prices of goods sold through ration shops are based on administered prices. Prices of certain goods like steel, fertilizers, sugar etc. are statutorily fixed.

14. Dual Pricing

Where a commodity is simultaneously covered under the administered prices as well as market prices, it is called double pricing. Part of the output is subjected to administered prices and rest is sold in the free market. Generally, administered prices are lower than the free market prices. Prices of sugar and cement are regulated by dual price system. The levy price is fixed below the open market price. A major part of the production is sold through public distribution system.

TYPES OF PRICING POLICIES

I. Pioneer Pricing Strategy

1. *Skimming price*

This is used in pricing a new product for which some consumers are willing to pay higher initial price. It is supported by large promotional expenses. This policy is advisible when (a) new product is introduced,

(ii) there are few producers, (c) demand is inelastic, and (d) the product is sophisticated used by rich and affluent customers. After sales have been made to these prime customers, and competition has entered the market, the innovator reduces the price of the product. This is advisable in case of products having high prestige value.

2. *Penetration price*

It involves setting a low initial price on a product to attract as many buyers as possible. The underlying idea is to widen the market at the very outset. The widened market and consequently the mass production is expected to reduce the cost of production. This policy can be adopted in the following conditions :

(a) Higher price elasticity of demand for the product.
(b) Volume of production is very high.
(c) The market will not accept high price.
(d) There is strong threat of potential customers.
(e) The product is mass consumption item.

II. Pricing at Maturity Stage of Product

Once the product enters 'maturity stage' the primary strategy is changed. At the stage of market maturity and saturation, the situation is that of oligopoly. At such a stage, price war is fatal for the firm. The firm needs to reduce the price to the extent the demand elasticity of the product permits it. It will keep the customers with the firm and discourage further entry of potential customers.

III. Pricing Established Products

Product Line Pricing

A multiproduct firm can maximise total contribution if it gives due consideration to place and function of each item in the product line. For instance, if products are complementary, the firm could adodpt the policy of 'loss leader' to achieve broader penetration. A consumer may be lured by the low price and once in the show room, he may be convinced to buy a more expensive model. Different types of product line pricing are:

(a) Full cost pricing (discussed already).
(b) Pricing based on elasticity of demand e.g. in the case of affluent sections which are price insensitive, the firm can put

up high margin on those products.

(c) Conversion-cost-pricing i.e. the cost of converting raw materials into finished products are used as the basis of product line pricing. Margin is added to the conversion cost of the product.

IV. Other Policies

(i) *One-price versus Negotiated price (single price policy)*

Under it, all buyers have to pay the same price for the product regardless of the quantity being purchased or any other market factors. Yet the prices of many large consumer durables such as appliances, automobiles, furniture etc. are all basically negotiated.

(ii) *Resale Price Maintenance*

It is the price fixed by the manufacturer for the wholesalers and retailers. It ensures the dealers a good margin and the consumer can buy good quality products at fair price. For it, manufacturers of drugs, detergents etc. fix the retail price and print it on the package. Since resale price includes cost of inefficient retailer for not selling the goods quickly, it is invariably fixed somewhat higher than it should be. Its advantages are :

(a) it prevents competition among distributors and hence there is no undercutting of prices;

(b) it is advantageous for small firms who face no competition from large firms;

(c) it dispenses with the need to sell any product as loss leader;

(d) the customer need not bargain.

The drawbacks of Resale Price Maintenance are :

(a) It is heavily tilted in favour of the seller and deprives the consumers of the advantages which may have accrued to him from competition.

(b) It may promote inefficient firms.

(c) It cuts at the root of competition so highly essential for efficiency.

Legal Aspects of RPM

In India, the RPM is prohibited under Sections 39 and 40 of the MRTPA, 1969. Section 33(1)(f) declares a stipulation as to resale price a restrictive trade practice. Every such agreement must be registered. Section 39 of the Act provides that any term or condition of sale seeking to establish a minimum price for sale of goods shall be void. The object of Section 39 is to curb the tendency of monopolists or dominant firms to prevent competition by insisting on the wholesaler or retailer to sell at a price stipulated in the agreement. It further forbids a supplier from notifying or publishing a price calculated to be understood as minimum price. To sum up, no person can dictate the minimum resale price to a wholesaler or retailer.

Section 40 prohibits a supplier from withholding supplies to a wholesaler or retailer on the ground that latter is likely to sell at a price below the minimum price either directly or indirectly. A supplier is deemed to withhold supplies from a dealer if :

(i) he refuses to supply those goods to the order of the dealer; or

(ii) he refuses or fails to supply those goods to the dealer except at prices or on terms and conditions as to credit, discount or other matters which are less favourable than the normal terms; or

(ii) he treats the dealer in a manner less favourable than that in which he normally treats other dealer in respect of time or methods of delivery.

RPM is, therefore, void and visited with liabilities under Section 51 of the MRTPA, 1969.

PRICING APPROACH IN SMALL BUSINESS

W.W. Haynes made a survey of 88 small firms in the U.S.A. in 1962 and reached certain conclusions regarding the pricing approach to be adopted by small firms. The firms covered under the survey were of two types namely : (a) Small manufacturers and (b) Retailers.

The following were the pricing pracitces of small business :

1. Small firms do not always follow full cost pricing rather than adjust prices according to changes in market conditions.
2. Cost is considered only as a reference point and not as a pricing variable.
3. Pricing decisions of the firms are rarely dependent on accounting techniques. Rather the firms rely on incremental principles for pricing.
4. Unlike large firms, small firms do not aim at target rate of profit.
5. These adopt different mark-ups for different products.

6. These firms are more concerned about their image and price their products so as to improve their image.
7. These prices are determined on the basis of trial and error. For instance, incremental principle of pricing was not followed due to the following reasons :
   (a) they lacked information and expertize;
   (b) they are content with getting a reasonable level of profit;
   (c) they aim at things other than maximisation of profit e.g. goodwill, market share etc.

FACTORS AFFECTING PRICING DECISIONS

1. Internal Factors (Cost Factors)

These include (i) price policy; and (ii) product costs. The significance of costs lies in the fact that product price should not be less than its cost if the price policy is to earn reasonable profit. Thus, cost is the chief determinant of price. The costs establish a floor below which a firm will not price its products. The internal factors are largely controllable.

2. External Factors Or Non-cost Factors

As compared to internal factors, the external factors are largely out of the control of the company. These are discussed below :

(i) *Demand*

Demand for the product is one of the most important consideration in pricing decisions. The demand is determined by : (a) price ; (b) availability of substitutes ; (c) income of buyers ; (d) tastes and preferences of buyers ; (e) number and size of competitors ; (f) number and size of buyers etc. For proper product pricing, the characteristics of demand should be kept in mind. The entrepreneur should establish a relationship between demand and adjustment in prices.

(ii) *Degree of competition*

Market structure influences the pricing decisions. Market structure consists of following basic elements :

(a) Number of competitors ;
(b) Size of each competitor ;
(c) Degree of product differentiation ;
(d) Ease of entry ;
(e) Nature of competition (whether pure, monopolistic or oligopolistic) ;

(iii) *Age of Industry*

Price in new industry tends to be more flexible then in old and well established industries.

(iv) Supplies of raw materials i.e. proportion of raw material cost into the total cost.

(v) *Nature of buyers*

For instance, where the number of buyers is quite large, they exert less influence on prices. Similarly, affluent buyers do not resist price increases.

(vi) *Economic condition of different market segments*

As economic conditions of different markets vary, discriminatory pricing could be used with advantage.

(vii) *Price Control* by government.

(viii) *Nature of the product*

Price increases in essential consumer products are opposed by consumers whereas those in the luxury or capital nature products may not have any resistance.

PRICE DISCRIMINATION

When same product is sold at differential prices to different buyers, it is called discriminatory pricing. The product is basically the same but may have light or illusory differences. For example, different classes in trains are charged differently though all passengers undertake the same journey.

Conditions in which differential pricing is possible

Price discrimination is possible in following circumstances :

(i) Differences in price elasticities due to differences in preference of buyers, their income and location, ease of availability of substitutes.

(ii) *Market segmentation*

The market is divided into different segments according to differences in price elasticities of customers. A different price is paid for each market segment. Segmentation is done with reference to the following :

(a) *Segmentation by geographical location :* It is done in the case of international trade where domestic and export prices of a product differ significantly.

(b) *Segmentation based on size of purchase order* e.g. bulk buyers are charged at a lower price due to their higher bargaining power.

(c) *Segmentation according to purchasing power* e.g. doctors charge different fees from different customers.

(d) *Segmentation on the basis of time of purchase.* This is done to achieve optimum utilisation of capacity. This is applicable in case of products like fans, refrigerators etc. Firms quote lower off-season prices.

(e) *Segmentation according to social and professional status of the buyers.*

Prices charged from private companies, government and educational institutions differs from each other.

It is not always easy to find out best way of market segmentation and the price to be fixed.

VARIOUS WAYS OF OPEN PRICE DISCRIMINATION

1. Time Price Differentials

Demand has a time dimension. The demand may shift in fairly short intervals. For instance, demand for telephone facilities is more in day time rather than at night. Following three conditions must exist before this differential can be exercised.

(a) Buyer must have strong preference for buying the goods at a particular time.

(b) During slack period, seller should be able to sell at a price that is sufficient to cover at least the incremental cost of product.

(c) It should not be possible to store the product/service.

2. User Price Differentials

In this case, the seller divides the market into different segments according to demand elasticity based on buyer's use of the product and charge different prices from different segments.

3. Quality Price Differentials

In several cases, quality becomes a significant determinant of demand elasticity. The seller has, therefore, to create differences in quality to sell the product e.g. by changing the appearance of the product.

4. Quantity Differential

When seller discriminates on the basis of quantity, it is called 'quantity differentials'. There are three types of quantity differentials:

(a) *Cumulative Discounts* i.e. the discounts provided by the seller on the basis of total quantity bought by a particular buyer during a period of time. These discounts are aimed at encouraging bulk buying, buyer loyalty. and forward planning of output.

(b) *Quantity Discounts :* These discounts are related to the size of single purchase. The object is to encourage bigger orders which reduces his cost of selling, packing and delivery etc.

(c) *Functional Discounts* : These are distributed according to trade status of distributor in the channel of distribution e.g. wholesaler, retailer.

5. Geog raphical Price Differential

Price differential could be based on buyer's location. Broadly speaking, the seller may quote one of the two types of prices.

(a) prices at point of origin of the goods called F.O.B. price.

(b) prices at the point of their destination called 'Delivered Price'.

(a) F.O.B. Pricing

When seller charges a uniform price from all the buyers buying similar quantity of a particular quality of goods, it is called F.O.B. Price. It is quoted in either of the following two ways :

—seller quotes mill price and buyer has to choose his own mode of transport and pay for it.

—seller quotes a price which includes mill price and actual transportation and cost of delivery of goods at buyer's place.

In both the cases, seller's return remains the same except that in latter situation he handles some additional work of packing, delivering and maintaining records of delivery.

(b) Uniformed Delivered Pricing

The seller charges same delivered price at all locations. It involves discrimination because the buyer who is located nearer to seller pays less than the one who is located far away. It is effective in case of commodities having national market and wherein the cost of transportation is less compared to value of the product.

(c) Basing point pricing

When delivered price is quoted on the basis of a basing point, it is called 'basing point pricing'. It includes : mill price plus transportation charges. The transport cost is not based on actual freight but on the basis of transportation cost from some designated production centre. The basing point may be either "single" or "multiple".

If freight charged is higher than the actual freight, it is called 'Phantom Freight'. On the other hand, if freight charged is less than the actual freight, it is called 'Freight Absorption'.

6. National Area Price Differentials

When price charged in domestic market is different than that charged in foreign market. This difference may be due to difference in nature of competition in both the markets or government regulations.

7. Cash Discount

When price concessions are offered on the basis of promptness of payment, these are called 'Cash Discounts'. Thc objcct of thcsc discounts is to have a comfortable liquidity position and to minimise bad credit risk. A buyer who wants to buy a credit has to pay more to cover up risk of default.

CHAPTER XX

RISK MANAGEMENT

Risk to small business exist in many forms. Unless taken proper care these risks can cause the failure of business. Control of risk is also necessary for survival and growth.

METHODS OF RISK CONTROL

Following are the three ways to control risk :

1. **Avoid/Reduce the risk**

   This can be done by following techniques :

   (a) Substitution of high risk materials and use of low risk materials and processes.

   (b) Screening high risk items e.g avoiding indiscriminate extension of credit and screening high risk individuals to reduce bad debts .

   (c) Eliminating high level risk. For instance by requiring employees to wear safety equipment while performing hazardous jobs.

   (d) Adopting good management practices which are the best bet against risk e.g. periodic inspection and training, good hiring procedures. Even where risks are shifted to others as in the case of insurance, good management practices can still reduce risk and lower the cost of insurance to business. Insurance costs can be reduced by installing sprinkler system, properly placing fire extinguishers, burglar alarms etc.

2. **Assume the risk** which are impossible to avoid. There are many risks which small business may face on a continuing basis. Good management practices can come to the risk even in this case. For instance, while stocking lady's garments, it is better to study the market and evaluate customer tastes.

3. **Shift the risk**

   This can be done by:

   (i) *Sub-contracting* those functions which are too time consuming or beyond the capabilities of business such as a building contractor awarding the electricity work to another.

(ii) *Hedging* : It is adopted in commodity markets to meet the risks arising from price fluctuations.

(iii) *Insurance* i.e insuring the risk by undertaking to pay premium.

Types of Insurance

(a) Fire insurance policy to guard against loss due to fire and lighting. Both building and its contents are insured. By paying additional premia, coverage can be had even against explosions and riots.

(b) Theft—both outside (such as burglary, robbery) and inside (embezzlement, employee theft).

(c) Automobile insurance.

(d) Life insurance on owner's own life or the life of principal officer. Many owners of small business may find insurance policy to be a cheap source of debt capital.

The policy could be (i) whole life policy or (ii) endowment policy i.e. if the assured dies during the period specified , his survivor is paid the face value of policy. If he does not die, he is paid the face value of policy at the end of specified period.

LOCATIONAL ANALYSIS

Significance of firm's location to its economic viability needs no emphasis. Two critical factors entering locational analysis are :

(i) Analysis of potential site.

(ii) Choice of specific location.

Locational analysis is a dynamic process and continues over the entire life of the firm. General location is based on convenience or cost e.g availability of vacant building, proximity to owner's residence, low rent. But low rent should not be the sole criterion. Following variables need probing while deciding about the location.

1. **Trade Area Analysis** i.e. an analysis of the geographic area that provides a major portion of the continued patronage to a business. It consists of a consideration of the following:

   (a) *Primary trading area* from which the firm can serve the consumer better from the point of view of convenience and accessibility. Such a location contributes towards a major part of the sales volume.

(b) *Secondary trading area* is the zone beyond primary area on which firm can exert strong pull but suffers a drawback from the point of view of convenience and accessibility.

(c) *Tertiary area* is not capable of being defined in geographical terms. It consists of customers who patronise a shopping place for reasons not connected with proximity eg. strong attachment to a particular shop.

2. **Study of population** characteristics to ascertain the following:
   (a) age distribution of general population and of potential customers ;
   (b) number of one person households and family households in that area ;
   (c) rent structure ;
   (d) age composition of families.
3. **Income level** of residents in trade area and disposable personal income (i.e. proportion of income available for expenditure). Discretionary buying power is that portion of one's own income that is not required for purchasing basic necessities but is likely to be expended on luxury items. To determine purchasing power and sales potential, a firm should undertake the following.
   (a) Determine the number of household units in the trade area from census data.
   (b) Multiply the number of household units with the average household income.
   (c) It would provide the total purchasing power (total disposable income).
   (d) Multiply the total purchasing power with the percentage of disposable income spent on a "particular item".
   (e) It would give the total potential purchasing power for that item.
   (f) Estimate of the percentage household income that will be spent in the particular store.
   (g) Estimate the projected sales.
4. **Occupational analysis and level of education**

Occupational and educational survey discloses the type of employment in the area and also the stability of employment.

5. **Analysis of competition**

It will provide a view of the nature, location, size, quality and quantity of competition in a given trade area. It will also provide a glimpse of the actions of the competitors.

6. **Site, history and future** i.e. history of failure or success of the location. It would suggest whether site has poor location or the management was incompetent or that there is a need for further investigation.
7. **Community attitudes.** i.e. Community outlook of the community with reference to the type of commodities sold by the small entrepreneur.

Accessibility of Location

Accessibility is integral to any site analysis. It refers to ease and safety of approach to the store e.g traffic congestion may discourage customers from patronizing a particular site. The accessibility can be gauged from a study of traffic pattern and traffic arteries.

Site Economics : For each type of business, there is an optimum location. For instance, locational analysis may reveal optimum site from the point of view of accessibility, population, income levels etc. But the occupancy cost may be prohibitive. Occupancy cost includes purchase price, lease/rental, utilities, maintenance, taxes etc. Unique requirements of each firm must be studied while evaluating economic feasibility of the site relative to occupancy cost.

Traffic Analysis : It is a basic factor in location analysis for many types of business. Traffic study is helpful for two reasons. Firstly, the traffic count measures the amount of pedestrians and vehicular traffic passing a site that represent potential customers. Secondly, it serves as a measure for comparing relative desirability of sites under consideration.

In making **pedestrian traffic count**, decide : (i) Who is to be counted, (ii) When shall the count take place, and (iii) When it shall take place. The purpose of the study is to find out the number of potential customers passing by the proposed site during the working hours of the store. It may be noted that heavy traffic volume is of little value if it does not represent potential customers. For instance, a ladies garment botique would be more interested in knowing the number of women passing by the site. The pedestrians must also be categorised according to age and the purpose of passing by the site. Other considerations in determining traffic flow are the season, month, week and day. From all these details, a reasonable estimate of the sales volume can be made. The information generated would be of the following type :

(i) Characteristics of individuals who are most likely to be store customers (from pedestrian interviews).

(ii) Number of such individuals passing the site during store house (from traffic counts).

(iii) Proportion of passerby who will enter the store (from pedestrian interviews).

(iv) Proportion of those entering who will become purchasers (from pedestrian interviews)

(v) Amount of average transactions (from past experience).

Automobile Traffic Count

The sales potential of many firms depends on quality and composition of automobile traffic passing the site. Automobile traffic may be classified on the basis of kind of trips taken e.g (a) work trip, (b) planned shopping trip, (c) pleasure trip. Restaurants, service stations etc are located along heavily travelled highways. Drycleaner's shop would find the location or work bound side of the street more favourable whereas grocery store would find homeward bound side more suitable.

PHYSICAL FACILITIES

Total store planning should be a high priority item for a small business owner. The building's exterior and interior features should be carefully studied from the standpoint of establishing its suitability for serving the needs of customers as also of the store owner.

1. New Building versus Purchasing existing building

Some stores prefer to construct their own building because of the possibility of incorporating efficient features. Exteriors and anteriors would be designed to match its special requirements. On the other hand when it is planned to acquire an existing building, the suitability of location as well as to meet the requirements of the business must be ascertained. Cost of remodelling is considerably less than constructing a new facility. Besides the process is faster than undertaking a new construction.

Buy versus Lease

In small towns and cities where real estate values are not excessive, the owner may choose to buy. It facilitates modification of the building without having to seek permission of the landlord. There is a further advantage of appreciation in value. Depreciation of building can be charged to tax. But it has the drawback of heavy capital outlay and limit on mobility.

Leasing has the advantage of saving in capital outlay and sparing of funds for current operations. The drawback is that the owner may not renew the lease. Modification in the building would require landlord's permission. If economic conditions deteriorate, lease payments may put severe strain on firm's finances.

Space Requirements : In assessing space requirements, the following considerations must be borne in mind.

(i) Display windows

People enjoy window shopping and this fact must be exploited to the advantage of the firm. 'Display' not only acts as promotional strategy but also projects store's image. Attractively designed displays catch the eye of casual shopper causing him to stop, look, enter and purchase merchandise. Thus effective provision must be made for display.

(ii) Store sign

A properly placed sign guides customers. However guard against the following:

(a) Improperly designed sign, (b) Wrongly placed sign where it is not readily visible, (c) Unreadable signs because of faded lettering, (d) Signs that convey wrong image.

INTERIOR FEATURES OF THE STORE

Interior of the shop must both be appealing and inviting. Small business owner should pay attention to those features that help create favourable shopping environment.

(a) *Flooring :* It must bc sturdy, good looking and durable.
(b) *Walls and ceiling* : Walls must be of sufficient strength to support the requirements of the building. Ceilings and walls must have matching colour.
(c) *Lighting and fixtures* : Lighting requirements must be studied from the point of view of nature of store. Proper lighting enhances the environment and helps the customers to merchandise clearly. Lighting must be diffused and not glaring.

(d) *Colours scheme :* Colours can be used to give certain visual effects such as making a building appear larger. Warm colours should be used in youth-oriented shops (e.g. children's clothes, toy stores, sportswear). Soft colours lend themselves to overall store decor.

(e) Other facility requirements such as rest room, toilet, shelves etc.

LAYOUT

Layout is a critical factor in efficient operation of the store. The term 'store layout' is used to denote "spatial arrangement of selling and non-selling departments, aisles, fixtures, display facilities and equipment in proper relationship to each other and to fixed elements of the structure". It should make merchandise accessible to customers.

In small retail firm, two types of layout plans are commonly used. These are discussed below :

(i) Grid Layout

It is a rectangular store arrangement pattern that features a main aisle and secondary aisles that are located at right angle to main aisle. Main aisles carry a large share of traffic and provide best location for convenience goods, seasonal merchandise etc. *Shopping goods* may be displayed on secondary aisles and *specialty goods* in a less travelled area.

Such a layout is conducive to low building costs. It is adapted to situations where structural columns are numerous and closed together. It minimises floor space requirement and allows display of greater amount

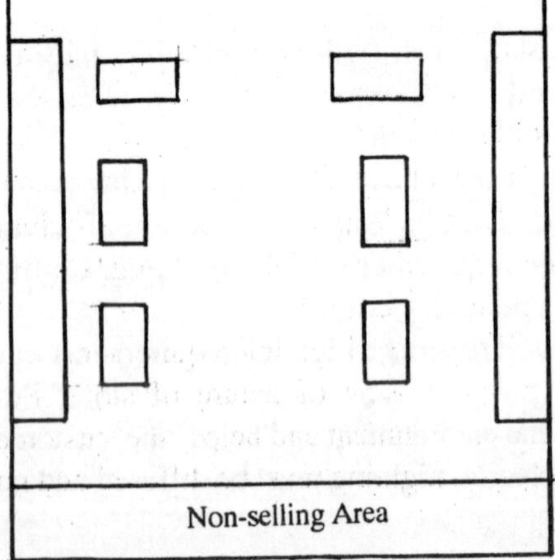

Fig. 1. Grid Layout

of merchandise. It also facilitates standardised display and makes it easier for customer to become familiar with the layout.

(ii) Free Flow Layout

It is a store layont which could be circular, octogonal, U-shaped etc. It has, therefore, no uniform pattern of arrangement. It has considerable flexibity because display counters can be added, removed, or rearranged without disrupting overall layout pattern. The customers can move from one area to another and have access to variety of merchandies. This is the most commonly used layout plan. It is less expensive and better suited to the needs of small business.

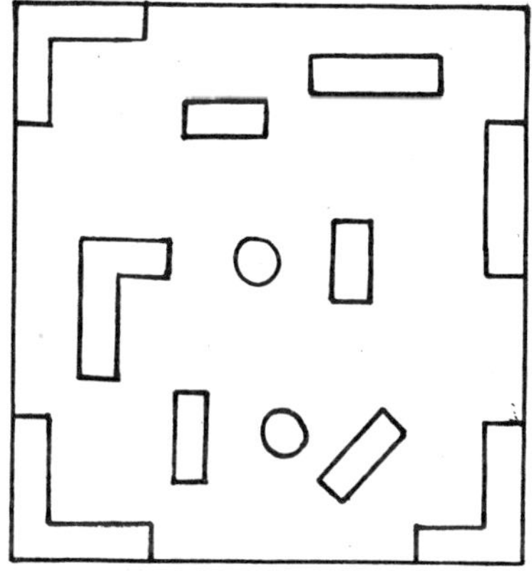

Fig. 2. Free Flow Layout

MANUFACTURING FACILITY LAYOUT

It refers to the efficient arrangement of manufacturing facilities. Attention is paid to use of equipment and location and space requirements of support services e.q maintenance, receiving shipping and storage. Benefits of good factory layout are : (i) Lower cost of manufacturing, (ii) Most efficient use of floor space, (iii) Reduction of manufacturing bottlenecks, (iv) More effective control, (v) Better service to customer (vi) Economical material handling.

Types of Manufacturing Layout Plans

1. Process Layout

It is used in case of job order production i.e. goods are manufactured according to customer specification. In it, similar equipment is located in one area e.g all drills, or lathe would lie in one area. All work of a particular type is sent to a particular department. Its advantages are : (i) Superior control of intricate processes, (ii) Greater utilisation of production facilities, (iii) Lower capital investment in equipment, (iv) Adaptability to frequent rearrangement of operation squence, (v) Improved specialised services, (vi) Lower per unit cost.

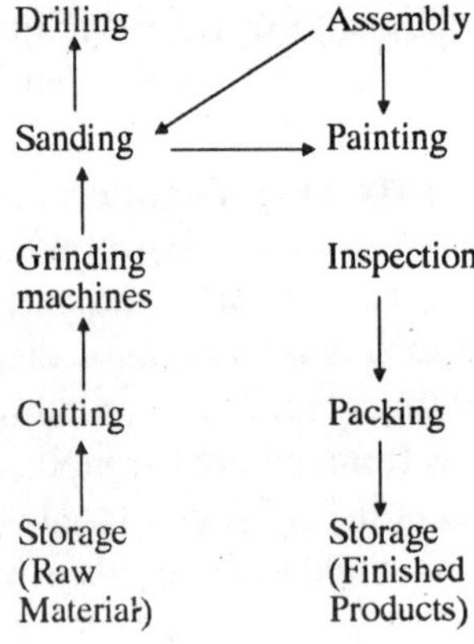

Fig 3. Process Layout.

2. Product Layout

It is used in mass production of goods in which all equipment needed to produce a specific product is arranged in sequence in an assembly line.

Storage of raw material —Product A / Saw→ Drilling → Sanding Machine → Assembly → Painting → Storage of finished product

Storage of raw material —Product B / Lathe→ Milling → Sanding Machine → Assembling → Varnishing → Storage of finished product

Fig. 4 . Product Layout.

The raw materials enter the production process and roll out as finished products. There could be considerable duplication of machinery. Therefore, it is an expensive system for small business. Its advantages are :

(i) Simplified control and reduced costs.
(ii) Reduction in material handling costs.
(iii) Smoother flow of material.
(iv) Reduces floor space required for goods in process.
(v) Reduces investment in work-in-process.
(vi) Ensures job specialisation.

CHAPTER XXI

MARKETING

Role of Marketing

Improved marketing is central to a small firm's industrial strategy. Unfortunately, many small firms assume that the only requirement for success is to open and wait for customers. Perhaps, it is due to severe limits on their resources. It is seldom recognised that marketing is a complex process affected by internal and external factors. Internal variable includes firm's financial position, management capability, personnel resources, products offered. External variable includes general economic conditions, characteristics of population, social and cultural factors, competition, government regulations etc. Therefore small firm's success depends on the ability to plan, organise, staff and control marketing activity in relation to internal and external environment. In this context, marketing is the performance of business activities that direct the flow of goods and services from the producer to the consumer. This is based on the assumption that the firm matches its product to what the customer wants. But this assumption gets translated into reality in the case of a small firm because of close affinity between the owner and his customers. It provides him a powerful basis for developing a dialogue between the producer and the consumer. The other in-built advantages enjoyed by a small firm in the field of marketing include : realistic marketing planning, shorter lines of communication, flexibility, ability to act quickly and decisively. For these reasons, marketing is considered to be a small firm's route to profits.

Concept of Marketing

Simply stated, marketing is the process of integrating and coordinating the following :

- identifying and measuring the needs of customers for the type of products or services that the firm is equipped to provide.
- translating the perceived needs into products or service development.
- developing and activating a plan that makes the product or

service available.

- informing prospective customers about the availability of the product/service and stimulating their demand at a price that generates satisfactory profits for the firm.

MARKETING FUNCTION

The functions that must be performed in the marketing process are as follows :

1. Buying and Selling

Exchange process involves buying in ancticipation of customer demand and searching for materials that will satisfy those needs. Selling function includes determination of potential customers and using a combination of sales techniques to stimulate demand for those goods or services.

2. Transportation and Storage

It involves the movement and handling of goods. Not all goods are sold at the same time they are manufactured. Storage is done so that goods are available at the time and place they are needed.

3. Risk-taking, Standardization and Grading

Stored goods are subject to several types of risks. They may undergo spoilage, obsolescence, destruction. Consumer preferences may change leaving the business owner with a large quantity of unsold goods. Some of the risks can be shifted through insurance coverage. But the most effective means of dealing with risks is the adoption of good managment practices.

Standardisation and grading enable consumers to make a comparison of the products. Standardization establishes uniformity of specifications in the matter of colour, weight, composition etc. Grading is done in the case of products that cannot be produced uniformly e.g. fruit, egg.

MARKETING PROCESS—STEPS

1. Identification of potential changes taking place in firm's market that could materially affect the firm's business.

2. Identification of Customer Needs

The first step in marketing should be to identify the needs of customers the firm intends to serve. Many firms simply focus an introducing technical perfections inthe product without assessing customer reactions. Many of the products introduced with lot of fanfare and financial back up have been found to have no customer. Perhaps, the firm went ahead with the assumption that market exists for them. Neglect of user needs is a common weakness both with large and small firms and particularly with the latter on account of resource constraints. The small firm is advised to proceed only on the basis of definite information collected with the help of a following exercise.

(i) Sources of Information about Markets and Customers :

There are two broad sources of market intelligence viz.,

(a) *Primary sources* which the company develops for its own specific requirements, and

(b) *Secondary* sources i.e. the published reports of trade association, government agencies, and others. These are not geared to the requirement of an individual firm.

Primary Sources

From a marketing perspective, the three primary sources of information are :

- *Internal Records of the Firm* : These consist of invoices, inventory audit, reports of salesmen etc. Invoices can be used to collect customers' addresses which would reveal the geographical market area, concentration of customers in a given area, their social characteristics and purchasing pattern. Sales records do not describe the total market but they provide important clue about firm's market standing. Salesmen's reports may be persued to discover new business opportunities or competitive weaknesses.
- Mail surveys, telephone interviews and personal interviews of actual or prospective customers.
- Information derived from direct observation of customers and competitors.

Secondary Sources

A number of publications provide overwhelming useful marketing information Industry. Specific data are published by trade and professional associations.

(ii) Pinpointing the Real Customers

The potential customers must not only be recognised but placed into proper categories as follows :

(a) Users (who consume the product/service) ;
(b) Buyers (who actually purchase) ;
(c) Decider (who decides what should be purchased) ;
(d) Influencer (who has some influence on the purchase process);
(e) Informer (who controls the flow of information to the decision groups).

A typical customer may play several of these roles. Costlier the item to be purchased, more actors playing different roles will get into the process. To illustrate, suppose the family decides to buy a TV set. All the family members would be the users. But the actual buyer could be the husband. Deciders could have been the husband and wife both. The children could be the influencers on the decision-makers. Any member could act as informer by providing or withholding information from decision making group. Generally, the role of buyer and decider could have been performed by the same individual. But in case of complex products, the purchaser's influence may be reduced particularly in case of organizational purchases. For successful marketing, the entrepreneur will endeavour to identify the roles played by different members in the decision process.

3. Market Segmentation

It is the grouping of customers into segments so that each segment has similar needs, characteristics and requirements. It helps a firm to relate its products to those requirements of the target group. A small firm may focus on a segment that may not be found attractive by a large firm. Segmentation could be on demographic (i.e. age, sex, religion), geographic, psychographic or social basis. Good segmentation must meet the following criteria :

(a) Needs of customs must be both identifiable and measurable.
(b) Firm must have the capacity to develop products that will satisfy the customer's choice in the particular segment.
(c) The segment must be economically worthwhile.

Procedure for market segmentation is described below :

(i) Ascertain firm's capabilities

It must know what set of needs it can satisfy. For instance, the small firm may be willing to sell its products to foreign buyers. But it must ascertain whether it has the necessary financial, promotional or distributive capabilities.

(ii) Ascertain the competition

Identify the characteristics and extent of competition in the various segments. All other conditions being equal, it should focus on that segment which has the least competition or the segment which are too small for large firms.

(iii) Focus on the segment chosen

For a small firm, the segment chosen on the criteria of customer characteristics such as geographical region, demography, has been found to be more suitable.

4. Marketing Decision Variables

Next step is the development of marketing strategy in relation to various decision variables which are classified as follows :

I. Controllable Variables

(a) Target Market segments
  * Location
  * Target customers
  * Timing

(b) Products offered
  * Type of product
  * Range of product
  * Design features
  * Quality

(c) Price
  * Price level
  * Price variables (discount)
  * Maintenance

(d) Advertisement and Promotion
  * Advertising level

* Advertising media
* Sales promotion

(e) Distribution
* Channels
* Number of sales outlets
* Warehousing facility

(f) Servicing

II. Marketing Uncontrollable

(a) Resource availability
* availability of required materials.
* cost and quality of required material
* material

(b) Competition—direct and indirect

(c) Economic conditions—total market size, economic trends, income situation.

(d) Socio-cultural conditions—societal values, life style, fashion consciousness

(e) Political and legal conditions
* Political risk situation
* Legal regulation

(f) Technological situation—state of technology, rate of technological change.

Decision about the Product

Product decisions have become quite important because the length of time for which a product can remain profitable has considerably shortened. Frequent technological innovation and entry of new products have contributed to the shortening of life of a product. Such factors pose a problem beyond the financial capabilities of a firm. The product features amenable to manipulation by a small firm are :

(a) Performance and functional features i.e. firm's ability to perform, durability, reliability and precision.

(b) Use characteristics i.e. ease in handling and serviceability.

(c) Aesthetic qualities e.g. style, design, colour etc.

(d) Extrinsic features e.g. uniqueness of product, status value etc.

Product Life Cycle

In addition to the above, product life cycle is equally helpful in deciding about the appropriate marketing strategy to be adopted. Consider the following 'Life Cycle Product'

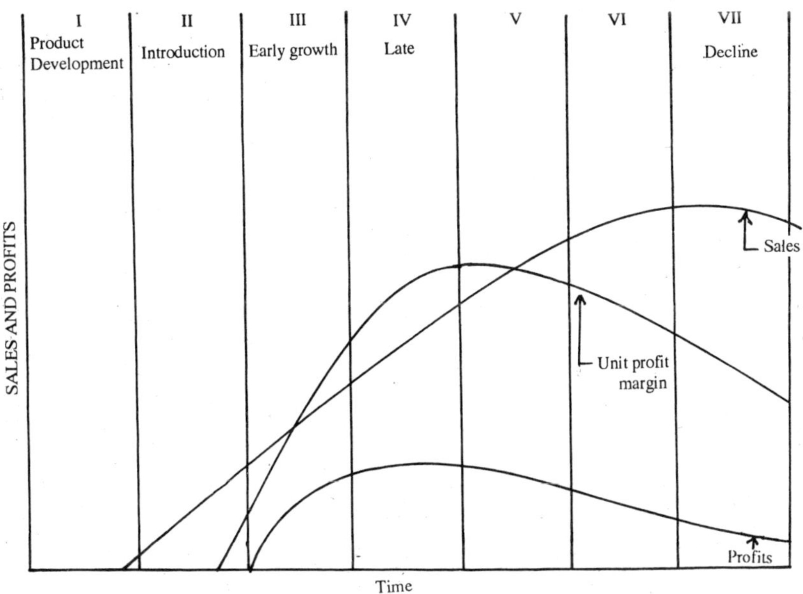

Fig. 1: Diagram showing effect of Life Cycle on Sales and Profits.

An idea about the stage the existing product is would give an idea about its sales and profits. Of course, the stages are arbitrary yet an understanding of the stage of market position of the product can be useful in planning the product strategies. Based on this, a firm can maintain a balanced product-mix with different life stages. The assortment of products will help firm know as to which of them would need development modification or elimination.

5. Marketing Mix

It is the integration of the four elements noted below to service the needs of target market :

(a) Product Mix

Correct combination of product and service. It will cover product depth (i.e. model, size, style, colour) and product breadth (i.e. number of product lines carried).

(b) Promotional strategy to inform customer about firm, products/service etc. through personal selling, sales promotion etc.
(c) Physical Distribution i.e. the chair of distribution to be adopted. It forms the subject matter of a separate chapter.
(d) Pricing.

Below are discussed two of the above.

PRODUCT MIX

It refers to number of different products offered by a company. It is not uncommon to find small firms selling multiple products. Product mix is done to optimize profits. The advantages of product mix are :

(i) It enables the firm to serve different segments of the market.
(ii) It gives relatively steady sales and profits to the firm.
(iii) The firm can keep all its bases covered.

Its demerits are :

(i) It makes greater demand on firm's resources in the form of increased investment in production facilities and inventory.
(ii) Marketing problems.

Therefore, the firm should weigh the pros and cons of a wider versus narrow product mix. The ultimate decision would rest on such considerations as the available resources, existing and future market opportunities and strategies of competitors. Philip Kotler* has suggested the following indicators of firm's suboptional porduct mix :

(a) disproportionately high percentage of total profits from a few product ;
(b) insufficient product breadth to exploit sales force;
(c) excessive productive capacity on a chronic or seasonal basis;
(d) steadily declining sale or profits.

Development of new products

Small firms should consider the frequent introduction of new or improved product as part of their market strategy. The procedure for generating new product ideas and implementing them is described below :

(i) Making creative search for new product ideas.

---

* Marketing Management 2nd Ed. Prentice Hall, Englewood of Cliffs, N.J. (1974), 444.

(ii) Scrutiny of the ideas for their worthwhileness.
(iii) Evaluating whether the idea is compatible with firm's objectives.
(iv) Establishing technical and market feasibility.
(v) Reviewing internal resources and capabilities.
(vi) Product Development and product testing.
(vii) Test marketing.
(viii) Commercial sales.

STATE ASSISTANCE IN MARKETING

To help the small industries in the marketing of their products, a large marketing network has been created as depicted in the following

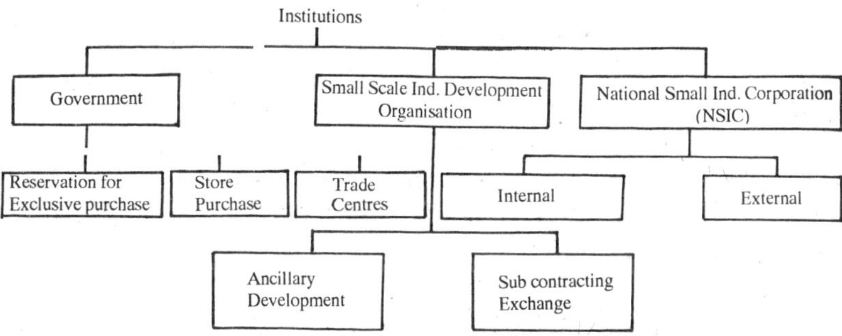

Fig. 2. Diagram showing Institutional Market Support to Small Scale Industries.

diagram.

From a perusal of the above, it becomes clear that, there is a three-fold institutional support for SSIs. This is as follows :

1. Aid by Government.
2. Aid by Small Scale Industries Development Organisation.
3. Aid by National Small Industries Corporation.

The kind of assistance given by each of these is described below :

1. Marketing Assistance by Government—Central and State

(i) *Reservation of items for Exclusive Purchase*

One of the foremost elements of support programme is the reservation of products of the small sector for exclusive purchase by the government. The reservation started with and items in 1968, went upto 334 items in 1977 and presently stands at 412 items (See Annexure A). Even in South Korea, 110 items have been reserved for the small and medium sector. Other reservations are as follows :

(a) 22 items for purchase for defence requirements ;
(b) 14 items for purchase by DGSD upto 75 percent of the requirements ;
(c) 28 items for purchase upto 50 percent of the requirements.

Besides reservation for exclusive purchase, Directorate General of Supplies and Disposal (DGSD) gives preference upto 15 percent over the lowest quotation received from the large scale industries. To enjoy these facilities, registration must be made with the DGSD.

(ii) *Purchase by State Organisations*

A number of organizations in the states purchase the requirements of government departments through limited or open tenders. For instance, State Small Industries Corporation assist the small units by submitting tenders to various state government agencies. It frees the small units form complicated procedures and formalities. State emporia act as distribution outlets for small units. Sale outlet is provided by consumer cooperative stores and super bazars. Several autonomous bodies in the state like Electricity Boards, Municipalities, Universities, Tourism Corporations etc. buy their requirements from small units.

(iii) *Central Government Stores Purchase Programme*

Stores Purchase Programme of the Central Government which is administered through Directorate General of Supplies and Disposal (DGSD) provides an outlet for the products of small industrial units in the country. DGSD procures store requirements of various central government departments, public sector organisations, and semi-government bodies. For the purpose of purchase, DGSD has divided purchases into following six groups.

Group I : Items which are of no concern to small-scale units and can be procured only from large scale units.

Gropup II: Items which can be manufactured by large-scale firms but permit substantial scope of purchase from small-scale units.

Group III : Residuary items which both types of firms can supply. Product of small firms enjoy 15 percent price preference over the price quoted by large-scale firms.

Group IV : Group V and Group VI items are those which have

been reserved for exclusive purchase from small scale units.

Other special concessions provided to small units are as follows :

(1) Free supply of application form for initial registration/renewal.
(2) There is no registration fee.
(3) Free supply of tender forms.
(4) No security deposit for taking/accepting forms in case of small units registered with NSIC and whose competency has been certified by NSIC.
(5) A price preference upto 15 percent in case of Group III items, Best price preference is not given in the following cases :
    (a) Where competition is among small units
    (b) Where items are reserved for exclusive purchase from small units.
    (c) Where tenders are received both from small and large units but lowest offer is from the former.

(iv) *Trade Centres*

These have been established by the Central Government to cater to marketing needs of small units. These centres provide an integrated marketing system, collect and disseminate information regarding all types of small industrial units in the region alongwith the details of products and prices. These provide a focal point for sellers and buyers– both national and foreign. These also provide library-cum-documentation service. About 50 percent of the total expenditure of these centres is met by the Central Government (excluding the cost of lands and buildings) subject to the maximum limit of Rs. 2 lakhs per year for a period of 5 years. There are about 17 trade centres already working in the country.

2. Marketing Support by Small Industries Development Organisation

SIDO provides marketing assistance to small units through the promotion of ancillaries, provision of marketing intelligence, establishment of trade centres and motivation of small entrepreneurs to encourage them to participate in the purchase programme of Central and State Governments. It also holds exhibitions and seminars and publishes information. Some of these services are mentioned below :

(i) Ancillary Development

SIDO in collaboration with Bureau of Public Enterprises promotes ancillary industries in order to help in the marketing of products of small units. Efforts are made to promote a mutually beneficial relationship between small and large industries through ancillarisation. For this purpose, it holds exhibitions and seminars and arranges buyer-seller meetings.

(ii) Sub-contracting Exchanges

A total of 16 sub-contracting exchanges have been set up to help small units in securing sub-contracts from large and medium units. These have been set up at the Small Industries Services Institutes (SISIs)

Functions of sub-contracting exchanges :

(i) Registration of spare capacity available with small units.

(ii) Approaching larger units to induce them to award sub-contracts to small units.

(iii) Helping small units develop new capacity for manufacturing items required by large units.

3. Marketing Assistance by National Small Industries Corporation

NSIC provides marketing assistance to small units in two ways :

Firstly, by encouraging participation by the small units in Government's Stores Purchase Programme, and

Secondly, by impressing upon large industries to obtain more and more of their requirements from small scale units.

Other service include : (a) free supply of tender forms, (b) issue of competency certificate to small units so that they do not have to pay any security deposit for participating in government purchasing, (c) taking up the grievances of small units against DGSD for redressal.

NSIC has it registered office at New Delhi and regional office at Bombay, Calcutta and Madras.

For the purpose of facilitating international marketing by small units, NSIC provides following types of assistance :

(a) Survey of Markets.

(b) Market research and marketing intelligence.

(c) Provision of necessary technological inputs so that standardised production is ensured.

(d) Establishment of raw material banks to meet the requirements of small sector.

(e) Establishment of 'External Marketing Assistance' to encourage export of small industry products.

To encourage exports by the small scale sector, following incentive schemes have been made available to them :

(i) Liberal imports of raw materials, components, spares and capital goods.

(ii) Allotment of indigenous raw materials to exporting units .

(iii) Cash subsidies.

(iv) Concessional railway freight.

(v) Facility of duty drawback.

ANNEXTURE A
LIST OF ITEMS RESERVED FOR EXCLUSIVE PURCHASE FROM SMALL SCALE SECTOR

Items reserved for exclusive purchase from small-scale industrial units are indicated as at the end of March-89

1. Animal driven vehicles
2. Anklets Web Khaki
3. All Badges cloth embroidered and metals.
4. Attache/ cases
5. Aluminiun Utensils
6. Ammeters/ohm meter
7. Automobiles Head light
8. Augur (Carpenters)
9. AAC/ACSR Conductors upto 19 stand
10. Absorbant Cotton
11. Agricultural Implements
    (a) Hand operated tools and implements
    (b) Animal driven implements
12. Bags/ice head
13. Bandage cloth
14. Barbed Wire
15. Basket cane (Procurement can also be made from State Forest Corpn. and State Handicraft Corporation)
16. Belt leather and Strips
17. Benzyl Benzelete
18. Blacksmith hearth
19. Boot Polish
20. Bone Meal
21. Boxes made of metal
22. Boxing Boots
23. Boots and Shoes of all types excluding canvas shoes
24. Brass dampers
25. Brass padlocks
26. Brief cases
27. Brooms
28. Buckets
29. Brushes
30. Beam scales (upto 30 Mds.)

31. Battery charge Engine driven only
32. Button meal
33. Blotting paper
34. Blow Moduled Containers
35. Cans (made up of G.I. sheets for milk and measurings)
36. Cash bags
37. Caps cotton
38. Caps Woollen
39. Caps Waterproof
40. Casing and capping
41. Ceiling rows upto 15 amps.
42. Centrifugal steel plate blowers
43. Copper sulphate
44. Coir mattress and matting
45. Chains lashing
46. Chapals and sandals
47. Coir fibre and Coir yarn
48. Community Receivers
49. Cone & Valves (for water fitting only)
50. Conduit pipes (Metallic)
51. Cotton Wool (Non absorbant)
52. Cotton Hosiery
53. Cotton Cord Twine
54. Crates Wooden
55. Cumblies
56. Curtains mosquito (civil requirements only)
57. Coir mattresses & cushions
58. Copper Naphenete
59. Corrugated Board Paper
60. Centrifugal pumps suction & dilivery 150 × 150 mm.
61. Crucibles upto and including 15 amps.
67. Drums & Barrels
68. Domestic Utensils other than stainless steel
69. Domestic Electrical Appliances
    Toasters Electric, Electric Iron, Hot Plates, Elect. Mixers and Electric-Lighter. Electric Oven, Juice Extractors.
70. Dustors cotton all types except the items required in Khadi.
71. Dust shield leather
72. Dust bins

73. Domestic (House wiring) P.V.C. Cables and wires Aluminium conforming to the prescribed ISI specifications and up to 10,000 mm. sq. nominal cross section. This would not be applicable to defence requirements.
74. Electric Call Bells
75. Electric Buzzers
76. Electric soldering iron
77. Eyelets
78. Expanded metal
79. Electric Transmission Line. Hardware like steel; cross barcross, arms clamps, arching arm, brackets etc.
80. Exaust Muffilers (Except in the case of original equipment manufactures)
81. Film spools cans
82. Football boots
83. Film polythene
84. French Polish
85. Garments (civil requirements only)
86. Gas Mantals
87. Gauzecloth
88. Ghamellas
89. G.I. Pad locks
90. G.I. Bath Tubs
91. G.I. Buckets
92. Glass ampoules
93. Gauze surgical all types
94. Gun Metal Bushes
95. Gun cases
96. Graphite crucibles upto No. 200
97. Grease Nipples & Grease guns
98. Glue
99. Gum Tape
100. Hand drawn carts all types
101. Handles wooden and bamboo (procurement can also be made from State Forest Corpn. and State Handicraft Corpn.
102. Hand Lamps
103. Hand Numbering Machine
104. Hand Gloves
105. Hand Pressess

106. Hide and country leather of all types
107. Horse and Mule Shoes
108. Hob nails
109. Holdalls
110. Hypodermic needles
111. Invalid wheeled chairs
112. Insecticides Dust and sprayers (Manual only)
113. Iron Clad switches (upto 30 MPH)
114. Keys Woodden
115. Kit bags
116. Kodali
117. Kullahs
118. Lace leather
119. Lint Plain
120. Lanterns Posts & bodies
121. Lathes
122. Lamp signal
123. Latex form sponge
124. Lamp holders
125. Leather bags
126. Leather boxes
127. Leather harness
128. Leather washers
129. Low-cost Radio (medium wave and community Radio Receivers)
130. L.T. Porcelain Insulators & Fuse grips
131. Magnesuim Sulphate
132. Machine Screws
133. Metal clad switches
134. Mail bag (Canvas dassoti & Jute)
135. Manhole covers
136. Metal polish
137. Miniature bulbs (for torches only)
138. Metric weights
139. Washers
140. Machine Shop Vises
141. Nail Tip heel ruatles
142. Nail cutters
143. Newar

144. Oil Stove (Wick Stove only)
145. Ordinary bench vices
146. Ovens electric (domestic type)
147. Paper conversion products, paper bags & celops, Ice-cream cups, paper cup and saucers.
148. Paint remover
149. Pillows (cotton)
150. Patient coats and Pyjamas
151. Plaster of Paris
152. Postal Lead seals
153. Piles fabric
154. Plug
155. Pouches
156. Postal weighing scales
157. Pump hand
158. PVC footwears
159. Polythene bags
160. Palm Rose Oil
161. Plastic Cane
162. Playing cards
163. Quilts, Razais (cotton)
164. Rags cotton
165. Railway Platform drinking water
166. Razors
167. Rubber Balloons
168. Rivets of all types (including bifurcate except for defence requirements).
169. Rolling shutters
170. Room Coolers (Desert type)
171. Scientific Laboratory glasswares (Barring sophisticated items) like Peakers Burette, Pipette, Conical flask, Round Flask Measuring Cylinder, Filter Funnel, Reagent Bottles.
172. Squirrel Cage Induction Motors upto and including 10 KW 440 volts 3 phase.
173. Stoneware Jars
174. Sanitary Towels
175. Soap Yellow
176. Soap Liquid
177. Soap soft (Civil requirements only)

178. Stapling machine
179. Steel wool
180. Spectacle frames
181. Sodium Silicate
182. Surgical gloves (Except Plastic)
183. Sanitary Plumping Fittings
184. Sanfasteners (excluding 4 psc. ones)
185. Safety matches
186. Scissors cutting (ordinary)
187. Shoe laces
188. Sign boards painted
189. Shellac
190. Skin sheep all types
191. Skiboots & shoes
192. Sole leather
193. Soap washing or laundry soap (civil requirements only)
194. Sockets
195. Spicked boots
196. Steel racks
197. Steel stools
198. Steel trunks
199. Stockinotte
200. Stone and stone quarry rollers
201. Suitcases
202. Steel desks
203. Shelves steel
204. Silk ribbon
205. Street light fittings
206. Steel windows and ventilators
207. Student Microscope
208. Standard Wire
209. Safcty Pins (and othcr similar products likc papcr pins, staplc pins etc.
210. Tack metallic
211. Cotton tapes and laces
212. Tarpaulins (civil requirements only)
213. Teak Fabricated round blocks
214. Tentage Civil/Military & Salitash jute for Tentage
215. Tin Trays

216. Tip Boots
217. Tent Poles
218. Tin can unprints upto 4 gallons capacity (other than can OTS)
219. Tyres & Tubes (Cycles)
220. Tiles
221. Toilets Rolls
222. Transistorised Insulation-Testers
223. Umbrellas
224. Utensils cooking including stainless steel, utensils except spoon desert.
225. Wooden Shelves
226. Wood Wool
227. Wooden Plugs
228. Wooden ammunition boxes
229. Wheel barows
230. Wicks cotton
231. Wire adjusting screws
232. Wooden packing cases of all sizes
233. Wire nails and horse shoe nails
234. Woollen Hosiery
235. Screws excluding High Tensile
236. Welded wiremesh
237. Wooden Chairs
238. Waxed Paper
239. Water proof papers
240. Wire netting and gauze thicker than 100 mesh size.
241. Wire Bushes and Fibre Bushes.
242. Wind shield wipers (Arms & Blades only) except in the case of Original Equipment Manufacturers)
243. Diesel Engine upto 15 H.P. (Slow speed)
244. Voltage Stabilisers
245. Paper Tapes (Gummed)
246. Clinical thermometers
247. Drawing and Mathematical Instrument
248. Aluminium builders & hardware hinges
249. Aluminium Drop/Towerbolts
250. Zinc Sulphate
251. Nickle Sulphate
252. Steel Measuring Tape

253. Zip Fasteners (Metallic)
254. Emergency Lamp
255. Electric flash gun
256. M.S. Tie Bars
257. Padlocks
258. Railway Carriage Fans (Transferred to group 9 list)
259. Bolts & Nuts (except High Tensile and Other special types)
260. Cirplips
261. Cloth Sponge
262. Cloth Covers
263. Cotton Cases
264. Cotton Packs
265. cotton Pouches
266. Cotton sling
267. Cotton Straps
268. Forges Bay Nets
269. Cotton Carriers
270. Cotton Bags
271. Badges Cloth (including embroidered)
272. Sleeping Bags
273. Wooden Pins
274. Wooden Veneers
275. Mallet wooden
276. Chrome Tanned (Semi finished Buffalows & Cow)
277. Rubber Hoses Armoured (Unbrained)
278. Rubber Cord
279. Potassium Nitrate
280. Soap Carbolic
281. Insecticide Fluid
282. Disinfectant Fluid
283. Foot Power
284. Table Knives (excluding cutlery)
285. Steel Bed stead
286. Boxes kit
287. Badges Metallic
288. Tin Seal Holders
289. Line Equipment
290. Safe meat & milk
291. Fuse Cut Outs

292. Roof Light Fittings
293. Railway Carriage Light Fittings
294. Chokes for Light Fittings
295. Ambulance Stretcher
296. Monometer
297. Whistle
298. Dyes
    (a) Azo dyes (DIRECT & Acid)
    (b) Basic Dyes
299. Silk Webbing
300. Lanyard
301. Sodium Nitrate
302. Lisasorb
303. Funnels
304. Nail Copper
305. Boxes Tin for Postage Stamps
306. Lockers
307. Letter Boxes Round
308. Tyres for Postal use
309. Cloth Jaconet
310. Cotton Ropes
311. Canvas Product
    (a) Water Proof Delivery bags to spec. No. IS-1422/70.
    (b) Bonnet Covers & Radiators Muff. tp spec. Drg. Lv. 7/NSN/IA/130295.
312. Cotton Canvas Bags
313. Water Proof Covers
314. Water Proof Bags
315. Haver Sacks
316. Rubber Tubing (Excluding braided tubings)
317. Dimethyl Phthalate
318. Dibutyl Phalate
319. Polythene Pipes
320. RCC Poles Prestressed
321. Graphite Crucible (upto No. 500)
322. Tublar Poles (Revetted Tubular Poles)
323. Brass Wire
324. Measuring Tapes and Sticks
325. Claw Brass and Wires

326. Shovels
327. Bench Vices
328. Blots Sliding
329. Steel Chairs
330. Valves Metallic
331. Studs (excluding high tensile)
332. Wires Fencing and Fittings
333. Hinges (other than Door fittings)
334. Happs & Stapples
335. Iron Dhobi
336. Horse Clipping Machines
337. Heaters Convectors upto 2 Kw-IS-4238/67.
338. Switches Tumbler
339. Fuse Unit
340. Link Clip
341. Trolley
342. Pully Wire
343. Cutters
344. Hose Pipe Clips (Transferred to Group VI)
345. Push cook gravity loath (Transferred to Group V)
346. Microscope for normal medical use
347. Scales Weighing
348. Castor Oil
349. Linseed Oil
350. Helmet non-metallic
351. Wax Sealing
352. Rail Screws
353. Plate Screws
354. Screw Spikes
355. Hydraulic Jacks below 30 ton capacity
356. Other Wodden Boards
357. Rust & Scale preventings/Removing composition
358. Nylon Stockings
359. Tin Mess
360. Cord Twine Maker
361. Cordage Others
362. Cotton Singlets
363. Cotton Beltings
364. Braces

365. Textiles manufacturers other than N.E.C. (not elsewhere classified)
366. Wodden Boxes and Cases N.E.C. (Not elsewhere classified)
367. Camois Leather
368. Rubberised Garments Cap and Caps etc.
369. Oil Bound Distemper
370. Bituminous Paints
371. Soap Curd
372. Nylon Tapes and Laces
373. Drilling Clay
374. Hand Lamps Railways
375. Privy Pans
376. Bowls
377. Metallic containers and drums other athan N.E.C. (Not elsewhere classified)
378. Taps
379. Brackets other than Railways
380. Pans Lavatory Flush
381. Battery Eliminator
382. Lightning Aresters-upto 22 KV
383. Lubricators
384. Hand Pouched Rice (Polished and Unpolished)
385. Honey
386. Palmgur
387. Pappads
388. Biscuits
389. Varnish Black Japan
390. Candle Wan Carriage
391. Wodden Boxes for Stemps
392. Coir Rope hawserlaid
393. Equipment Camflags Bamboo Support
394. Post Pocket (Wodden)
395. Wodden Flush Door Shutters
396. Cleansing Powder
397. Napthelene Balls
398. Hammers
399. Screw Drivers
400. Zip Fastners (Non-Metallic)
401. Pressure Die Casting upto 0.75 Kg.

402. Glass & Pressed wares
403. Sluice Valves
404. Fire Extinguishers
405. P.V.C. Insulated Aluminium Cables (upto 120 sq.mm.) (ISS : 694)
406. Enamel Wares & Enamel Utensils
407. Rakes Ballast
408. Transformer Type Welding sets conforming to IS : 1291/75 (upto 600 amps.)
409. Pickles & Chutneys
410. Water Tanks upto 15,000 litres capacity
411. RCC Pipes upto 1200 mm. dia.
412. Steel Almirah
413. PVC Pipes upto 110 mm.
414. Items reserved for purchase from Small Scale Industrial Units upto 75% of the requirements by Directorate General of Supplies and Disposal (as at the end of March 1988).
    1. Railway Carriage Fans
    2. Push Cock Gravity Loath
    3. Formation signs
    4. Rubber Mattresses
    5. M. Vitamin Tablets
    6. Glass Lookings
    7. Pin Split Tapers
    8. Filing system including filing cabint
    9. Carbon dioxide crash tenders
    10. Coupling Universal
    11. Hospital & Aseptic furniture
    12. P.V.C. Pipes upto 110 mm. dia. (Transferred to Gr-IV)
    13. Carbon Paper
    14. Laminated Jute Bags

ITEMS RESERVED FOR PURCHASE FROM SMALL SCALE INDUSTRIAL UNITS UPTO 50% OF THE TOTAL REQUIREMENTS BY D G S & D

1. Hose Pipe Clips
2. Coir Ropes Others
3. Cellulose Lacquers & Thinners
4. Paint Ready Mixed
5. Varnishes excluding Black Japan
6. Oil Paste
7. Fire Bricks
8. Flushing Cisterns
9. Power Transfromers
10. Weigh Bridges
11. Dry Distemper
12. Red Oxide
13. Wagon Black
14. Graphite Paints
15. Aluminium Paints
16. Yarn Worsted
17. Lead sheets
18. Lead Tubes
19. Lead Pipes
20. Lead Wool
21. Lead Tablets 17.5 mm. dia.
22. Pencils
23. P.V.C. underground aluminium cables upto 35 mm. sq. mm (ISS-1544)
24. Typewriter ribbons
25. Rectifier Type Weldings Sets confirming to IS 4559/68 with amendment Nos. 122.
26. Duplicating Machine
27. Printing Jobs
28. Jams, Jellies, Marmalades, Sauces & Preservatives

CHAPTER XXII

CHANNELS OF DISTRIBUTION

The ways in which producers can get linked with consumors are varied. The main challenge before a small scale entrepreneur is to select the best channel for his product. The outstanding feature of good distribution channel is that the product should move efficiently and at minimum cost from production point to the ultimate consumer.

Channel of distribution may be defined as the set of marketing institutions (i.e middlemen) which participate in the distribution of goods, from the point of production to the point of consumption. It is a route along which goods move from producer to consumer.

KINDS OF CHANNELS

Broadly speaking there are two main types of distribution channels viz,:-

1. *Direct Channel* : It is a route in which there are no middlemen and the marketing functions are performed by the producer. Good pass directly to the cousumer.
2. *Indirect Channel :* It is a route where more than one middlemen link producer and consumer. In other words, in this kind of channel, middlemen perform the marketing functions.

In practical terms, there are five-channels in the case of consumer goods. However, in the case of " Industrial goods," there could be four channels. These are depicted in the following figure (see Fig. 1 on p. 290).

I. Channels Of Distribution For Consumer Goods

(a) Manufacturer→Consumer [Direct Selling]

This is the simplest shortest and absolutely direct channel where no middlemen are involved. Manufacturer may advertise his products in newspapers, magazines, television etc and solicit directly from customers.

Main advantage of this channel is that it is fast and economical. The manufacturer has full control over the product's distribution besides direct contact with customer. The drawback of this channel is that the

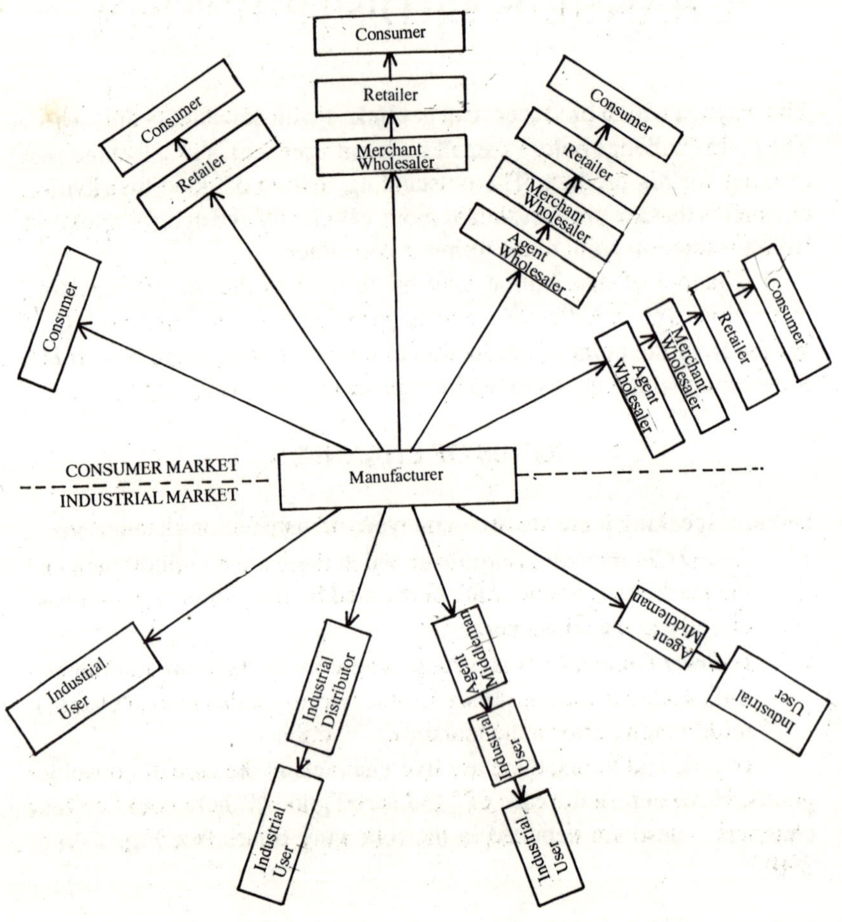

Fig. 1 Channels of Distribution

manufacturer does not have expert services of middlemen at his disposal.

Reasons for adopting this channel are: need to reduce marketing costs, closer control over market, proper market monitoring,desire to secure uniformity in terms of sale etc.

(b) Manufacturer→Retailer→Consumer

It is called one stage (simple indirect) channel because only one retailer is involved. The retailer is quite large such as a departmental store, chain store. The manufacturer himself performs the functions of a wholesaler. He also performs the functions of a financier of inventories besides arranging their storage and transport. Automobiles, appliances shoes, apparels etc. are suitable for this channel.

(c) Manufacturer → Merchant wholesaler → Retailer → Consumer.

It is a two stage distribution channel because of the involvement of two middlemen namely wholesaler and retailer. This is the traditional channel used mostly by manufacturers of consumer goods like soaps, detergents, cosmetics etc. Reasons for recourse to this channel are ; (a) the manufacturer has a narrow product line, (b) there exist strong wholesalers who are capable of providing specialised and adequate promotional support.

(d) Manufacturer →Agent wholesaler→Merchant wholesaler →Retailer→Consumer.

This is a three stage distribution channel because of the existence of three middlemen namely agent wholesaler, merachant wholesaler and retailer. This is capable of securing the widest possible distribution. The services of agent wholesaler are availed for despatch of goods to merchant wholesalers. This is the practice with TV manufacturers, textile mills etc.

(e) Manufacturer→Agent wholesaler→Retailer.

Sometimes manufacturer finds it difficult to get wholesalers at reasonable terms and excludes them. He uses agent wholesaler to reach retailers.

II. Channels of Distribution For Industrial Goods

The channels used for industrial goods differ from those used for consumer goods because the industrial users generally buy in bulk quantites. Consequently, there is no retailing. The four principal channels used for industrial market are :

(a) Manufacturer → Industrial User (Direct Setting)

Manufacturers of heavy or expensive industrial products like computers make use of this channel. This channel is preferred because number of customers is small and considering the nature of products, these require close collaboration between manufacturer and users.

(b) *Manufacturer→Industrial Distributor→Industrial User [One stage channel]*

This channel is used by the manufacturers of small machine tools, accessories etc because such goods are used by a number of customers.

(c) *Manufacturer→Agent Middleman→Industrial Distributor→Industrial User [Two stage distribution channel}.*

This is used by those manufacturers who do not have an efficient and economical sales organisation at their disposal and customers are widely scattered.

(d) *Manufacturer→Agent Middleman→Industrial User.*

In it, agent middleman are used to reach customers. The middleman are entrusted with the performance of marketing functions. This channel is adopted when it becomes difficult to get distributors to buy product at reasonable terms and conditions.

FACTORS AFFECTING THE CHOICE OF CHANNEL OF DISTRIBUTION

Different considerations which go into the selection of a channel are described below.

I. Consumer or Market Characteristics

(a) *Nature of market - whether industrial or consumer.*

Industrial users prefer to deal directly with the manufacturer. On the other hand, consumer good buyers make their purchases from retail stores. Products sold to both types of markets use more than one channel.

(b) *Geographic location of customers.*

Direct selling is used where customers are located in narrow area. But where there is large geographical dispersal of customers, indirect channel will have to be employed.

(c) *Size of the market* particularly in the case of mass consumption products like groceries, indirect channel can deliver goods better.

(d) *Size of purchase order :*

In case of large orders such as refrigerators, direct selling is convenient. But where the purchase order is small, intermediaries prove more useful.

(e) *Customer idiosyncracies* e.g. desire for credit, amount of personal relationship involved also determines the choice of channel.

II. Product Characteristics

(a) Price of product

Lower the unit value of the product, longer is the channel. More expensive the goods, shorter and direct is the channel.

(b) Technical complexity of the product

Complex products are sold directly because of the need to provide dependable service such as installation, maintenance etc. For standaradized products, longer channel may be preferred.

(c) Bulk and weight of the product

Bulk and heavy products are marketed directly to minimise transportation cost unlike the products with high value and lesser weight like wrist watches, cameras etc.

(d) Perishability of the product

Perishable and fashion products follow shorter channel e.g. eggs fish, jams etc.

(e) Complementarity of product

If one product needs use of another both can be sold through the same channel e.g. VCRs and cassettes.

(f) Brand loyalty

If product commands low brand loyalty and is easily substitutable, direct selling is profitable. For instance, toothpaste, soaps, detergents etc.

(g) Standardisation of products

Standardised products are capable of passing through a longer channel.

III. Company Characteristics and Policies

(a) Financial position of the company

Where the manufacturer is financially strong, he can develop his own marketing forces, grant credit and therefore sell directly. On the other hand, firms lacking adequate financial resources cannot afford to bypass middlemen.

(b) Nature of activity

Production-oriented enterprises cannot develop marketing expertise overnight and have to depend on middlmen.

(c) Range of products

For a single product firm, direct selling is an expensive luxury. However, a firm with broad product lines can market directly to retailers.

(d) *Desire of control over products*

Firms desiring to have greater control over products prefer to sell directly.

(e) *Marketing policy*

Some manufacturers prefer middlemen in view of their services like grant of credit, intimate relationship with market demonstration channels etc. Aspects like adequate after sale service may compel the manufacturer to sell directly.

IV. Middlemen Characteristics

(a) *Availability of middlemen.*

(b) *Provision of marketing services by middlemen.*

Unless middlemen are able and willing to provide marketing services like assembling, storage, transportation etc, management may not be able to exercse his choice.

(c) *Middlemen's preferences and company's ability to comply with them.*

For instance some wholesalers may like to have a sole agency for a particular territory but the company may not able to agree to it.

(d) *Cost of intermediaries.*

Selection of channel is guided by its capacity to provide efficient distribution at lowest possible costs.

(e) *Customs and traditions in a particular trade also dictate the choice of a paraticular channel.*

(f) *Legal restrictions.*

For instance, distilleries can market their output through licensed liquor shops only.

V. Distribution Strategy

The term 'strategy' denotes whether a manufacturer likes to have intensive or exclusive distribution. These are described below :

(a) *Intensive mass distribution*

Company desiring to have mass distribution has to have recourse to all the available outlets. This strategy is adopted in case of mass consumption items like cigarettes, candy, chewing gum etc. But many wholesalers or retailers do not like to promote a product which is being handled by everybody else.

(b) *Selective distribution*

It consists of selecting only those outlets that can best serve the manufacturer's interests. It is used for products like sewing machines, electronics, refrigerators etc. Selection of this channel facilitates cooperative advertising between the middlemen and manufacturer and avoidance of price cutting.

(c) Exclusive distribution

It is an extreme form of selective distribution where manufacturer allocates a market area to a particular middleman. Exclusive agencies are common in marketing such articles as automobiles, electrical appliances, branded men's clothing etc. It ensures aggressive selling.

MIDDLEMEN

Also called 'intermediaries', they constitute a link between producers and consumers. Their role is to facilitate the transfer of products to the final consumer.

Types of Middlimen

1. Agent Middlemen

Known as 'functional middleman' he assists in the transfer of title to goods. He acts as an agent of the owner of the goods and receives his remuneration in the form of broker age or commission. He is engaged to sell in markets located outside the jurisdiction of the manufacturer's sales force.

Agent middlemen can be sub-divided into following categories :

(a) Commission agents

They sell on behalf of the owner. For the purpose of sale they take possession of the goods, make necessary arrangements for storage and ensure the transfer of title to the buyer. In return for their services, they get a commission on sales.

When they have large amount of authority and liability on consigned goods, they are called 'factors'.

If a commission agent assumes liability for collecting the debts, he is called a "Del Credre agent".

(b) Brokers

They negotiate sale and purchase on behalf of other parties and get a brokerage as a certain percentage of the value of goods brought and sold.

(c) Forwarding and Clearing Agents

They operate mainly in the field of export and import trade to collect, forward and deliver goods, bring them to docks, perform customs formalities, insure and ship goods on behalf of exporters. Clearing goods receive goods from abroad on behalf of importers, examine their quality and quantity, and transport them to importer's place.

(d) Auctioneers

They undertake to auction goods on behalf of sellers and perform the related functions of displaying goods, selling to highest bidder and transfer ownership.

2. Merchant Middlemen

These intermediares take title to goods, bear the risk and perform various marketing functions and hope to make profit in the process. They fall into two broad categories.

(i) Wholesalers
(ii) Retailers

These are discussed below:

I. Wholesalers

A wholesaler is a business unit which buys goods in large quantities and sells them to retailers and others. He does not sell in significant amounts to ultimate consumers. He operates between manufacturer and retailer. They are of following varieties.

(a) Manufacturer wholesaler

He combines manufacturing with wholesale business. He may sell other manufacturers products as well.

(b) Retailer wholesaler

He buys in large quantities from manufacturers and sells directly to ultimate consumers.

(c) Pure wholesaler

He does the job of wholeselling exclusively. He buys from different manufacturers in large quantities and sells to retailers.

Functions performed by wholesalers

1. *Assembling* the goods from different manufacturers.
2. *Warehousing* – to create 'time utility'and helping in adjusting demand with production.
3. *Financing* : He finances retailers by selling on credit and helps manufacturer by buying goods in large quantities.
4. *Grading and packaging* according to quality, size, shape, contents etc.

5. Providing marketing information and advice to manufacturer and retailer.
6. *Transportation* : He transports goods from production center to retailer's place.
7. Risk bearing in the form of price fluctuation, demand slackness, deterioration etc.

SERVICES OF WHOLESALERS

1. Services to Manufacturers :

(a) Securing orders from widely scattered retailers and helping manufacturer to concentrate only on production.

(b) Storage of goods so that the manufacturer is saved the expenses of incurring warehousing expenses.

(c) Participation in manufacturers' sale promotion and advertising campaign.

(d) Risk transfer through the placing of bulk orders with manufacturer.

(e) Reducing working capital requirements of manufacturer by buying against cash or advance payments.

(f) Relieving the manufacturer from undertaking marketing research.

2. Services to Retailers :

(a) They need not hold large stocks of variety of goods.

(b) Grant of credit.

(c) Benefit of specialisation.

(d) Prompt execution of orders.

(e) Advice on matters of product display, sales promotion etc.

(f) Reducing retailer's need for market intelligence.

II. Retailers

The word 'retailer' has been derived from the French word, retailer i.e. "to cut off a small piece". In commercial parlance, it means " a merchant middleman who sells products primarily to ultimate consumers". He stands nearest to ultimate consumer and is the last link in the distribution chain. As he comes in contact with cousumers, he meets people with varied choices, temperaments and tastes. It compels him to carry a wide assortment of goods to beable to cater to variety of customers.

Functions of Retailers

The functions discharged by a retailer include: assembling, grading and packaging, financing, marketing information and risk bearing.

Services by Retailers

1. Assembling a wide variety of goods at convenient points.
2. Keeping ready stock of wide assortment of goods.
3. Bringing new products or their varieties to the knowledge of consumers.
4. Offering expert advice to consumers regarding suitability of products.
5. Extending credit facilities and free home delivery.
6. Saving the manufacturer from the hassle of direct marketing.
7. Undertaking sales promotion activities through window display and counter display.
8. Acting as chain link between consumers and wholesalers.
9. Saving the consumer from the need of having large stocks of different types of goods.

Types of Retailers

Retailers are of two principal types, viz :–

(i) Large Scale Retailer, and

(ii) Small scale Retailer

The diagram given below shows the broad classifiction of retailers.

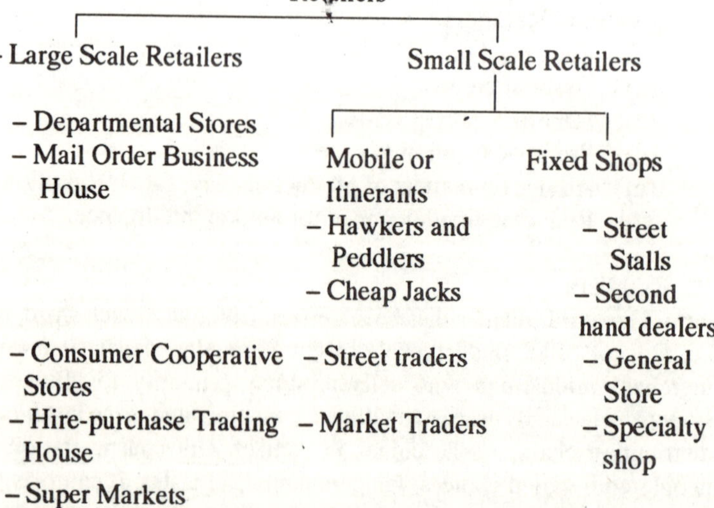

One price stores

Diagram Showing Retailer Classification

1. Large Scale Retailers

(i) Departmental Stores :

It is a large scale retail organisation having number of deparatments under the same roof. Each deparatment deals in a particular line of merchandise.

((ii) Multiple or Chain Shops

It denotes a retail organisation that controls a number of stores under a common ownership and management selling similar products and operating in different areas of either the same city or country e.g. Bata Stores, Snowhite Drycleaners.

(iii) Mail Order Houses

These are retail enterprises which carry on business through mail without involving any face to face contact between the buyer and the seller.

(iv) Cousumer Cooperative Store

These are run on voluntary basis by the consumers who organise themselves on the basis of "one person, one vote". Sales are made at market prices and profits are distributed among members as 'dividend' besides bonus which is calculated on the basis of purchases made by a member.

(v) Hire-purchase Trading House

It is a retail organisation which sells goods on instalments. The possession of goods is immediately handed over but ownership is transferred only on the payment of final instaliment. It buyer fails to pay any instalment, the goods are taken back and the moneys paid untilthen are treated as hire-charges.

(vi) Super Markets

It is a large scale departmental store offering a wide variety of consumer goods namely food items, grocerils drugs, cosmetics, and other household goods on a self-service basis. There appeal lies in careful display, low margin, wide variety and self service.

(vii) One -price shops

These are retail establishment dealing in a large variety of low-priced goods of daily use, selling all wares at a single price. Goods are sold on "cash and carry basis".

2. Small Scale Retailers

(A) Mobile or Itinerant Retailers

These retailers keep moving from one place to another to sell their goods. They sell such product as vegetables, milk, eggs, bread etc. These include:-

(i) Hawkers and Peddlers

They sell goods from door to door carrying goods on carts, as animals or on their heads and it is the oldest method of retailing.

(ii) Cheap Jacks

They hire small shops in residential locations and do not stick to a particular place. They shift to places where they have better prospects.

(iii) Street Sellers

They display their goods in busy street corners or on pavements e.g. in Connaught Place or Flora Fountain. They sell daily use items like handbags, shoes, utensils, decoration items etc.

(iv) Market Traders

They sell their products in weekly/fortnightly or monthly markets. They also operate in vacant verandhas of fixed shops after these shops are closed.

(B) Fixed Shop Retailers

They operate from properly established shops and include the following :

(i) Street Stalls

There are located at busy streets. The stall is an improvised structure –a table or temporary platform to display the goods which include cheap products like toys, pens, hosiery garments etc.

(ii) Secondhand Goods Shops

They deal in secondhand goods like books, clothes, furniture etc.

(iii) General Store

Also called 'variety store', they are located in residential areas and carry all kinds of products of daily use. It may be a single line store (dealing in one type of goods e.g. shoes) or multiple line store.

(iv) Specialty Store

These deal in single line merchandise e.g. toiletries, bakery, children's wear etc.

Elimination of Middlemen

Middlemen occupy a key position in the marketing system. But in recent years a great deal of controversy has developed regarding their usefulness. Below is given the arguments for and against the retention of middllemen.

Case for Retention of Middlemen

1. They render a number of marketing services which can not be provided by any other ageney in such an efficient and economical manner. Their services include assembling, storage, transportation, grading and packaging, grant of credit etc.
2. They relieve the manufacturers from the problemd of looking after the marketing and thereby enable then to focus on production alone.
3. They provide specialised services in the distribution of products which is an indispensable function.
4. In view of the large scattering of consumers, their services cannot be dispensed with.

Case Against Middlemen

1. They push up prices. In many cases, middlemen's share constitutes 30 to 50 percent of the price.
2. They do not provide services commensurate with the share of profits cornered by them.
3. Compared to manufacturer who has to bear such risks as strikes, depression, change in fashion, a middleman takes away a larger share of profits.
4. It is not always impossible for the manufacturer to sell directly to consumers. Middlemen are therefore, superfluous in the chain of distribution.
5. They rersort to anti-social activities like hoarding, artificial scarcity creation and black marketing etc.

Conclusion however is that middlemen cannot be eliminated altogether from the marketing scene. But there is always a scope for rationalisation of the marketing process through the reduction in the number of middlemen.

CHAPTER XXIII

FRANCHISING

Franchising is a means of marketing a product or service with a view to achieving a greater and faster rate of expansion than would otherwise be possible. The owner of a product–whether an organisation or an individual entrepreneur known as franchisor develops a type of business but let others called 'franchisee' run it for royalty payments.

DEFINITION

The International Franchising Association has defined franchise as, "a continuing relationship in which franchisor provides licenced privilege to do business plus assistance in organising, training, merchandising and management in return for consideration from franchisee".

It is thus a method for owner (franchisor) of a product or service to obtain retail or wholesale distribution through licensed affiliated dealers (franchisees). The franchisor grants the franchisee the exclusive right to distribute a product a service in a specific geographical area on specified terms alongwith an option for renewal.

Franchising style of distribution is similar to a large chain store so that all franchised outlets have an identifying trade mark, standard symbols, standardised products, uniform business practices etc. The franchisee finances on his own. Franchisor receives a fixed sum for allowing use of trade name and providing training. The franchisee is essentially paying for a reliable and proven business backed by professional advice and national sales promotion drive. Noted examples of franchised products are fast food operations like Wimpy, Nirulas, Essex Farms, Snowhite Drycleaners, etc.

Most things can be franchised from weighing machines to trucks. A good franchise can prove beneficial both to the franchisor and the franchisee and the economy as a whole.

TYPES OF FRANCHISIING ARRANGENTS

1. **Product and Trade Name Franchise**

   Herein the franchisee aquires the identity of the supplier. He concentrates on one product line of the franchisor and identifies the business with him.

2. **Exclusive Distributorship** is used for products that are purchased rather infrequently e.g autos. The manufacturer signs an exclusive agency contract with a distributor giving the latter an exclusive right to sell goods within designated geographical area. The distributor agrees to certain stipulations of the manufacturer e.g. adequate level of inventories, prices to be charged, services to be provided etc.

3. **Conversion franchising** permits independent business owner who is already established to get affiliated with a franchisor and realize the benefits of franchising relationship.

4. **Combination franchising.**

   Herein two franchisees share a location and management.

5. **Formal Franchising:**

   In it there is fully integrated and continuous relationship between franchisor and franchisee. The relationship covers total operations of the franchise including product or service, trade market, strategy, quality control etc. The most common form of such franchise are the fast food restaurants such as McDonald.

ADVANTAGES OF FRANCHISING

1. Management Training

Franchisors provide extensive amount of management training to franchisees to help them overcome their weakness. Prior to opening a franchise, the franchisee is given training as well as counselling once the franchise become operative. Pre-opening training is most comprehensive designed to instruct franchises in professional and profitable operation of business. The areas covered during training are : storage management, accounting, sales promotion, advertising, inventory control etc.

2. Availability of Established Brand Named Products

Under franchising, the franchisee acquires the right to use the brand name or trade mark of the franchisor. Identification with an established name ensures ready marketability.

3. Standardized Goods and Services

Franchisor's reputation largely depends on the quality of products/ services provided by the franchisee. To ensure that goods or services are consistent in all the franchised outlets, the franchisors provide the raw materials and keep close control on the standard of products.

4. Advertising by the franchisor provides extensive sales promotion.

The advertising in done by the franchisor. Alongwith the product advertisement, the names of franchisees are also given.

5. Financial Assistance

Franchisors offer wide range of financial assistance to franchisees e.g. short-term credit, lower down payment, free counselling, flexible repayment terms etc.

6. Established Business Methods

Franchisee does not have to build business from ground up Rather he buys business that has proved its success. He can capitalise on the accumulated knowledge, experience and skill of the franchisor that are based on sound business principles. He can avoid many of the pitfalls encountered by small business owners. He also profits from franchisor's goodwill in providing consumer accepted products.

7. Volume Purchasing Power

Joint cooperative purchasing is useful both to franchisor and franchisee. Mass high quality purchases lower costs of products.

8. Higher Success Rate

Owning a franchise does not guarantee success but historically success ratio is much higher for franchisees than for independently owned businessmen.

9. Uniform Control System

Franchisor assists in keeping uniform type of control over franchising operations e.g. prescription of standardised reporting procedures and forms. For instance, standardized inventory control enables franchisee to maintain more accurate count of merchandise available and needed.

10. Income Potential

Joining of proven business style with franchisee's initiative provides more favourable income earning potential than independent business operation.

LIMITATIONS OF FRANCHING

1. Franchising Fees and Royalties

Franchise cost include licence fee and fees for initial processing of franchisee's application. It is payable when franchise agreement is signed and is not refundable. Other costs include down payment on equipment, building decoration, office furniture, advertising of grand opening, cash reserves for operating the franchise. Franchisee will have to bear travel and living expenses while undergoing training. In addition, royalty payments to franchisor are based on predetermined percentage of sales. This is payable for continuing the use of franchisor's trade mark, trade name and other related items.

2. Conformity to Standaradised Operations

There is no autonomy to run the business as is the case with independent business owners. Franchisors have varying degree of control over franchisee's operations to ensure quality and uniformity of standards of product/service.

3. Restricted Freedom of Purchasing

Franchising establishes specifications and quality standards for all items used in franchise. Franchisee has the option to buy directly from franchisor or open market or distributors licensed by franchisor.

4. Limited Product Line

Franchisor controls the product/services marketed through franchisee's outlet. The franchisee cannot introduce other products except those introduced by the franchisor.

5. Restriction on Sale of Franchise

Sale, transfer, assignment of ownerrship interest must be approved by franchisor. Even where transfer is approved, the new owner is required to conform to the requirements of franchise.

6. Termination or Expiration of Agreement

Length of franchise agreement varies from one year to perpetual agreement.

SUCCESS IN FRANCHISING

There are no ready made formula to indicate the success of a franchisee. But it has been seen th at franchisees with no previous experience in the operative area of franchise are the most suitable. The reason is that individuals new to business have no preconceived idea. They are more receptive to training and more grateful for the opportunity provided by franchising. Research in U.K. has shown that franchisees come from variety of backgrounds—accounting, chemists, plumbers, firemen etc. and most had no previous experience of self employment. A great majority felt that franchising gave them a feeling of independence and escape from working for someone else.

Basic quality required of a franchisee is the ability to manage his own outlet and mantain amicable working relationship with franchisor and acting as a part of large organisation.

International Franchising Association (IFA)

It was founded in 1960 as a non-profitable association that represents franchising companies in the U.S.A and around the world. It serves as a spokes person from franchising companies, serves member companies and those interested in franchising, sets standards of business practices, serves as a medium for exchanging experiences and expertize and offers educational programmes for top excutives and managers. IFA has developed a Code of Ethics for enhancing mutual trust and confidence between franchisors and franchisees and set high standards of business ethics and conduct.

BIBLIOGRAPHY

1. Aitken, Huge G.T., *Exploration in Enterprises.* Harvard University, Cambridge, Mass (1965).
2. Alexander, P.C., Industrial Estates in India—Small Industry Extension Training Institute, Asia Publishing House (1963).
3. Allen, Louis L., *Starting and Succeeding your own small Business* Grossat & Dunlap, N.Y. (1968).
4. Anyon Jay G., *Entrepreneurial Dimensions of Management,* Livingstone Publishing Co., Wynnewood Peirs (1973).
5. Anderson, Dennis. *Small Industries in Developing Countries—Some Issues,* World Bank Staff Working Papers, 518. Washington D.C.
6. Apparao, P.B., *Personnel Management in Small Scale Industries.* Deep & Deep Publications, (1988).
7. BCCI, Role of *Organised Industry in the Effective Development of Small Scale Industry,* (1979)
8. Bala, Sashi, *Management of Small Scale Industry (Problems, Government Policy, Assistance Finance, Production, Marketing, Labour Management),* Deep and Deep Publications (1983)
9. Bangera, L.C., *Entrepreneurial Role in Nursing Sick Units,* The Financial Express, 26 August, 1980.
10. Basso, Lee L., *Cost Handbook for Small Manufacturers.* L.B. Associates, St. Louis (1964).
11. Baty, Gordon B., *Entrepreneurship—Playing to Win,* Reston Publishing Co., Reston Va. (1974).
12. Baumback, Clifford M and Mancuso Joseph R., *Entrepreneurship and Venture Management,* Prentice Hall, Englewood Cliffs ; N.J. (1975).
13. Behari, B., *Rural Industrialisation in India.* Vikas Publishing House, Delhi (1976).
14. Collins, Orvis and Moore David G., *The Organization Makers.* Appleton Century Craft ; N.Y. (1970).
15. Copulsky William and McNulty Herbert N., *Entrepreneurship and the Corporation.* AMACOM ; N.Y. (1974).
16. D. Sahal (Ed.). *The Transfer and Utilization of Technical Knowledge.* Lexington Books, Lexington, Mass (1974).
17. D.J. Storey (Ed.), *The Small Firm—An International Survey,* St. Martin Press, London.
18. Desai, Vasant. *Problems and Prospects of Small Scale Industries,* Himalaya Publishing House, Bombay (1983).

19. Deshpande, Manohar, *Entrepreneurship of Small Scale Industries.* Deep and Deep Publication, New Delhi (1984).
20. Dhananjaya A., *Critical Appraisal of Small Enterprises Promotional Activities in Delhi,* ILO (1974),
21. Development Commissioner SSI, *Industrial Design Aid to Small Industries.*
22. Dhar, P.N., *Small Scale Industries in Delhi (Study in Investment, Output and Employment Aspects).* Asia Publishing House, 1958.
23. Dhar, P.N. and Lydall, H.F. *The Role of Small Enterprise in Indian Economic Development,* Bombay.
24. Dominguez, John R., *Venture Capital.* Lexington Books, Lexington Mass (1947).
25. Douglas, McGregor. *The Human Side of Enterprise.* McGraw Hill, N.Y (1960).
26. Drucker, Peter F., *Innovation and Entrepreneurship.* Harper & Row N.Y. (1980).
27. Deeks, John S., The small Firm Owner Manager, Praeger, New York.
28. "The Big Problems of Thinking Small, Taking on the Business of Small Company" *Dun's Review,* February 1978.
29. Fitzgerald, C.T., *Organising for New Product Evolution in Small Technically Based Manufacturing Companies,* MIT Press, Cambridge, Mass.
30. Friedman, Thomas and Solman Paul. *Life and Death on the Corporate Battlefield.* Simon and Schuster, N.Y. (1982).
31. Galbraith, John K., *The New Industrial Estate.* Houghton Mifflin, Boston (1974).
32. Gild, George. *The Spirit of Enterprise.* Simon and Schuster. N.Y. (1984).
33. Goyal, S.K., *Small Scale Sector and Big Business.* Indian Institute of Public Administration (1984).
34. Ghosh, P.K., *An Investment into the Development of Occupational Choice.* Ph.D. Thesis, Univ. of Manchester (1962).
35. Hann, H. H de., *The Industrial Distribution of Labour Force in India 1961-71 (Part II).* Centre for Development Planning Discussion Papers, Rotterdam (1980)
36. Jain, R., *Planning a Small Scale Industry : Guide to Entrepreneurship,* SS Books Association, (1976).
37. Kilby, Peter (Ed.), *Entrepreneurship and Economic Development,*

The Free Press N.Y. (1971)

38. Khan, R. R., *Management of Small Scale Industry*. S. Chand, New Delhi (1979).
39. Kirzmer, Israel M. *Competition and Entrepreneurship*. University of Chicago Press, Chicago (1973)
40. Lakdawala, D.T. and Sandesara, J.C., *Smáll Industries in a Big City*, Bombay (1960).
41. Liles, Patrick R., *New Business Ventures and the Entrepreneur*. Richard D. Irwin, Harward, Ill. (1974).
42. Mancuso, Joseph. *Fun and Guts : The Entrepreneurial Philosophy*. Addison and Wesley, Reading, Mass (1971).
43. *Entrepreneurship and Venture Management* Prentice Hall, Englewood Cliffs (1975)
44. Mathur, S.P., *Economics of Small Scale Industry*. Sundeep Prakashan, Delhi (1979).
45. McClelland, D.C., *The Achieving Society*. Vakils Feffer and Simons, Bombay.
46. Mansfield, Edwin. *Industrial Research and Technological Innovation*. W.W. Norton (1968).
47. Mazumdar, Dipak, The Issue of Small Versus Large in the Indian Textile Industry : An Analytical and Historical Survey. World Bank Staff Working Papers, Washtington, D.C.
48. McGregor, Douglas, *The Human Side of Enterprise*.McGraw Hill, N.Y. (1960).
49. Ojha, P.D., Finance for Small Scale Enterprises in India, *RBI Bulletin*, Nov. 1982.
50. Palmo, Michael, The Application of Psychological Testing to Entrepreneurial Potential. *California Management Review* 13, Spring 1971.
51. Pathak, H.N., *Small Scale Industries in the Next Decade*. IIM, 1978.
52. Pessiemier, Edgar A., *New Product Decisions*. McGraw Hill, New York (1966).
53. Pickle, Hall B., *Personality and Success : An Assessment of Personal Characteristics of Small Business Managers*, Small Business Administration (1984).
54. Pickle, Hall B. and Abrahamson Royce L., *Small Business Management*, Hamilton, New York (1976).
55. Rao, V.S.P., *Human Resource Management in Small Industry*. Unpublished doctoral thesis submitted to Andhra University (1990).

56. Rao, P.A., *Self-Employment Schemes in Urban & Semi-urban Areas: Organisation and Management.* Mittal (1989).
57. Rao, Lakshman. *Industrial Entrepreneurship in India.* Chugh Publications, Allahabad (1986).
58. Sahoo, K.M., *Industrial Democracy.* Deep & Deep Publications (1989).
59. Sundesara, J.C., "Sale and Technology in Indian Industry". *Oxford Bulletin of Economics and Statistics,* August. 1966.
60. *Efficiency of Incentives for Small Scale Industry* (1982).
61. Sameeuddin, *Entrepreneurship Development in India.* Mittal Publications (1989).
62. Satyanarayan, T., *Financing of Small Scale Industries.* Himalaya Publishing House, 1989.
63. Sharma, R.A., *Entrepreneurial Change in Indian Industry,* Sterling , N. Delhi (1985).
64. Schabacker Joseph C., *Cost Planning in Small Manufacturing Company.* Small Business Administration, Washington D.C. (1960).
65. "Size and Technology in Indian Industry". *Oxford Bulletin of Economic and Statistics,* August 1966.
66. Schollhammer, Hans and Kuriloff, Arthur H., *Entrepreneurship Small Business Management,* John Wiley and Sons, New York (1979).
67. Steinhoff, Dan, *Small Business Management Fundamentals.* McGraw Hill. New York (1974).
68. Steinmataz, Lawrence et al., *Managing the Small Business.* Richard Irwin, Homewood Ill. (1968).
69. Smith, Norman R., *The Entrepreneur and His Firm. The Relationship Between Type of Man and Type of Company.* Michigan State University Press (1967).
70. Sinha, Ramesh P., *Some Problems of Small Scale Industries,* N. Delhi (1985).
71. Smith, Norman R., *Small Industry in India : Evidence and Interpretation of Indian Planning and Economic Policy.* Gujarat Economic Association, Ahmedabad (1981).
72. Singh, Nagendra P., *Management of Entrepreneurial Development Programmes : Case Study of Voluntary Agencies.* SIET (1977).
73. Socider, William. *Encouraging Entrepreneurship in the Large Corporation.* Research Management. May 1981.

74. Tulsi, S. K., *Incentives for Individuals.* Economic and Scientific Research Foundation.
75. Vepa, Ram K., *Modern Small Industries in India : Problems and Prospects.* Sage Publications (1988).
76. Vesper, Karl H., *Entrepreneurship and National Policy.* Heller Institute of Small Business Policy, Chicago (1983).
77. Vinze, M.D., *Women Entrepreneurs in India,* Mittal Publications (1987).
78. Wriston, Walter D., *Risk and other Four Letter Words.* Harper and Row, New York (1986).

INDEX

Wisdom